Relations of Global Power

RELATIONS OF GLOBAL POWER

NEOLIBERAL ORDER AND DISORDER

EDITED BY **GARY TEEPLE**
& STEPHEN McBRIDE

A Garamond Book

University of Toronto Press

LIBRARY AND ARCHIVES CANADA CATALOGUING IN PUBLICATION
Relations of global power : neoliberal order and disorder / edited by Gary Teeple & Stephen McBride.

"A Garamond Book."
Includes bibliographical references and index.
Also issued in electronic format.

ISBN 978-1-4426-0365-3 (pbk.).—ISBN 978-1-4426-0364-6 (bound)

1. International economic relations. 2. International relations. 3. International organization. 4. Neoliberalism. I. McBride, Stephen II. Teeple, Gary, 1945–

HF1359.R454 2010   337   C2010-905832-1

We welcome comments and suggestions regarding any aspect of our publications— please feel free to contact us at news@utphighereducation.com or visit our Internet site at www.utphighereducation.com.

North America
5201 Dufferin Street
Toronto, Ontario, Canada, M3H 5T8

2250 Military Road
Tonawanda, New York, USA, 14150

ORDERS PHONE: 1-800-565-9523
ORDERS FAX: 1-800-221-9985
ORDERS E-MAIL: utpbooks@utpress.utoronto.ca

UK, Ireland, and continental Europe
NBN International
Estover Road, Plymouth, PL6 7PY, UK
ORDERS PHONE: 44 (0) 1752 202301
ORDERS FAX: 44 (0) 1752 202333
ORDERS E-MAIL: enquiries@nbninternational.com

The University of Toronto Press acknowledges the financial support for its publishing activities of the Government of Canada through the Canada Book Fund.

Typesetting by Em Dash Design.

Printed in Canada

RECYCLED
Paper made from
recycled material
FSC
www.fsc.org   FSC® C021757

Contents

Acknowledgements

All books are the products of the work of many people; edited books even more so. It is not possible to mention all of those who generously lent their support in various ways, but we would like to extend a special thanks to those who laid aside time from very busy schedules to help complete this volume.

In particular, we want to thank the many readers who gave their time to help with the assessments and editing: Alison Ayers, John Calvert, Bill Carroll, Marjorie Griffin Cohen, David Fairey, Megan Humphrey, Marilyn Gates, Fernando De Maio, Ben Muller, Peter Prontzos, Mark Leier, Jim Sattler, and Ingo Schmidt. We would also like to express our appreciation to the anonymous reviewers appointed by the press who provided detailed and helpful comments. And we must also acknowledge the financial support and sponsorship provided by the Centre for Global Political Economy at Simon Fraser University.

The contributors also deserve special thanks; they waited a long time while we struggled with our own work schedules and long searches for contributors to fill gaps in the coverage that we wanted filled. In this, we were not entirely successful, despite our efforts.

We owe a great debt to Anne Brackenbury, Executive Editor at the University of Toronto Press. She encouraged us with our proposal, pressed us with deadlines, expedited production, and was a constant support through the whole process. Martin Boyne did the copy-editing, and we thank him for his many perceptive comments and questions, and his quick responses.

Finally, we would like to thank our respective families for their continued understanding and support, in particular Monica Escudero and Jan Keeton. The completion of this volume will provide some respite from our associated preoccupations.

Collaboration is an involved process fraught with possible differences and difficulties, but for us it has been a very positive experience, one in which we found a large degree of like-mindedness and comradeship, while sharing the workload. The collaboration proved to be rewarding and fraternal.

Gary Teeple and Stephen McBride
Vancouver

Introduction
Global Crisis and Political Economy

GARY TEEPLE and STEPHEN McBRIDE

The financial crisis that threatened the global economic order between 2007 and 2009 tarnished the image of neoliberalism as the common sense informing the management of the global political economy. The emergency, not to mention the panic-driven practical response of governments and international organizations to the looming crisis, was a repudiation of the neoliberal conventional wisdom. Far from relying on market forces to take care of the situation, governments stepped in and advanced huge sums of money to stave off financial and economic collapse.

To most observers, neoliberalism's concept of the political economy as self-regulating and requiring only minimal state intervention was exposed as a dangerous fantasy. Yet with the immediate crisis behind them, the authors of neoliberal globalization show all the signs, like the Bourbon monarchs, of having learned nothing and forgotten nothing. If not advocating exactly a return to "business as usual," policy makers show resistance to jettisoning the neoliberal certitudes of minimal government and reliance on private markets. Indeed, the budget deficits and debts incurred in bailing out a faltering capitalist system are now being used as a rationale to further reduce the role of the state in society. As the contributors to this volume make clear, however, if the push to return to pre-crisis normality succeeds, it will not be to the unregulated free capitalism of neoliberal rhetoric, but rather to the set of institutions that embed a particular set of power relations and that confer great benefits to some social actors and work to the disadvantage of others. In short, neoliberal globalization has always been underpinned by a set of institutions, formal and informal, public and private, global and national, that reflect the power relations between social classes and states.

If the recent crisis was unusually severe, and the prospects of recurrence remain real, it is important to remember that economic crises have been regular and inevitable occurrences in the capitalist mode of production, not least in the era of neoliberal globalization that began to be recognized as such in the 1980s and 1990s. From about 1980 to 2008, the long struggle to impose the neoliberal model was never free of economic crises—and every crisis was used to further erode working-class living conditions or standards in order to extract ever more surplus for private accumulation. In Latin America, the 1980s are often referred to as "the lost decade," a period of debt crises throughout the region that flattened economic growth and increased unemployment. In Japan in 1989, a large real-estate and stock-market bubble burst, leading to a nearly decade-long recession. In 1994, the Mexican peso fell, and along with it living standards were degraded for much of the working class and peasantry, and the effects were felt throughout Latin America. In 1997, the financial crisis struck many nations in southeast Asia, creating impoverishment for millions. These were but some of the major crises that took place in the era of global neoliberalism, without mentioning the many short recessions during this period, or specific American crises such as the "dot-com bubble" in 1995–2001, the S&L bailout, the collapse of Enron in 2001, and WorldCom in 2002, to name some of the most significant (Burrough & Helyer 1999; Cruver 2002; Glasberg & Skidmore 1997; Kindleberger 2005; McLean & Elkind 2004).

In seeking to understand the neoliberal order, most of the contributors adopt a political economy approach. Economics and politics in isolation from each other cannot provide meaningful explanations. To be sure, the political and the economic have to do with different forms of allocation of social resources, but they are intrinsically related—neither can exist without the other. Politics has to do with the relation between the state and different economic forces; in fact, the very existence of the state depends on economic activity that provides the resources that allow it to function. Economics has to do with the market, which has always required rules and regulations to maintain the property relations that define it and to defend it against its own unequal consequences. In short, the state distributes economic resources according to publicly determined policies, while the market, bound by politically defined property relations, distributes according to ownership and the price mechanism. Political policies are informed by economic and class demands, and all economic demands are framed by political decisions. The political and the economic are very much opposite sides of the same coin: there is no market free of politics and no politics free of economic considerations. Their study in separate disciplines flies in the face of an integrated reality.

Historically, however, there is a periodic shift of emphasis from one to the other—a waxing and waning of the use of the state to bolster market relations or mitigate the rules that define them. In capitalism, the chief purpose of both the state and the market is capital accumulation, but there is a difference in the distribution of benefits between classes. On the one hand, greater prominence given to state allocation allows for more resources to classes and strata that do not have direct economic power; on the other hand, more power bestowed on the market allows the classes and strata that control and own the means of production to allocate resources more for their own benefit.

In the following chapters there is frequent reference to Keynesianism and neoliberalism—conflicting political policies that are also economic policies—as the background to the analyses. Both can be understood as "regimes of accumulation" (Kotz, McDonough & Riech 1994), as a relatively coherent set of institutions and policies that emphasize the role of the state or the market respectively and that characterize a given period. Neither of these regimes was free of the possibility of crises of accumulation.

The mid-1970s saw the high point in the development of the Keynesian welfare state in the industrial world and a low point in the postwar rate of profit. Up to this time, a particular constellation of factors—postwar reconstruction, the threat of socialism, national liberation struggles in the developing world, the opening of the former colonies to international capital expansion, the high demand for labour, new technology, and a rise in union membership, among others—had given the working classes in the developed world a certain degree of economic and political leverage to command high wages and increasing amounts of state redistribution. Inflation and stagnation were the results: inflation, in part because the conditions that allowed labour to demand an increasing share of the total social product remained in place, in part because postwar working-class living standards and expectations had acquired the status of normalcy, and also because the US was printing money to offset its balance-of-payments deficit and to pay for much of the Vietnam war; and stagnation, in part because, in this context of declining profits, capital was losing its incentive to invest. Neoliberalism was to be the "answer" to the welfare state and state "interference" in the accumulation process.

The advocates of neoliberalism promoted the myth of the free market, in which an "invisible hand" transformed the pursuit of individual interest into public good. It battled with the Keynesian orthodoxy of the postwar era that endorsed the "mixed economy," i.e., the state enterprise and provision of goods and services to supplement the operation or offset the shortcomings of the marketplace. In practice, neoliberalism comprised a set of policies intended to dismantle postwar Keynesian practices that had created stagnation for capital accumulation by the 1970s. The policies were aimed at shifting the growing working-class share of the total social product back to corporations and the private accumulation process, and were accompanied by the construction of a new set of institutions and practices to replace or modify those aligned with Keynesianism.

Sometimes these neoliberal policies were introduced individually and incrementally, at other times as omnibus bills, attacking the welfare state on all fronts in comprehensive pieces of legislation. In the name of minimal government and priority of the market and private property, public services in health care, education, social security, and infrastructure were cut, downgraded, or shifted to the private corporate sector and charities. State enterprises were sold off at fire-sale prices. The corporate share of the tax base was gradually shifted to the working classes. In some jurisdictions, legislation was passed to limit government powers to tax and borrow, forcing a retrenchment of the public sector and limiting further expansion. Government regulations and oversight in the economy were loosened or abandoned. Working-class organizations and rights were systematically undermined through legislative and judicial restrictions and, in the developing world, through the frequent use of illegal, violent means. Workers' pensions were increasingly privatized, putting them at risk in the stock market, and wage increases were often capped by government, preventing workers from escaping the inflation-induced erosion of living standards.

In the battle of ideas, the forces behind neoliberalism made wide use of the mass media and the proliferation and authority of conservative corporate-financed think tanks to promote their message. The world was subjected to constant refrains about the benefits of competition and the marketplace, the undemocratic and anachronistic nature of trade unions, wealth creation through stock-market investing, the inefficiency of everything governmental, and fanciful notions such as supply-side or trickle-down economics and flat tax proposals. Accompanying the ideological messages were measures aimed at the working classes to promote an attachment to private property and hence capitalism. A sizeable portion of public housing in the UK, for example, was sold off at deep discounts early in the Thatcher regime, while in the US, "subprime mortgages" were made available in the early 1990s under Bill Clinton.

Neoliberalism attempted to dismantle the Keynesian welfare state in order to "free" capital for private accumulation. It brought deregulation, privatization, and retrenchment of the public sector, anti-union policies and practices, wage controls, pension "marketization," and the subsidization of corporations and the rich—but certainly not without pervasive and abiding resistance. The Washington Consensus, another label for global neoliberalism or structural adjustment programs, promised a better world. Unleashing the powers of private enterprise, it was argued, would produce social and political stability and modernization for developing countries, and a higher standard of living. In actuality, it brought a series of economic crises and uncertainty, unprecedented social and economic inequality, high rates of individual, corporate, and national indebtedness, and the destruction of small farmers and peasantry (Madeley 1999; Wallach and Sforza 1999).

The increasingly unregulated financial sector nevertheless continued to build itself a vast house of cards, based on numerous and complex instruments of "structured finance," that is, money without any link to real commodities or "productive activity," in the form of an array of "securitized new products"—all of them profoundly speculative in nature. A mountain of credit and debt built on incalculable risk engulfed the world's financial sector and stretched well beyond the roughly $70 trillion in world gross product (CIA 2009)—a speculative bubble of a staggering and insupportable size, producing unprecedented financial insecurity for individuals and corporations worldwide. The first article in this collection, by David Kotz, examines the link between this rise of the financial sector and neoliberalism. More generally, Kotz introduces the concept of social structures of accumulation (SSAs)—"the complex of institutions which support the process of capital accumulation"—and uses it to analyze the shift from Keynesianism to neoliberalism, within which financialization has played such a central role.

While the Washington Consensus and the domestic implementation of neoliberal policies brought increasing amounts of national deregulation to produce a less regulated international exchange, transnational frameworks arose to provide a degree of predictability to the global economy. These supranational structures have increasingly diminished some of the powers of national constitutions, incrementally shifting sovereignty from the state to supranational organizations or agreements or to private actors such as corporations or investors. They include generalist international agencies such as the United Nations, as well as more specialized agencies such as the International Monetary Fund (IMF), the World Bank, the World Trade Organization (WTO), and the Bank of International Settlements, all of which changed their roles and assumed greater disciplinary importance for national states; common markets, trading blocs, and customs unions, such as the European Union (EU), the North American Free Trade Agreement (NAFTA), or the Southern Common Market, MERCOSUR; and agencies for the harmonization of standards, such as the Codex Alimentarius, the ISO (International Organization for Standardization), or the Universal Postal Union. Alongside these institutions of global economy governance, global security treaties—such as NATO, United Nations peacekeeping operations, the North American Aerospace Defense Command (NORAD), the Organization for Security and Co-operation in Europe, and the Australia, New Zealand, and United States Security Treaty (ANZUS)— continued into the post–Cold War period and often assumed new functions and roles. These are but a few of the numerous international mechanisms that provide frameworks of supranational law and practice, often with embedded corporate privilege and limited democratic access. The second chapter, by Stephen McBride, examines these new global institutions, using examples drawn from the global financial architecture, the WTO, NAFTA, bilateral investment treaties, and the domestic realm. A common theme is that by locating important decisions in institutions remote from public and popular influence, democracy is diminished as private authority is enhanced. Chapter 3, by Claire Cutler, focuses on the numerous systems of private authority that have arisen to steer corporate and state activities. In tracing the rise of the private, by referencing the proliferating studies of private modes of governance and regulation in the global political economy, Cutler makes a persuasive case that the phenomenon is highly significant but is largely bereft of theoretical analysis. Many accounts of private authority adopt an essentially apolitical and functionalist rationale that diverts attention from the shift in power that the rise of private authority represents and serves to "depoliticize" the issue. Her chapter points to the need to overcome such technocratic accounts and instead analyze critically the distributional consequences and the democratic legitimacy of private governance arrangements in the global political economy. This will involve an analysis of the underlying interests and purposes that are served by private authority and will inevitably challenge those existing theorizations of international relations that have been blind to the implications of private authority.

Implementation of the Washington Consensus enhanced the expansion and the operations of transnational corporations (TNCs) in the developing world. The issue of national sovereignty came into question as laws and regulations regarding foreign investment were pressed on dependent nations by global agencies or industrial states. TNCs, moreover, often interfered in the political affairs of the host country, engaged in illegal activities, practiced transfer pricing, caused environmental destruction, violated exchange controls, refused the disclosure of information on accounts or operations, ignored employment policies and violated both workers' rights and a range of human rights, among other questionable and illegal activities (UNCTC 1990). In reaction to this "new reality," the developing world demanded a code of conduct for TNCs, in pursuit of a New International Economic Order (NIEO). These efforts failed, and Kavaljit Singh's chapter addresses the issue of the regulatory mechanisms that replaced them. Singh notes the privatization of authority over corporate conduct by way of voluntary codes of conduct and self-regulation (sometimes involving co-regulation with civil society actors). Such devices serve to camouflage the extent of deregulation, and, in the wake of the financial crisis, Singh makes a case for state intervention to ensure adequate regulation.

The chapters by Bob Russell and Mark Thomas deal with the control of labour in the neoliberal era. The period was characterized by globalization of production and distribution chains, a phenomenon triggered by revolutionary changes to the labour process, and particularly to the technology component. Computer-based means of production, first introduced in the late 1970s, have increased productivity and the speed of communications over the last three decades to such a degree that national or even regional markets are no longer large enough to absorb local production. The new means of production are often said to be based more on knowledge than on skill; the processes are continuous, operating without reference to cultural, national, religious, or human considerations; and increasingly, as robotic automated systems, they can operate with few or no humans at the point of production. Russell examines information and communication technology and its relation to the global production and labour processes. He notes a number of managerial paradoxes or contradictions, such as TNCs' efforts to generate employee commitment while pressing ahead with flexible and global production processes that confer little or no security on labour. To make this possible, part of the deregulation demanded by neoliberal or structural-adjustment policies was aimed at the reduction or non-enforcement of labour standards. Since at least the nineteenth century, there have been attempts to create transnational public policies for labour, beginning with the abolition of the slave trade and regulations on prison, female, child, and forced labour. Efforts to increase regulation of labour exploitation grew with the creation of the League of Nations in 1919 and its associated International Labour Organization (ILO). Lately, there have been moves to restrict "social dumping"—the export of goods and ser-vices whose labour component is either poorly or not protected by ILO or other international standards—by using domestic standards to block or impede these imports, or by demanding compliance with interna-tional standards such as ILO or human rights principles, or by inserting a "social clause" that sets out certain standards for all signatories, among other mechanisms. In his paper, Thomas critically surveys the multi-level governance regime that emerged involving state, international, and pri-vate authorities. Of particular interest is the evaluation of ILO regula-tions and corporate codes of conduct regarding labour.

Changing technology and the construction of a global economy brought more unemployment and underemployment, accompanied by the intensification of work for those employed. Of the world's total labour force of about 3 billion, in a population of about 6.7 billion, approximately 30 per cent are unemployed or underemployed (CIA 2009). In 2007, moreover, the IMF reported that the globalization of labour, coupled with technological change and the decline of labour standards, had produced a pervasive declining trend in labour's share of total income (IMF 2007). The ILO estimates, moreover, that about 250 million children are employed around the world. In 2009, the ILO reported that almost half a billion workers in 2008 did not earn more that $1 per day, and about 1.3 billion or 43.5 per cent of the global labour force earned less than $2 per day (ILO 2008). Such are the con-sequences of global neoliberalism.

Moreover, the social conditions of labour were also under sustained attack as states reduced their commitment to the provision of health care, education, and social security. In a sophisticated critique of neolib-eral thinking on these issues, David Coburn challenges the notion that there is an automatic relationship between economic growth (even sup-posing that neoliberal policies were to produce such an effect) and good health. The level of economic development certainly matters, but so too does the type of socio-economic development and the priorities of gov-ernment. Coburn's article examines the links between public health and the retrenchment of welfare regimes. With increasing inequality and ris-ing unemployment, a deterioration in global health could be expected. Indeed, the rise of class inequality within states at all levels of devel-opment means that class inequalities in health are at very high levels.

In the attempt to remove barriers to private capital accumulation, neoliberal policies have been aimed at dismantling or undermining the rights spelled out in the Universal Declaration of Human Rights and its two main Covenants—on Civil and Political Rights and on Economic, Social, and Cultural Rights. Many key rights constitute obstacles to unmitigated accumulation practices: for instance, civil rights for citizens as consumers and owners/occupiers, political rights allowing criticism of the operation of TNCs, not to mention legislation constraining the role of TNCs, and economic, social, and cultural rights that imply access to state-supported education, health care, and social security. Because human rights, for the most part, are realized and enforced at the national level, the development of a transnational political economy has allowed for the violation of the very rights or principles that defined capitalism in an earlier stage of national development. The article by Tony Evans addresses the questions of what human rights are and what their fate might be in a global economy. A central point is that the practice of rights is built on relations of power.

Closely related to limitations on human rights is the militarization that has accompanied globalization. The post–Cold War period failed to produce the anticipated "peace dividend," and neoliberal globalization was accompanied by massive arms sales. According to the Stockholm International Peace Research Institute, between 1997 and 2007, world military expenditures rose about 37 per cent; in 2008, total expenditures amounted to almost $1.4 trillion, surpassing the peak spending of the Cold War (SIPRI 2007). The United States, the leading force in promoting neoliberalism, spends close to one half of this total. Conventional arms-sales transfers amounted to about $42 billion in 2007, up from $38 billion in 2006; the US and Russia accounted for more than one half of this total, most of which goes to developing countries (Grimmett 2008). Most of the world's nations increased their military budgets in 2008, and over a dozen significant armed conflicts have persisted in developing nations, fuelled by such arms transfers. James M. Cypher's chapter explores the importance of military power in maintaining a world open to capital investment.

Keynesian policies in the postwar era mitigated the harshness of class antagonisms through state redistribution of social resources to the working classes. Neoliberalism, however, comprises a set of policies openly advancing the interests of one class at the expense of another, moderated only by the supposition that benefits will "trickle down" to those lower in the social hierarchy. Resistance to these policies, it follows, has been considerably greater than protests in the Keynesian era. Demonstrations, strikes, and riots began when these policies were first imposed on parts of the developing world by the World Bank and the IMF in the 1960s and 1970s (Walton & Selton 1994; Payer 1974, 1982); this resistance grew in the 1980s and 1990s when the same policies were increasingly introduced into the industrial world, depressing the living standards of the populations of the North. The responses to the crisis to date can be summed up largely as socialization of the corporate losses at the expense of the taxpayer, with the continuation of neoliberal policies undermining the living standards of the working classes. In the absence of formal political alternatives, extra-parliamentary protest and social unrest become the main avenues of political expression. The article by Elaine Coburn provides a survey of the key movements that have countered the growth of neoliberal globalization.

In the final chapter, Gary Teeple offers an analytical overview of the crisis of 2007–09. He attempts to dissect what happened in this period using the main themes and concepts found in the book, namely, regimes of accumulation, financialization, globalization, military Keynesianism, and the consequences of neoliberalism.

REFERENCES

Burrough, Bryan, and John Helyer. 1999. *Barbarians at the Gate: The fall of RJR Nabisco*. New York: Harper and Row.

CIA. 2009. *The World Fact Book* February. <https://www.cia.gov/library/publications/the-world-factbook/geos/xx.html>.

Cruver, B. 2002. *Anatomy of Greed*. New York: Carroll and Graf.

Glasberg, D.S., and D. Skidmore. 1997. *Corporate Welfare Policy and the Welfare State: Bank Deregulation and the Savings and Loan Bailout*. New York: Aldine de Gruyter.

Grimmett, R.F. October 23, 2008. Congressional Research Service Report to Congress: Conventional Arms Transfers to Developing Nations, 2000–2007.

International Monetary Fund. 2007. *World Economic Outlook*.

ILO. "Global Employment Trends 2008." <http://www.ilo.org/public/english/employment/strat/globa108.htm>.

Kindleberger, Charles P. 2005. *Manias, Panics, and Crashes: A History of Financial Crises*. New York: Wiley.

Kotz, D., T. McDonough, and Michael Riech (eds.). 1994. *Social Structures of Accumulation*. Cambridge: Cambridge University Press.

Madeley, John. 1999. *Big Business, Poor Peoples, the Impact of Transnational Corporations on the World's Poor*. London: Zed Books.

McLean, B., and P. Elkind. 2004. *Enron: The Smartest Guys in the Room*. New York: Portfolio.

Payer, Cheryl. 1974. *The Debt Trap, The IMF and the Third World*. Harmondsworth: Penguin.

——. 1982. *The World Bank: A Critical Analysis*. New York: Monthly Review Press.

Stockholm International Peace Research Institute (SIPRI). <http://yearbook2007.sipri.org/chap8>.

UNCTC. 1990. *Transnational Corporations, Services and the Uruguay Round.*
New York: United Nations.

Wallach, L., and M. Sforza. 1999. *Whose Trade Organization? Corporate
Globalization and the Erosion of Democracy.* Washington, DC: Public
Citizen.

Walton, John, and David Selton. 1994. *Free Markets and Food Riots: The
Politics of Global Adjustment.* Oxford: Blackwell.

1

Financialization and Neoliberalism

DAVID M. KOTZ

The neoliberal era is now more than a quarter-century old, dating from around 1980. Among the unsettled issues concerning neoliberalism is its relation to the growing role of "finance" in the economy that has accompanied neoliberalism. The aim of this chapter is to contribute to our understanding of this relation.

A common view is that the rise of neoliberalism is explained by the growing role and power of finance in the political economy of capitalism. According to Dumenil and Levy (2004: 1–2), "... neoliberalism is the expression of the desire of a class of capitalist owners and the institutions in which their power is concentrated, which we collectively call 'finance,' to restore ... the class's revenues and power...." Some analysts view the rise of what might be called "financial dominance" as the underlying development that explains not only the emergence of the neoliberal order but also the associated form of globalization in this era (Dumenil & Levy 2005: 17).[1]

This chapter presents a different view. The changing role of finance in the economy in recent decades can best be captured, not by the idea of dominance by the financial sector, but by the concept of "financialization," which suggests an expanding role for finance in economic activity. It will be argued here that the immediate cause of the financialization process of recent decades is found in neoliberal restructuring, rather than financialization explaining the rise of neoliberalism. However, financialization also has deeper roots that are unrelated to neoliberalism. This interpretation of the relation between financialization and neoliberalism clarifies what would otherwise be puzzling differences between the form of financial dominance that arose in the late nineteenth/early twentieth centuries and the financialization of the current neoliberal period.

The first section explains what is meant by neoliberalism, relying on the social structure of accumulation theory, which explains the periodic changes that take place in the institutional structure of capitalism. The second section explains what is meant by financialization followed by a section that considers the origins of financialization and neoliberalism, as well as the relation between the two. In light of this, the next section analyzes the differences between financial dominance in the late nineteenth and early twentieth centuries and the financialization of the neoliberal era. The final section offers concluding comments.

NEOLIBERALISM AND SOCIAL STRUCTURES OF ACCUMULATION

The particular institutional form of capitalism has changed periodically since capitalism emerged several centuries ago. Neoliberalism can be understood as the latest institutional form of capitalism. The social structure of accumulation theory offers an analysis of the periodic changes in the capitalist institutional structure (Kotz, McDonough & Reich 1994; McDonough, Reich & Kotz 2010). A social structure of accumulation (SSA) is interpreted here as a coherent, long-lasting capitalist institutional structure that promotes profit-making and forms a framework for capital accumulation.[2]

According to the SSA theory, each SSA functions effectively at promoting profit-making for several decades, but at some point it ceases to do so. This brings a period of crisis, which eventually gives rise to a new SSA. Each SSA exists at the level of global capitalism as well as within individual countries, although with some institutional variation across countries. The construction of the post–World War II SSA was completed by the late 1940s and worked effectively through to around 1973. That SSA was characterized by active state regulation of economic activity both within states and in the global system, well-developed welfare states, significant capital–labour cooperation, and a co-respective, or restrained form of competition among large corporations. The postwar SSA was a significant departure from the past, when the state had played a more limited role in the economy and individuals were left largely to fend for themselves. This postwar system is often referred to as "regulated capitalism" because of the historical break entailed by the great expansion in the role of the state in that period.

Around 1973, the postwar SSA entered a period of crisis, and in the late 1970s a new SSA began to take shape, initially in the US and the UK. It came to be called "neoliberalism," since its main features resemble the pre–Great Depression "free-market" version of capitalism. In most of the world, although not in the US, the term "liberal" refers to the view that the state should stay out of the economy.

The neoliberal SSA was well established by the early 1980s (Kotz & McDonough 2010). This SSA represented a sharp break from the previous one. Its main features are the removal of barriers to free movement of goods, services, and especially capital, throughout the global economy; a withdrawal by the state from the role of guiding and regulating economic activity; the privatization of state enterprises and public services; the slashing of state social programs; a shift to regressive forms of taxation; a shift from cooperation between capital and labour to a drive by capital, with aid from the state, to fully dominate labour; and the replacement of co-respective behaviour among large corporations by unrestrained competition. Neoliberalism has an associated ideology of worship of the so-called free market along with a denial of any positive role for the state apart from its coercive functions.

The neoliberal SSA has entailed a major restructuring of the global capitalist system, as well as a transformation of domestic institutions in the US, the UK, and many other countries. However, some capitalist countries have moved only marginally toward the neoliberal model, such as the Scandinavian countries and Japan.[3] The neoliberal institutional structure qualifies as an SSA, since it is a coherent, long-lasting capitalist institutional structure that has brought a rising rate of profit in the leading capitalist countries[4] and has formed a framework for capital accumulation.[5]

FINANCIALIZATION

A literature has arisen recently about the phenomenon of financialization. Definitions of this awkward term vary among authors. Perhaps the best, and most inclusive, definition is given by Epstein (2005: 3): "... financialization means the increasing role of financial motives, financial markets, financial actors and financial institutions in the operation of domestic and international economies." To clarify this definition, it may be helpful to explain what is meant by "finance." Finance has to do with the movement of purchasing power between actors in the economy, either in the form of extension of credit or the assumption of ownership rights over an asset that is expected to yield payments over time.[6] Since capitalism reached its corporate stage, securities have become the representation of both ownership and creditor status. As securities became tradable, financial markets arose in which the status of owner or creditor could be bought and sold. In recent times increasingly complex types of securities have been created and traded, including "financial derivatives" whose value is tied to the value of other securities.

Therefore, financial activity includes dealings in stocks and bonds, mortgages, financial derivatives, futures, foreign exchange, and many other types of assets, as well as making old-fashioned loans. Financial activity is traditionally distinguished from non-financial economic activity, which refers to the production, storage, and distribution of goods and the production of those services classified as non-financial based on having a purpose not directly related to financial activity (such as haircuts or education).

The wording of the definition of financialization given above suggests a quantitative expansion of the role of finance in the economy, but it is not clear whether this means that the role of finance changes qualitatively. That is, does financialization imply a change in the relation between the financial and non-financial sectors of the economy? If such a change does accompany the "increasing role" of finance as stated in the preceding definition, what kind of change is it? Possible changes include the following: finance becomes more powerful in relation to the non-financial sector, or the link between finance and the non-financial sector becomes either tighter or looser.

To address this question, we will examine the historical background of the emergence of financialization in the neoliberal era, drawing largely on the US case. During the 1920s, the financial sector in the US was largely unregulated, and the later part of the decade saw widespread financial fraud and speculative excess. At the end of the 1920s the stock market collapsed, followed by the banking system a few years later. As the Great Depression wore on, the view became influential that the excesses of unregulated finance had been a major factor responsible for the severity of the Depression. This view greatly influenced the new regulation of finance that became part of the postwar SSA. Financial institutions in developed capitalist countries were typically state owned or closely regulated by the state in the postwar SSA. In the US there were state controls on interest rates, financial institutions were segmented by type of business permitted, entry into financial markets was closely regulated, and banks were protected by the state against failure. These tight regulations forced the financial sector to concentrate on promoting capital accumulation in the nonfinancial sector.

Starting in the 1970s, activity in financial markets and the profits of financial institutions began to rise relative to non-financial economic activity and profits. Foreign-exchange transactions in the world economy rose from about $15 billion per day in 1973 to $80 billion in 1980 and $1,260 billion in 1995. World trade in goods and services was 15 per cent of the value of foreign-exchange transactions in 1973, but by 1995 it had fallen to less than 2 per cent, implying that the explosion in currency trading was primarily for financial transactions, not for the purchase of internationally traded goods and services (Bhaduri 1998: 152). In the US, the value of all financial assets rose from about 150 per cent of GDP during 1960–80 to over 300 per cent of GDP in 2003 (Orhangazi 2008: xii). The pre-tax profits of financial corporations in the US rose from an average of 13.9 per cent of all corporate profits in the 1960s to 19.4 per cent in the 1970s, fell slightly to 17.2 per cent in the 1980s, and then rose to 25.3 per cent in the 1990s and 36.8 per cent of all corporate profits during 2000–06 (US Bureau of Economic Analysis 2008).[7] Dumenil and Levy (2005: 38) found that in France the rate of profit of financial corporations was far below that of non-financial corporations in the early 1980s, but by the late 1990s the financial profit rate had far surpassed that for non-financials. Epstein and Jayadev (2005: 51–52) found that the share of national income received by financial institutions and holders of financial wealth was much higher in the 1990s than it had been in the 1970s in a majority of OECD countries studied.[8]

The change in the role of the financial sector in the neoliberal era has not just involved a quantitative expansion of its activities and profits. In this era financial institutions, particularly the giants among them, have broken out of their role as servants of non-financial capital accumulation to pursue their own profits through financial activity. They have done so increasingly through activities based in the financial market, rather than just making loans to institutions outside of the financial sector. The creation and sale of new financial instruments largely replaced the long-term loan relationships with the non-financial sector that had predominated in the regulated capitalist SSA.

THE RELATION BETWEEN FINANCIALIZATION AND NEOLIBERALISM

It is widely recognized that a radical shift took place from state-regulated capitalism to neoliberal capitalism around 1980. It is also well known, at least by specialists, that during the neoliberal era a process of financialization has taken place in capitalism. However, determining the origins of these two developments, and the relation between them, is not a simple matter.

One view is that financialization arose independently of neoliberalism. There are several variants of this position. Paul Sweezy (1994) argues that the tendency toward stagnation, which in his theory is inherent in the monopoly stage of capitalism, led to a shift in investment from the real sector, which had declining investment opportunities due to developing stagnation, to the financial sector starting in the 1970s. There followed an explosion of financial activity that we have come to know as financialization. John Bellamy Foster (2007) took Sweezy's analysis one step further, arguing that the financialization resulting from the stagnation tendency of monopoly capitalism led in turn to neoliberalism: "What we have come to call 'neoliberalism' can be seen as the ideological counterpart of monopoly-finance capitalism ..." (9).

In his sweeping analysis of the history and pre-history of capitalism, Giovanni Arrighi (1994) argues that a series of cycles referred to as "long centuries" (or regimes of accumulation) have characterized modern Western economic history. First was the long fifteenth to sixteenth century dominated by Genoa, and last (so far) is the "long twentieth century" dominated by the US. Each regime of accumulation eventually enters a crisis phase, as overaccumulation and increasing competition result in declining profitability in trade and production. The crisis phase is marked by a shift of investment from trade and production, due to its declining profitability, into finance (Arrighi 1994: 214–15). In this view, contemporary financialization is a reflection of the crisis in the US-dominated long twentieth century, analogous to the period of finance capital in the late nineteenth and early twentieth centuries that reflected the crisis of Britain's "long nineteenth century." However, Arrighi does not specifically link neoliberalism to contemporary financialization.[9]

As was noted above, Dumenil and Levy (2004) hold that growing power on the part of financial capital, associated with financialization, led to neoliberal restructuring as a means to benefit financial capital. However, this view suffers from serious problems. If neoliberalism represents the victory of financial capital, or of some broader category of "finance," then two questions arise: over whom was this victory won, and how was finance able to achieve such dominance? Let us consider the first question first. If an identifiable financial capitalist interest was able to bring about neoliberal transformation by defeating an identifiable non-financial capitalist interest, there should be evidence of a battle between the two. Non-financial capital, presumably embodied in the giant non-financial corporations that now straddle the globe, would surely have put up a good fight, if neoliberal restructuring had not been in their interest. Yet no one has found evidence of such a fight.

Neoliberalism first took root in the US and the UK at the end of the 1970s. In the US the shift toward neoliberalism appeared to have unified support from the capitalist class, apart from a few mavericks. A major part of big capital had earlier supported the regulated capitalist SSA, in alliance with organized labour (Kotz 2002). It was the desertion of that alliance by big capital in the 1970s which made it possible for neoliberal restructuring to proceed so quickly, since labour was too weak to stop the shift to neoliberalism on its own. In the UK, when Prime Minister Margaret Thatcher began neoliberal restructuring in 1979, there was some division within the capitalist class over it, but it did not pit financial against non-financial capital—initial opposition arose from old-line, aristocratic sections of finance and industry reacting to Thatcher's emphasis on upward mobility (Harvey 2005: 31).

Some advocates of the view that financial dominance explains neoliberal transformation define "finance" so broadly that this claim becomes consistent with the absence of any visible struggle between financial and non-financial segments of capital. Dumenil and Levy (2005: 21–22) define finance as "both institutions (the financial system: commercial and investment banks, pension funds, insurance ...) and individuals, [that is,] capitalists—or a fraction of capitalists since some capitalists are more 'financial' than others." The capitalists specified to be excluded from "finance" include the "small shareholder or the owner of a small firm" who "does not actually belong to finance," and also corporate managers ("finance can be used to refer to capitalist owners as opposed to management"). Thus, it appears that finance includes not only financial institutions but also all large-scale owners of capital, excluding only small business, small shareholders, and managers. That is, finance turns out to more or less coincide with big capital, perhaps with small financial institutions thrown in.

If big capital as a whole supported neoliberalism, then it is not surprising that there was no visible battle within the capitalist class over its installation. Small business has always predominantly supported a liberal regime—in the US it was the main opposition to the New Deal and the institutions of postwar regulated capitalism. Furthermore, high-level corporate managers have become fabulously rich in the neoliberal era, as management pay has skyrocketed in countries that underwent neoliberal restructuring; this suggests that no opposition to neoliberalism should be found from that quarter.

However, if "finance" is defined so broadly that it includes all of big capital, the claim that neoliberalism represents the victory and interests of finance has no explanatory value. Big capital has been part of every ruling coalition since capitalism reached its monopoly stage. Most of big capital supported, even if reluctantly, the interventionist, welfare-state, strong trade-union SSA following World War II. By defining "finance" so broadly that the absence of any big battle within capital is understandable, we are left without an answer to the question of why big capital deserted regulated capitalism in favour of neoliberal restructuring in the late 1970s.

If finance is defined more narrowly to refer to an identifiable financial capitalist segment of capital, then the second question raised above must also be answered: how did financial capital achieve a dominant position? According to this view, presumably non-financial capital was dominant in the postwar SSA. In the US, banks and other financial institutions complained throughout that period about the restrictions on their activities. It was not until after neoliberal ideas became dominant toward the end of the 1970s, including the new belief that regulation was harmful and free markets were always best, that the financial sector was deregulated by the US Congress, starting with the passage of two new laws in 1980 and 1982.[10] Financial deregulation set the financial sector free, allowing the process of financialization to develop. It appears that the beginning of neoliberal restructuring set the stage for financialization.

Figure 1.1 shows the pre-tax profits of financial corporations in the US as a percentage of total corporate pre-tax profits. Not until 1989, about seven years after financial deregulation, did financial profits begin to rise well above the 20-per-cent share of total corporate profits that had first been reached in 1970. After 1989, financial profits as a share of total profits displayed a marked upward trend, although with large fluctuations around that trend. Therefore, in the US, the period of rapid growth of financial profits relative to total profits came significantly after the neoliberal restructuring of the financial sector. This is consistent with our view that neoliberal restructuring led to financialization, rather than the alternative view that the growing power of the financial sector led to neoliberal restructuring.

However, financialization is not simply a consequence of neoliberalism. One can identify a strong tendency toward financialization within core processes of capitalism, once it has reached the stage of corporate capitalism. The rise of the corporate form of organization in the nineteenth century turned capitalist property from personal property into corporate property. Ownership of capital was transformed from direct ownership of enterprises to ownership of financial securities, which represents indirect ownership of enterprises.

[handwritten margin note: NEOLIBERAL RESTRUCTURING OF FINANCE]

FIGURE 1.1 Profits of Financial Corporations as a Percentage of Profits of All Corporations in the US

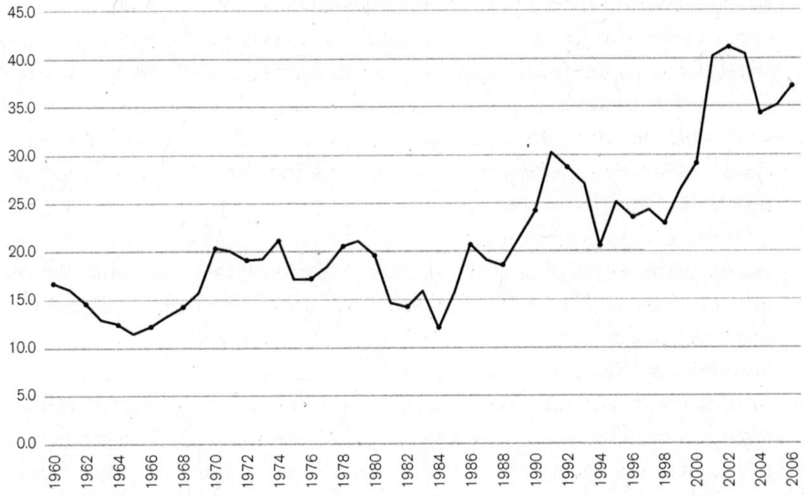

Note: Profits are before tax and with inventory valuation and capital consumption adjustments.
Source: US Bureau of Economic Analysis, 2008.

This offered an opportunity for capitalists to escape the chief problem they always face as individuals—the fearsome risks built into capitalism from the introduction of new technologies and new products.
Any fortune that is stuck in the form of an actual productive enterprise
is always in danger of eroding due to competition from new products
and new processes. Hence, capital is always looking for ways to escape
such risks. There are various ways to gain some protection against such
threats, including the pursuit of monopoly power or protection by the
state. However, shifting ownership of capital from real capital to financial capital is the best way to insulate against the inherent risks of the
capitalist marketplace. This is likely the reason why the Rockefellers'
huge fortune, born in oil, was soon shifted to finance and real estate.
Chase Manhattan Bank, the Rockefeller bank, was not tied to any particular company or industry. However, even banking faces some risks,
particularly if it involves medium-term loans to various productive enterprises. Holding, and dealing in, marketable securities promises still more
safety. The ideal is to hold wealth whose form can be changed instan-
taneously when any threat appears. In that way, capital remains safe,
with only workers bearing the risks of new products and new processes.[11] This explains the existence of an underlying tendency toward an
"increasing role of financial motives, financial markets, financial actors
and financial institutions in the operation of domestic and international
economies," the definition of financialization cited above.

The tendency toward financialization can be held in check by institutional arrangements, which ultimately reflect the relative power of various classes and groups at the time the institutions are formed. After World War II, financialization was largely held in check by the institutions of the postwar regulated capitalist SSA. However, the financialization tendency exerted pressure against the various regulations that hindered it during the postwar SSA. Toward the end of that period, financial institutions found various ways to partially get around the regulations. Once neoliberal ideas began to gain strength during the 1970s, the pressure that was rapidly building to tear down the regulation of the financial sector in particular joined with neoliberal arguments against regulation in general to provide the justification for rapidly granting bankers their freedom.

If the dominance of finance does not explain the rise of neoliberalism, what does? The context for the rise of the neoliberal SSA was the crisis of the postwar SSA. During the 1970s, that SSA was no longer working effectively at promoting profit-making. The world economy became very chaotic in that decade, with large fluctuations in prices of key raw materials, inflation rates, and currency exchange rates. As was noted above (in note 4), the rate of profit fell in the leading capitalist countries during that decade. The Keynesian techniques for management of the economy, which had seemed so effective in the 1960s, could not deal with a combination of high unemployment, stubbornly high inflation, and chaos in international currency markets. In that context, a search for a new institutional structure for capitalism began.

Harvey (2005) argues that neoliberalism was a response by ruling elites and classes to the threats and chaos they saw in the 1970s. He argues that neoliberalism was a project "to re-establish the conditions for capital accumulation and to restore the power of economic elites" (19). While neoliberalism was not effective in restoring the rapid accumulation of the regulated capitalist era, Harvey points out that it did restore the power and wealth of the elite, observing that the greatest beneficiaries in the US have been financiers, CEOs of large corporations, and owners of some new sectors such as computers, the internet, and mass media.

This analysis, which identifies the capitalist class as a whole as the promoter of neoliberalism, is consistent with the absence of a sharp battle between financial and non-financial capital over its introduction. However, observing that neoliberalism benefitted most of capital does not provide a full explanation for its emergence. It was in many respects surprising that a new version of the old liberal ideology and institutions returned at the end of the 1970s. There were good reasons why the liberal type of institutional structure was abandoned after World War II in favour of a regulated capitalist SSA, which produced the fastest economic growth in capitalist history. It is not obvious, however, that in the 1970s neoliberal restructuring was the only way, or the best way, to restore capitalist power. Some maverick capitalists in the US, such as investment banker Felix Rohatyn, advocated a new regulated capitalist institutional structure during the 1970s that would overcome the problems with the previous one. We need an explanation for why Rohatyn's position gained little traction.

One factor that led toward a new liberal SSA was undoubtedly a tendency to look to an imagined perfect past, before big government and strong trade unions hemmed in the actions of capital. The old-time religion of free markets—free of government regulation and the need to bargain with trade unions—was bound to exert some appeal for big capital. Strong trade unions raise wages and exercise some control over working conditions; a regulatory state taxes business and limits its freedom of action in the market. With profits falling, the desire to cut wages, gain control over working conditions, cut taxes on capital, and get out from under government regulations made the old liberal ideology appealing to capital. It is much more effective to cite the neoliberal liturgy that the regulatory state, high taxes on business and the rich, and strong trade unions undermine economic efficiency, discourage investment, and hinder economic progress, than simply to demand the right to pay lower wages, impose harsher working conditions, produce unsafe products, and shift the tax burden to those least able to shoulder it.

However, the appeal of an idealized past is not the only factor that was pressing toward neoliberalism. There were several factors in the concrete historical conditions of the 1970s that help to account for the rise of a neoliberal SSA at the end of the 1970s.[12] First, from 1948 to 1973, capitalism had become increasingly globally integrated. What began as relatively insulated national markets in the leading capitalist countries grew increasingly competitive, as firms from the US, Europe, and Japan invaded one another's markets. As a result, by the early 1970s, long-established relations of co-respective behaviour toward rivals broke down in markets, such as those for autos, steel, and electrical machinery, which had been dominated by a few giant corporations in each country. As monopoly power eroded, big capital could no longer afford to consider the long-run advantages of state regulations and trade unions, which had stabilized key relations of the system. Instead, fearing for their survival over the short-run in the new, more competitive environment, big business turned its attention to reducing its costs and increasing its control by any means possible. This provided a reason for big business to desert its previous coalition with labour, which had created and maintained the postwar SSA, and to join with small business, which had always opposed regulated capitalism. Increasing global economic integration had placed big business in the position of small business, which would encourage the former to adopt the outlook long held by the latter.

Second, the Great Depression had been a major factor in convincing big capital to support a regulated capitalist SSA after World War II. Its severity threatened the survival of capitalism itself. Fearing a return of the depression after World War II, it seemed that big government, along with concessions to the working class, was the only guarantee of the survival of the capitalist system. By the 1970s the Great Depression had receded into the past. Over time it came to be seen as a peculiar historical accident, one not likely ever to be repeated. A major reason for big business to support state regulation and a capital–labour compromise was no longer compelling.

Third, the threat posed by the alternative state socialist system in the late 1940s had passed. In the late 1940s the "socialist bloc" in Europe seemed very strong and was soon joined by China. Communist and Socialist parties had emerged with large popular followings in many leading capitalist countries. This created large incentives to compromise with labour in that period, to stave off the threat of revolution. By the late 1970s, the threat of socialist revolution had become remote in the West, as the Communist-ruled states seemed to stagnate and lose their earlier revolutionary fervour, while leftist parties in the capitalist countries had accepted a reformist role. Such institutions as welfare states and strong trade unions now seemed unnecessary as components of any new SSA.

The above factors can explain the emergence of a neoliberal SSA at the end of the 1970s, in the context of the crisis of the previous SSA. The neoliberal SSA was reinforced at the end of the 1980s, when the state socialist systems in Europe disappeared and China became increasingly integrated with world capitalism. In the 1990s, the stability of the neoliberal SSA was demonstrated when the coming to power of the Labour Party in the UK and the Democratic Party in the US, the twin birthplaces of neoliberalism, led to further reinforcement of the neoliberal SSA in those countries, rather than the turn away from it that had been suggested during the election campaigns.

Neoliberalism, therefore, does not represent the interest of financial capital alone. It represented the changed interests of a relatively unified capitalist class under the particular historical conditions prevailing during the period of crisis of the preceding state-regulated SSA in the 1970s. Financialization, a long-term tendency in capitalism, was held in check by the postwar SSA, and was released only after the neoliberal restructuring that began in the late 1970s. Once established, the neoliberal SSA presented a favourable environment for financialization.

FINANCE CAPITAL VERSUS FINANCIALIZATION

The late nineteenth and early twentieth centuries saw the rise to power of financial capitalists in some leading capitalist countries, particularly the US and Germany. This development led Rudolf Hilferding to propose the concept of finance capital (Hilferding 1981). As the financialization of capitalism has proceeded in recent decades, it may be tempting to see this as a new version of the finance capital of that earlier period.[13] Yet the historical record shows that they are two quite different social phenomena. The analysis of the relation between neoliberalism and financialization presented here sheds light on the differences between finance capital and financialization. The US case will be discussed for this purpose.

In the late nineteenth century, the New York bankers, led by J.P. Morgan and Company, gradually extended their control over a growing share of US industry, starting in the 1880s in railroads. In the 1890s, banker control was extended to manufacturing and communication, and after 1900 to electric power and light. By the middle of the first decade of the twentieth century, the New York banks controlled a major share of large non-financial corporations in the US (Kotz 1978: 24–39). The banks had representatives on the boards of the major corporations and often named the CEO. The bankers' aim, particularly that of Morgan, was the elimination of "excessive competition" and the establishment of "order." In pursuit of such objectives, the banks sought to expel two types of capitalists from control of large corporations. First, where possible they squeezed out the highly competitive entrepreneurs who had started many of the new large companies. The most famous example was Morgan's expulsion of the unreformable price-cutter Andrew Carnegie from the steel industry upon the formation of Morgan-controlled US Steel Corporation in 1901 (Josephson 1962). Morgan viewed such entrepreneurs as preventing orderly progress in industry by persistently engaging in destructive forms of competition. Second, Morgan sought to drive out financial speculators such as Jay Gould, who would buy up a controlling interest in corporations, loot their assets through various clever schemes, then sell out before the damage became known (Josephson 1962). Morgan and the other bankers thought the financial speculators were as dangerous to industrial progress as were the overly competitive entrepreneurs.

What developed was a merger of financial and industrial capital, with the banks serving as coordinating centres for newly formed financial groups—a relationship that Hilferding called "finance capital." One of the major financial groups emerged from the Standard Oil fortune, centred initially around National City Bank and later around Chase Manhattan Bank (Kotz 1978: 35–39). An important point about the finance capital of that period was that, while it had a monopolistic character that involved being cautious about investing in new industries, it was directed toward developing the real sector of the economy through maintaining close relationships between financial institutions and non-financial corporations. It is important to note the difference between the role of financial speculators such as Jay Gould, who engaged in pure theft, and that of Morgan and the other major bankers of that era, despite the association of both with the term "finance."

By the 1920s, the power of the New York bankers declined somewhat as new financial centres emerged in the Midwest and on the Pacific Coast and some large companies (such as the Ford Motor Company) arose outside the bankers' control. The later part of the 1920s, a decade marked by laissez-faire policies in the US, saw a resurgence of financial speculators, such as the Van Sweringen brothers of Cleveland and Samuel Insull of Chicago (Kotz 1978: 46, 48). The new speculators engaged in "financial innovation," creating holding companies in the railroad and power utility sectors and investment trusts (speculative forerunners of mutual funds). As a wave of speculative fever took hold in the late 1920s, even some of the old-line banks were drawn into financing speculative activities. Alongside the old system of finance capital, based on close financial–industrial relations aimed at industrial progress, was emerging a new system involving separation of finance from non-financial activity, in which financial operators sought purely financial profits independent of the progress of non-financial companies. Thus, it appears that a first round of financialization was taking hold in the second half of the 1920s in the US.

The economic collapse that began in the autumn of 1929 came to be blamed, not just on the financial speculators, but on the entire unregulated financial system. The eventual involvement of many old-line banks in financing speculative activities toward the end of the 1920s left them vulnerable to attack. This led to the postwar system of close regulation of the financial sector, forcing it once more to focus on serving real accumulation.[14]

After the deregulation of the financial sector began in 1980–82, the development that had been so prominent in the 1920s resumed, as the financialization tendency discussed above became free to operate again. The financial sector gradually shifted from loan-based financing of the non-financial sector to market-based and speculative activities. The financial sector became, not dominant over the non-financial sector as it had been in J.P. Morgan's day, but independent of it.[15] A growing share of corporate profits shifted to financial corporations, and many of the new fortunes gained were in speculative financial institutions such as hedge funds. The Enron scandal and the subprime mortgage debacle showed that the spirit of Jay Gould had reappeared in new forms.

CONCLUDING COMMENTS

This chapter has argued that a neoliberal SSA arose at the end of the 1970s for reasons not directly related to the process of financialization. It argues that the key causes, given the crisis of the previous SSA, were the increasing global economic integration of capitalism, the dimming memory of the Great Depression of the 1930s, the receding threat to capitalism from the rival state socialist system and from Socialist and Communist parties, and a decade later the disappearance of the state socialist system. According to this view, financialization is an ever-present tendency in corporate capitalism; once neoliberalism released the constraints against it, it developed rapidly in the favourable neoliberal institutional context. However, financialization has not involved a new dominance of the financial sector, but rather a growing separation of finance from non-financial activity.

Every stage of capitalism has its contradictions, which eventually bring a systemic crisis. The contemporary neoliberal, financialized form of capitalism has its particular contradictions (Kotz 2008). Some of these contradictions are located in the financialization process. While it has been argued that financialization involves the separation of finance from productive activity, such a separation cannot be complete. Ultimately financial profits are related to non-financial activity, and financial activity can have a large impact on the non-financial sector. For a time the expanding financial sector indirectly promoted capital accumulation in the system as a whole, by facilitating a rapid expansion of household borrowing, which made economic growth possible in the face of the wage stagnation produced by neoliberalism. However, the increasingly speculative character of the booming financial sector made it increasingly vulnerable. At this time the financial sector in the US has entered a period of crisis, which has spilled into the global financial system. At the same time, the possibilities for continued real economic growth within the neoliberal model appear uncertain. While history does not exactly repeat itself, the possibility exists for a combined financial and economic crisis within the neoliberal institutional structure. If this scenario does emerge, we may be entering a new period of institutional restructuring, whose end point cannot be foretold.

NOTES

1 Foster (2007: 9–10) also views neoliberalism as an outgrowth of the expanding role of finance. His interpretation is considered below.

2 This concept of an SSA differs somewhat from the dominant interpretation in the early SSA literature, which focused on the role of an SSA in promoting economic growth that is rapid by some historical standards. The traditional understanding of an SSA is criticized, and the SSA conception presented here is explained and justified, in Wolfson and Kotz (2010).

3 The most thorough neoliberal restructuring has taken place in the formerly Communist-ruled states of eastern and central Europe and central Asia. Neoliberal restructuring was imposed in much of Latin America and Africa, with the IMF and World Bank playing a key role. A number of developing countries in East Asia and South Asia, including China, have adopted hybrid institutional forms incorporating elements of both a state-directed development model and neoliberalism.

4 The rate of profit in the US, and for a combination of the UK, France, and Germany, declined from the mid-1960s through the end of the 1970s, at which time it began a long-term rise (Dumenil & Levy 2004: 24, figure 3.1).

5 Many studies have shown that the rate of economic growth has been significantly slower in the neoliberal era than it had been in the era of regulated capitalism, for the world economy and for the leading capitalist economies. Indeed, growth in most of the leading capitalist countries has been no faster in the neoliberal era than it had been in the crisis phase of the regulated capitalist era (Kotz & McDonough 2010).

6 Finance also refers to the shifting of wealth from one form to another, as in the exchange of one nation's currency for that of another.

7 From 2001–03, the profits of financial corporations constituted over 40 per cent of total corporate profits.

8 The large increases were found in Australia, Belgium, Finland, Korea, the Netherlands, the UK, and the US. In Germany the increase was smaller, and in Japan the share declined slightly.

9 A problem common to the analyses of Sweezy, Foster, and Arrighi is that, as Orhangazi (2007: 46–53) points out, it is not obvious why opportunities for profitable investment in the financial sector should be available when such opportunities have become limited in the real sector.

10 The two laws were the Depository Institutions Deregulation and Monetary Control Act of 1980 and the Garn-St. Germain Act of 1982, both of which gradually deregulated interest rates and loosened the restrictions that had segmented the financial sector.

11 Holding wealth in the form of marketable securities is safer in normal times. However, during a financial crisis some types of securities suddenly, and unexpectedly, become very risky, although no form of private-sector wealth is immune to a potential fall in asset valuations under such conditions.

12 The analysis of the rise of neoliberalism presented here draws on Kotz (2002).

13 While Arrighi (1994) views both periods as episodes of financial expansion that attend the crisis of a regime of accumulation, he does not explicitly suggest that the relation between financial and real sectors was identical in the two periods.

14 One study found that the major banks experienced a resurgence as centres of ownership and control over large non-financial corporations in the quarter-century following World War II (Kotz 1978: ch. 4). However, the banks did not achieve the same level of control as witnessed in the era of J.P. Morgan.

15 Sweezy (1994) and Foster (2007) make a similar observation about the difference between contemporary financialization and the era of finance capital. However, they do not analyze why the two cases are qualitatively different.

REFERENCES

Arrighi, Giovanni. 1994. *The Long Twentieth Century*. London and New York: Verso.

Bhaduri, A. 1998. "Implications of Globalization for Macroeconomic Theory and Policy in Developing Countries." In Dean Baker, Gerald Epstein, and Robert Pollin (eds.), *Globalization and Progressive Economic Policy*. Cambridge: Cambridge University Press. 149–58.

Dumenil, Gerard, and Dominique Levy. 2005. "Costs and Benefits of Neoliberalism." In Gerald Epstein (ed.), *Financialization and the World Economy*. Cheltenham, UK, and Northampton, MA: Edward Elgar. 17–45.

——. 2004. *Capital Resurgent: Roots of the Neoliberal Revolution*. Cambridge, MA, and London: Harvard University Press.

Epstein, Gerald. 2005. Introduction: Financialization and the World Economy. In Gerald Epstein (ed.), *Financialization and the World Economy*. Cheltenham, UK, and Northampton, MA: Edward Elgar. 3–16.

Epstein, Gerald, and Arjun Jayadev. 2005. "The Rise of Rentier Incomes in OECD Countries: Financialization, Central Bank Policy and Labor Solidarity." In Gerald Epstein (ed.), *Financialization and the World Economy*. Cheltenham, UK, and Northampton, MA: Edward Elgar. 46–74.

Foster, John Bellamy. 2007. "The Financialization of Capitalism." *Monthly Review* 58(11): 1–12.

Harvey, David. 2005. *A Brief History of Neoliberalism*. Oxford: Oxford University Press.

Hilferding, Rudolf. 1981. *Finance Capital: A Study of the Latest Phase of Capitalist Development*. London and Boston: Routledge and Kegan Paul.

Josephson, Matthew. 1962. *The Robber Barons: The Great American Capitalists, 1861–1901.* New York: Harcourt, Brace & World.

Kotz, David M. 2008. "Contradictions of Economic Growth in the Neoliberal Era: Accumulation and Crisis in the Contemporary U.S. Economy." *Review of Radical Political Economics* 40:2, Spring.

——. 2002. "Globalization and Neoliberalism." *Rethinking Marxism* 14(2): 64–79.

——. 1978. *Bank Control of Large Corporations in the United States.* Berkeley: University of California Press.

Kotz, David M., and Terrence McDonough. 2010. "Global Neoliberalism and the Contemporary Social Structure of Accumulation." In Terrence McDonough, Michael Reich, and David M. Kotz (eds.), *Contemporary Capitalism and Its Crises: Social Structure of Accumulation Theory for the Twenty First Century.* Cambridge and New York: Cambridge University Press. 93–120.

Kotz, David M., Terrence McDonough, and Michael Reich (eds.). 1994. *Social Structures of Accumulation: The Political Economy of Growth and Crisis.* Cambridge: Cambridge University Press.

McDonough, Terrence, Michael Reich, and David M. Kotz (eds.). 2010. *Contemporary Capitalism and Its Crises: Social Structure of Accumulation Theory for the Twenty First Century.* Cambridge and New York: Cambridge University Press.

Orhangazi, Ozgur. 2008. *Financialization and the US Economy.* Cheltenham, UK, and Northampton, MA: Edward Elgar.

Sweezy, Paul M. 1994. "The Triumph of Financial Capital." *Monthly Review* 46(2): 1–11.

US Bureau of Economic Analysis. 2008. *National Income and Product Accounts of the United States,* Table 1.14. Revision of January 30, 2008. <http://www.bea.gov/>.

Wolfson, Martin, and David M. Kotz. 2010. "A Reconceptualization of Social Structure of Accumulation Theory." In Terrence McDonough, Michael Reich, and David M. Kotz (eds.), *Contemporary Capitalism and Its Crises: Social Structure of Accumulation Theory for the Twenty First Century.* Cambridge and New York: Cambridge University Press. 72–90.

2

The New Constitutionalism
International and Private Rule in the New Global Order

STEPHEN McBRIDE[1]

In the era of neoliberal globalization, political economists have noted efforts to entrench the new world order by means of binding and enforceable provisions of international economic agreements that, in certain respects, have the qualities of domestic constitutions (Gill 1992; Clarkson 1993; McBride 2005: ch. 8, 2006). Constitutions have traditionally been viewed as attributes of sovereign nation-states, and mainstream constitutional scholarship has focused on their development over time within national contexts, their formal and informal (or written/codified, unwritten/uncodified) characteristics, and specific content in terms of institutional design, rights of citizens, and mechanisms of enforcement and amendment.

Additionally, the trend in such scholarship has been to focus on codified aspects and to neglect the older meaning of the word *constitution* as summing up the entire governmental order of a particular nation-state (McBride 2003). In large part this reflects both the increased tendency to entrench rights in written constitutions, and the emergence of post-colonial independent states, which required foundational constitutional documents. Even in the UK and its former dominions, formerly bastions of informal constitutional practices, rights inclusions (as with the Canadian Charter of Rights and Freedoms) and, in the case of the UK, involvement in the European Union (EU) have led to greater attention to the codified constitution. To a degree this has blinded constitutional experts to the impact of non-traditional measures, such as trade agreements, which have had a significant impact on the constitution when considered as the formal and informal rules and values that establish political institutions and condition the way they operate.

Thus, most constitutional discussion continues to focus on the nation-state level and, outside the EU at least, has neglected the quasi-constitutional nature of economic treaties to which nation-states are party. In focusing precisely on this aspect of international economic treaties, political economists have made a major contribution to literature on governance, pointing to instruments that are binding on states, if not on capital, and on which globalization depends.

A focus on institutions appropriate to further processes of capital accumulation can be found in various approaches to political economy, such as regulation theory and social structures of accumulation theory[2] (for example Kotz, McDonough & Reich 1994; O'Hara 2006). The general definition of a social structure of accumulation is "the complex of institutions which support the process of capital accumulation" (Kotz, McDonough & Reich 1994: 1). Although it is acknowledged that the form of such institutions may change, their importance in underpinning a successful capital accumulation process is a constant. If a particular SSA—"the ensemble of economic, political, and ideological institutions which serve to reproduce capitalist relations of production"—can no longer deliver, then crisis results, and this can be resolved only on terms consistent with continued capitalism by constructing new institutions to perform that function (McDonough 1994: 80). From this perspective, one of the great contributions of an appropriate institutional structure is to provide predictability on such issues as the distribution of rewards in society and on the location and functioning of decision-making authority (Fairris 1999: 1066; Kotz 1994: 64).

As SSA theory anticipates successive stages of capitalism, with corresponding institutional structures, the approach lends itself quite well to analyses of changes in the postwar era from a Keynesian to a neoliberal form of capitalism, and interpretations of that shift that posit a crisis in the accumulation process, specifically a crisis of "over-accumulation" (see, e.g., Harvey 2003, 2005, 2006). The institutional implication of this approach is that the Keynesian welfare state and national economic management institutions that had facilitated capital accumulation in the postwar period had come to be an obstacle by the 1970s. After a hiatus and a search for alternatives, the neoliberal institutional model emerged as the alternative in the late 1970s and 1980s. This period is coterminous with the discovery of "globalization" in academic and popular literature. The approach would similarly alert us to the possibility of further institutional change as a result of the crisis of 2007–09 and beyond.

To create profitable opportunities for capital, the neoliberal state (see Harvey 2005: ch. 3) reshaped institutions and engaged in "accumulation by dispossession" (Harvey 2003: ch. 4) in a number of ways. Privatization, deregulation, labour flexibility, capital mobility, and free trade are important weapons in the neoliberal policy arsenal. Limiting democratic governance through concentrating power in institutions that are well insulated from popular pressure is at the core of its institutional design.

The focus of this chapter is on the way neoliberalism has constructed new institutions that provide a constitutional framework for the new accumulation strategy associated with economic globalization. Before turning to the illustration and assessment of the provisions of international economic agreements, it will be useful to sketch the main themes identified in this analysis of the new constitutional order, particularly its implications for the exercise of authority at the nation-state level. These can be summarized as follows. First, the effect of the neoliberal rules is to insulate (private) capital from governmental (i.e., public) regulation. Second, key powers are institutionally located in ways that are remote from popular pressure and democratic influence. These locations are designed to be minimally accountable, or not accountable at all to popular representatives. Third, the agreements are designed to "lock in" the neoliberal content of globalization by embedding rules in international agreements that will be very difficult to change in the future. Finally, in many cases public authority is replaced by private, or a sharing of authority that was formerly exercised exclusively by public actors.[3] Underpinning these trends is the enhanced structural power of private capital. In this chapter I note this phenomenon (see Gill & Law 1989), but my focus will be on the institutional framework that facilitates that power and helped unleash it in the first place.

The essence of the new constitutionalism has been described as consisting of "efforts to insulate important economic agencies and agents from popular scrutiny and accountability, and thus to narrow democratic control of the economy" (Gill 1992: 269). Stephen Gill leaves no doubt that this reflects sustained activity on the part of capitalist elites (279). More systematically, the new constitutionalism accomplishes this by seeking to embed the neoliberal capitalist model as the universal model. Adam Harmes (2006: 727–37) outlines the use of "legal-juridical" institutions, which by definition are more remote from popular pressure than executive or legislative ones. They are still more remote if they are international rather than national, and private rather than public (McBride 2006). Similarly, Ran Hirschl (2004: 72–73) notes a global trend toward constitutionalizing enhanced judicial power that, he argues, is part of a broader process of political and economic elites wanting to insulate policy-making from democratic politics.

There have been previous efforts to "lock in" liberal approaches. Historically, the Gold Standard performed this function by ensuring that the adjustment costs of trade imbalances were borne by deflationary monetary policies at the domestic level, by means of measures that created unemployment. Thus labour ultimately bore the burden of adjustment. Similarly today, treaty guarantees of capital mobility create an exit option for capital. This disadvantages labour and ensures that states will compete to attract investment through the adoption of business-friendly policies. In effect, states that sign on to capital mobility provisions exert a self-disciplining effect that limits their potential policy choice (Harmes 2006: 740). Other institutional mechanisms include intellectual property rights (a protectionist deviation from the rhetoric of free trade), direct investor-to-state dispute-resolution mechanisms, and, domestically, central bank independence from political influences.

Taking seriously Ronald Reagan's comment that the Canada–US free trade agreement represented a "new economic constitution" for North America, Stephen Clarkson (1993) used the concept of "constitutionalism" to analyze the Canada–US relationship. Both the original free trade agreement and the later North American Free Trade Agreement (NAFTA) "constitutionalized" an earlier, less formal relationship by imposing limits on government actions, defining new rights (especially for capital), and establishing enforcement mechanisms and ratification and amendment procedures—all the paraphernalia, in fact, of a constitutional system. The effect, Clarkson argues, was asymmetrical in that the impact was much greater on Mexico and Canada than on the US, since both were essentially subordinate to the US.

More generally, the issue of whether the US is governed by the new constitutional arrangements has occasioned some debate. On the one hand, Gill (1992: 269, 279) considers that although the US is key to enforcing the new constitutionalism, its role is contradictory since it is not itself subject to its disciplines. This is partly because of the pre-eminent role of the US within the global political and economic system, and partly because of the vicissitudes of American domestic politics. On the other hand, some commentators clearly depict the US as being a part of the new constitutional system. For example, Chantal Thomas (2000) refers to an "international branch" of the US governmental system comprising the World Trade Organization (WTO), NAFTA, and other international agreements. This change, she argues, is so deep that it is "constitutional," amounting to "a fundamental change in the structure of American government," albeit without amending the text of the Constitution. McBride (2003) has similarly referred to "quiet constitutionalism" in Canada, whereby significant changes to the Canadian constitution, broadly defined, have occurred without being discussed or debated in constitutional terms because they have been implemented by means of international trade agreements.

Even before the 2007–2009 crisis, some commentators depicted global trade and investment governance as being in a state of disarray (Stiglitz 2002). This was because there had been no major breakthroughs in trade or investment negotiations since the Uruguay Round of the General Agreement on Tariffs and Trade (GATT) ended in 1994. Disputes—over agricultural subsidies and protection, intellectual property, and investment rules—as well as fundamental questions and protests regarding inequality and fairness in the global trading system, and the social dislocations associated with globalization produced paralysis in the further development of the world trading system. The perception of crisis in global economic governance has, of course, been heightened by the very real financial and economic crisis. Efforts to rethink, reform, or resist the existing structures may accelerate. However, it is also true that many aspects of the new constitutionalism have already been embedded in multiple and overlapping venues, and they will be hard to dislodge.

I will illustrate *global* new constitutionalism using two examples: the global financial architecture, on the one hand, and the trade governance through the WTO on the other. In reality, there are numerous other institutions also involved in the system of global economic governance. In some cases, like the Organization for Economic Cooperation and Development (OECD) and the International Labour Organization (ILO), their decisions lack enforcement mechanisms. In others, such as the International Monetary Fund (IMF) and World Bank,[4] policies have tended to be imposed on developing countries rather than on developed ones. However, the WTO has enforcement mechanisms that are binding on both developed and developing countries.

Regional analysis will focus on NAFTA. Though much more limited in scope than the European Union, the agreement can serve to illustrate the asymmetries of the new constitutionalism. *Bilateral* examples are often omitted entirely from discussions of the new constitutionalism, despite the plethora of bilateral investment treaties (BITs) that have emerged and the inclusion of investment chapters in bilateral free trade agreements (see Blackwood & McBride 2006). I discuss such agreements since they contain the same type of enforceable provisions that are found in broader agreements, and so, for the parties involved, the treaties' contents become binding as far as state actions toward the other signatory are concerned. Finally, I provide examples of *domestic* or *national* new constitutionalism. By this I do not mean how domestic institutions are affected directly by the provisions of international agreements. Rather, in some countries the constitutional order, formal or informal, has been changed in anticipation of entering the new global order or as a result of neoliberal globalist thinking.

GLOBAL NEW CONSTITUTIONALISM: THE FINANCIAL ARCHITECTURE

The "international financial architecture" (IFA) consists of a web of public and private forums, institutions, and organizations, which together play varied, overlapping, and/or discrete roles in the functioning of capital markets. This group includes international financial institutions (for example, the IMF, World Bank, the BIS,[5] and regional development banks[6]), private regulatory and standard-setting bodies (such as the International Accounting Standards Board and rating agencies), international organizations (various UN agencies), and multilateral forums (including the G7 and the OECD). Until the financial and economic crisis struck in the fall of 2008, proposals to change the IFA largely focused on increasing the oversight and responsibility of some bodies, such as private regulatory and standard-setting organizations, restructuring others, and creating new institutions in order to cover gaps left by the current patchwork composition of the IFA, such as creating a world bankruptcy court (Ocampo 1999).

Debates around the effectiveness of global financial governance gained importance in the late 1990s following a series of spectacular, and mostly unpredicted, financial crises in emerging markets (such as Mexico in 1994–95, East Asia in 1997–98, Russia in 1998, Turkey in 2000, and Argentina in 2001–03) (Kenen 2001). This prompted much discussion of the IFA, motivated in large part by the perception that crises in international capital markets might become chronic recurring events, and because of the tendency for contagion to spread to areas that were seemingly unrelated to the original investor panic (Auernheimer 2003). As a result, it became widely recognized that an overhaul (or at the very least, some alteration) of the IFA would be needed to ensure greater stability in capital markets. Clearly these efforts were overtaken by the magnitude of the crisis of 2008, though doubtless discussions will intensify as the crisis evolves.

The IMF is at the centre of the debate, as it is the institution that has taken on the bulk of the responsibility for providing the large sums of money required to bail out countries facing financial crisis, and it also designs (with the assistance of the debtor) the conditionality that is attached to this funding. Its policies have contributed to discrediting the neoliberal hegemony that is now more broadly under challenge. During the Asian financial crisis, tight monetary policies were imposed as a means of avoiding a currency collapse, yet high interest rates served only to create massive amounts of foreign currency debt and led to the bankruptcy of many local corporations since they could no longer meet their debt obligations (Story 2003: 27). Furthermore, as Story comments, fiscal tightening exacerbated the crisis domestically, yet it was deemed necessary in order to finance bank bailouts. Joseph Stiglitz, among others, has suggested that IMF recommendations compounded the crisis (Underhill & Zhang 2003), although it might be argued that, viewed as policies focused on bailing out investors and limiting the damage to confidence in international financial markets, they served their purpose, at least temporarily.

Until 2008, debate on the IFA and the IMF was largely monopolized by technocratic suggestions, such as enhanced standards and transparency, as well as by national policy-oriented suggestions that placed the onus on domestic reform within emerging market economies. For instance, initial suggestions for reform of the IFA were issued by the G7 following the Halifax summit of 1995, where it called for crisis prevention through the adoption of sound monetary and fiscal policies within each country, as well as enhanced surveillance of national economic policies, financial market events, and data dissemination (Pelaez & Pelaez 2005). Over the years this consensus grew, and it became standard for developing countries to be "urged to adopt measures such as tight national prudential regulations to manage debt, higher stocks of international reserves and contingent lines as a safeguard against speculative attacks, and tight monetary and fiscal policies to secure market confidence, while maintaining an open capital account and convertibility" (Akyuz 2000: 2). Surveillance of standards of best practice implementation falls to the IMF, as Article IV, section 3b, of its Articles of Agreement requires that its members submit information on monetary and fiscal policies, exchange-rate policy, and structural policies (Pelaez & Pelaez 2005: 69). The IMF is also responsible for publishing best-practice standards of its own.

However, technocratic and national regulations-focused proposals overlook larger structural problems with international financial markets. The problem of financial crisis and contagion is now clear, as is the inadequacy of the global governance arrangements in the financial sector. Globalization of financial markets and deregulation of capital flows were not accompanied by the creation of a corresponding set of institutions to match the new accumulation regime. Instead, older multilateral institutions created during an era of embedded liberalism were reformed on an ad hoc basis, and the newer bodies that did emerge were hardly sufficient to cover all the gaps and to meet new challenges given the speed, complexity, and information density of international financial markets. However, none of this is surprising given that the neoliberal regime, which relies on accumulation by dispossession, in large part generated through deregulated financial markets, required a replacement of public guidance and oversight with decentralized private authority. Thus, the crisis of global financial governance and the IFA is not the product of a technical failure of institutional design but rather a reflection of an underlying contradiction within the neoliberal regime of accumulation.

GLOBAL NEW CONSTITUTIONALISM: THE WTO

Together with the International Monetary Fund and the World Bank, the World Trade Organization stands at the centre of global economic governance. All three are firm advocates of what has become known as neoliberal globalization. The WTO's predecessor, the General Agreement on Tariffs and Trade (GATT), was equally as premised on liberal principles but was more limited in scope, less intrusive into national autonomy, and less able to enforce its decisions.

When the WTO emerged from the Uruguay Round, the last of successive rounds of revisions of the GATT, it marked a significant intensification of the liberalization of world trade, the extension of trade to new areas, and a greater capacity for enforcement.[7] Ostensibly the changes were in response to states' increased resort to non-tariff barriers, continued protection in agriculture, textiles, and services, and perceptions that enforcement mechanisms were inadequate (Cohn 2000: 214). The transformation has been described as one from a system of shallow or negative integration based on reciprocal reduction of border measures (GATT) into "'deeper,' positive or 'behind the border' integration which can require analysis of almost any national policy likely to have spillover or external effects across borders" (Wolfe 1996: 692–93). The driving force behind the enhanced agreement was the United States, which had resorted to aggressive trade tactics in the 1980s in response to both a persistent trade deficit and the pressures of its own multinational corporations for guaranteed access to foreign markets and investment opportunities. Picciotto (2003: 379–80) argues that the US has vigorously pursued the interests of its multinationals, especially in areas like pharmaceuticals and the media and cultural sectors, using the US Trade Representative's office and legislation such as Section 301 of the Trade Act. Since the EU adopted its own version of Section 301, now known as the Trade Barriers Regulation, European big business has been similarly protected in its quest for market access.

The WTO agreements "are almost entirely concerned with setting limits ... on national state regulation" (Picciotto 2003: 377) and go well beyond traditional trade issues such as tariffs and anti-dumping to permit challenges to national regulations on consumer, environmental or health-protection measures, efforts to regulate foreign investment, and cover services and other areas formerly beyond the reach of trade agreements. For the most part, the WTO was deliberately more intrusive into the affairs of nation-states, however, through proscribing measures rather than prescribing them. It featured strengthened dispute-resolution procedures (as compared to GATT), measures to increase transparency and achieve better coordination (such as the trade policy review mechanism), and an agreement to hold biannual ministerial meetings.

Under the WTO's dispute-settlement mechanism there has been a significant change in procedures. Once a member country initiates a panel hearing to determine if another country has contravened a WTO agreement, the panel acts quickly. Decisions can be appealed, but, once confirmed, the panel's decision must be implemented or compensation paid. Turning down a panel decision now requires a consensus. In the event that a country does not comply, the WTO can authorize retaliatory action (see Das 1998: ch. 21; Valihora 1998). Steven Shrybman (1999) identifies two themes that emerge from WTO panel decisions: "The first is the expansive reading given to rules that limit government options that might (even indirectly) interfere with trade. The second, the exceedingly narrow interpretation given trade provisions that might create space for environmental, cultural or conservation exceptions to the free trade orthodoxy" (17–18). These decisions express a hostility to state intervention in the economy that is characteristic of neoliberal understandings of the proper sphere for state action. They serve to reinforce domestic tendencies to neoliberalism and to raise the barrier for any governments contemplating an alternative economic strategy.

A number of policies that could be ingredients of industrial strategy, such as domestic-content regulations on foreign investment or the use of Crown corporations for non-commercial, public-policy reasons, are prohibited or rendered more difficult to use. Measures regulating national security, health, or the environment may be permitted as long as they are the least trade-restrictive measures that could accomplish their purpose. The WTO agreements apply to provincial and local governments, and the national or federal governments undertake to pursue reasonable measures to secure compliance, even where these are matters of provincial jurisdiction. The evidence principally suggests that trade agreements have had limited impact on the functioning of federal systems, though it is recognized that centralizing pressures are possible (Rocher & DiGiacamo 2008).

The architecture of the WTO reflects the neoliberal concern with constraining the state and freeing investors and markets from state intervention. In the case of the TRIPS (Trade-Related Aspects of Intellectual Property Rights) agreement, states must defend the rights of investors to enjoy their intellectual property rights. The WTO agreements serve to sustain and enhance neoliberal measures taken at the domestic level. As part of international law, they have a quasi-judicial and quasi-constitutional aura. Therefore, their impact is harder to challenge than ordinary domestic legislation. The WTO also serves to "legalize" formerly non-binding agreements that states had entered into by importing their provisions into the enforceable WTO agreements. Examples include the food standards established by the Codex Alimentarius Commission and various intellectual property agreements such as the Berne Copyright Convention and the Paris Industrial Property Convention (Picciotto 2003: 383–84).

Moreover, although the WTO is an agreement amongst states, and the dispute-settlement provisions require states to bring and respond to allegations that WTO provisions have been contravened, there is considerable role for private interests within the apparently state-to-state processes. This can take place through fact-finding exercises in which the providers of information are private interests (Cass 2001), presentation of *amicus curiae* briefs, and intense cooperation between states and corporations in preparing or responding to cases, a relationship that has been depicted by Shaffer (2003) as a public–private partnership.

REGIONAL NEW CONSTITUTIONALISM: THE CASE OF NAFTA

Under the WTO, states have the capacity to establish regional free-trade areas such as NAFTA and custom unions such as the EU. Such agreements must at least meet WTO standards, and, in reality, there would be little point to negotiating them unless they exceeded WTO standards of liberalization or coverage (Lee 2001: 3).

The inclusion in NAFTA of far-reaching investment protections established a linkage between trade and investment that had not previously been made in multilateral forums in a way acceptable to the US. NAFTA served as a precedent, and to some degree a template, for US bilateral investment treaties and investment clauses in free trade agreements. However, the unanticipated high incidence of investment complaints against the US itself, and the perception that foreign investors had more rights with respect to the US government than did domestic investors, provoked a partial rethink, and US policy has evolved. The change in policy is relatively minor and seems aimed primarily at modifying the balance between investment protection and retention of states' rights to regulate in the public interest by strengthening the rights of states to a certain extent (Gagné & Morin 2006).

NAFTA Chapter 11 covers, subject to certain reservations, all forms of investment interests. It prohibits a wide range of performance requirements and creates investor rights in dispute resolution. NAFTA embeds foreign investors' rights as equivalent to the rights of states in some areas and provides (in Article 1136.7) that investor-state disputes "shall be considered to arise out of a commercial relationship." This pre-commits the signatories to treat disputes between themselves and foreign investors as commercial rather than regulatory matters and to have such disputes settled according to what is essentially a private, international commercial-arbitration system. Article 105 commits the signatories to "ensure that all necessary measures are taken in order to give effect to the provisions of this agreement ... including their observance ... by state and provincial governments." Potentially this could have an impact on federal–subnational relations in federal states, although, so far, it seems merely to have stimulated greater cooperation between levels of government in the negotiation of such agreements. Chapter 11 prohibits a wide range of performance requirements and creates investor rights in dispute resolution. The lengthy list of prohibited performance-requirement measures includes requirements to export a certain proportion of goods or services produced, or achieve any specified level or balance of foreign-exchange earnings, or target specific export markets. The agreement bars domestic content or purchasing requirements, as well as provisions that would insist on transfers of technology.

The North American Free Trade Agreement thus inhibits the development of an industrial policy, other than free trade, in signatory states. As a result, investors may focus on areas of "natural" comparative advantage. The restrictions are widely held to be less onerous on the US than on Mexico and Canada, partly because Canada and Mexico have historically relied more on active state policies (see Bowles et al. 2008), partly because power differentials make it more feasible for the US to ignore the agreements if it is in its own interests, and partly because much US industrial policy has taken place under the national-security rubric—an area exempted from full coverage by NAFTA and the WTO (Schloemann & Ohlhoff 1999).

In addition, at the behest of the US, national sovereignty was retained through Article 1902, which reserves a country's rights to "apply its own anti-dumping law and countervailing duty law to goods imported from the territory" of other parties to the agreement. It was the desire to escape precisely this exercise of (US) national autonomy that motivated many to support the original FTA with the United States, although that agreement failed to deliver on the goal of rendering Canada exempt from the aggressive use of those measures by the United States. Article 1902 further guarantees that dispute panels will be applying national laws in these areas. Ortiz Mena (2002: 427) argues that the novelty of the system, first introduced in the Canada–US Free Trade Agreement, lies in its formal inter-state characteristics being embodied in a "private party system" in which the chief actors, apart from governments, are importers and exporters. The US has vigorously applied anti-dumping and countervailing duties—over a thousand investigations since 1980, with nearly 300 countermeasures currently in place (Macrory 2002: 3). The Softwood Lumber case affords numerous examples of opportunities for private political influence on the part of vulnerable but powerful economic interests (see Zhang 2007).

Cases normally begin when a domestic industry files a petition. This process has been described as a search "that sooner or later will provide a technicality that generates the 'right' result" (J. Michael Finger, cited in Gastle 1995: 740). This situation results from the provisions of Section 301 of the US trade law which, while not providing direct access, since US private interests must first request action by the US Trade Representative, nevertheless "affords substantial protection to the American private party" (Gal-Or 1998: 22). Indeed, the same point can certainly be made about Canada and Mexico. Chapter 19 provides for a review, if requested, by a binational panel selected from a roster of potential panelists. Private interests such as business have standing, as long as they would do so under the law of the importing country (NAFTA Article 19.04.7).

BILATERAL NEW CONSTITUTIONALISM

Bilateral Investment Agreements mushroomed in a context where periodic efforts to negotiate multilateral investment agreements foundered (see Blackwood & McBride 2006). After the setback at the Seattle WTO ministerial in 1999, multilateral trade initiatives at both the WTO and the Free Trade Area of the Americas (FTAA) negotiations made little progress, and the negotiation of bilateral trade agreements, increasingly including investment chapters, came to be viewed favourably by US trade authorities. After the WTO failure at Cancun, then-US Trade Representative Robert Zoellick commented, "The US strategy on trade has sought to press ahead on global trade liberalization through the WTO. And we hoped that others would, too. And the message we received in Cancun from them was, 'not now.' The US trade strategy, however, includes advances on multiple fronts. We have free trade agreements with six countries right now. And we're negotiating free trade agreements with 14 more" (US Department of State 2003).

With the earlier BITs, but more comprehensively with NAFTA, the settlement of investment disputes through the international commercial arbitration system underwent a significant transformation. In the past, states did agree to specific instances of binding arbitration but retained final authority because they did not concede general *a priori* consent to arbitration. In the case of many BITs, however, and then NAFTA, this is precisely what was conceded. The result was that investor–state arbitration is transformed "from a modified form of commercial arbitration into a system to control the exercise of [the state's] regulatory authority with respect to investors as a group" (Van Harten 2005: 608).

Earlier multilateral initiatives ended in failure or, at best, partial success. This is true whether the goal was to assert the rights and sovereignty of host countries, or to protect the rights of investors. The impasse over this issue is thus a long-standing one. The bilateral route can be effective, for capital, in securing far-reaching investment protection and limiting virtually any constraint on investment. It nonetheless falls short of providing the stability, predictability, and efficiency that a multilateral regime could provide. It is a "second-best" solution from the point of view of multinational capital and of capital-exporting states. And for the Americans, the variety of provisions in BITs, though certainly tending strongly toward liberating capital from state interference, nonetheless means the failure of their objective of using BITs to establish their own tough standards of investment protection as customary international law (see Sornarajah 2004: 158–59, 205–07; Smythe 1998; for a contrasting view see Lowenfeld 2002: 486–88).

The goals of US investment policy, expressed substantially in agreements such as NAFTA and the US BITs, and (less satisfactorily from the US viewpoint) in the WTO's Agreement on Trade-Related Investment Measures (TRIMS), have been consistent over a long period. Protection of US investors abroad is one goal, but it seems to take second place to a desire to establish the US view of investment rights as normal, customary international law. DeLuca (1994: 265) summarizes the official goals of the US BITs program as "reinforcement of the US view of international law, protection of existing US investments and reaffirmation of the importance of protecting American investment in US foreign policy." This finds expression in strongly protective stances on all of the key issues: the scope of investments that are covered and the breadth of the definition of investment; the degree of regulatory control that states retain; the standard of treatment to be accorded foreign investment; the right of or limits to establish an investment in the territory of the host state; the performance requirements that can be imposed on a foreign investor; issues of expropriation, nationalization and compensation, and the standards to be followed; whether recourse is available to international arbitration and whether general state consent to have investor-state disputes arbitrated outside the host country is granted.

There is some common ground between capital-exporting states, but the US is distinctive in its attachment to the right of entry, or establishment for foreign investors, and on the prohibition of performance requirements that host states may wish to impose on investors. In promoting this agenda the US has been aided by events in the global economy. Falling commodity prices, the onset of the global debt crisis, conditional lending by IFIs and private banks, the collapse of Bretton Woods, and the promulgation of the Washington Consensus—these all coalesced to create conditions amenable to the sacrifice of control over inward flows of foreign direct investment. A detailed account of the conditions giving rise to these events is not possible here, but their role in explaining the spread of BITs should not be underestimated.

The US is not alone in its view of what a good international investment-protection regime should look like. David Schneiderman (2000) uses the lens of new constitutionalism to analyze Canada's role as a participant in a number of bilateral investment treaties. He finds that Canadian policy has adopted the same stringent standards that have been characteristic of US trade and investment policy. He explores the degree to which the bilateral investment treaty between Canada and South Africa incorporates NAFTA principles. Schneiderman demonstrates how the agreement has constitutional implications for the Republic of South Africa because its provisions are discordant with the South African constitution's provisions pertaining to property rights. Similarly, a proposed free trade agreement between Canada and Colombia involved bartering "a slice of Columbia's sovereignty.... The proposed deal [would] require Colombia to enforce international labour standards under penalty of sanctions" (Frankel 2008: A13).

The great advantage of bilateral investment treaties for the developed countries is that favourable asymmetries of power can be used to extract maximum concessions from developing countries. Most BITs have been between developed (capital-exporting) and developing (capital-importing) countries. In multilateral negotiations, developing countries can unite to effectively resist at least some of the demands made by the developed world. In contrast, bilaterally their position is much weaker. Summing up the multilateral versus bilateral options for developing countries, Shadlen (2005) concluded that in both cases developing countries sacrificed policy autonomy in exchange for market access. In bilateral agreements the trade-off was intensified, and while developing countries might make more gains in terms of market access, they had to make much deeper concessions in their ability to regulate investment and intellectual property rights.

DOMESTIC NEW CONSTITUTIONALISM

Adjusting Constitutions

Adjustments in national constitutions in the face of globalization and trade agreements have been noted in the literature. For example, McBride (2003) has argued that Canada's domestic exercise of political authority was affected in four ways: already existing trends toward the dominance of decision-making by the executive branch were reinforced, the intra-bureaucratic hierarchy of ministries and agencies altered in favour of economic and trade ministries, federal supervisory power over provinces increased somewhat, and the courts lost jurisdiction in certain areas. Similarly, Schneiderman (2004: 69) has noted that national constitutional regimes are under pressure to foster the neoliberal globalization model and, based on an analysis of a number of Supreme Court of Canada decisions, considers that "the Court, has, on occasion, gone too far in tilting constitutional interpretation in ways consonant with the values of economic globalization by limiting unreasonably legislative power over economic subjects." Similarly, Kelsey (1999) reports that the Philippine Supreme Court interpreted the constitution in ways that ensured that imperatives of economic globalization would trump references to economic nationalism in the constitution. Canada's long-running saga of proposed constitutional changes (from the 1960s to the 1990s) was focused on the relations of English and French Canada, Quebec and the rest of the country, regional and federal-provincial issues. Even the entrenchment of rights and freedoms was partly based on these considerations, since the new Charter of Rights and Freedoms was conceived as a focus of national identity and, consequently, national unity in the face of secessionist tendencies. However, side-by-side with these concerns were others that spoke to the political economy of new constitutionalism. For example, when the federal government unveiled its post–Meech Lake constitutional proposals (see McBride 1993), they included measures that, viewed from a neoliberal perspective, would better enable Canada to compete in the new global economy (Canada 1991: 1) by deterring its governments from indulging in certain policy activities. Thus the mandate of the Bank of Canada would have been changed to one exclusively focused on inflation control, there would have been greater harmonization of federal and provincial fiscal policy to the dictates of monetary policy, and property rights would have been entrenched. This round of constitutional negotiations ultimately failed, but the inclusion of these proposals indicates how globalization has influenced constitutional thinking.

In Canada the federal level of government has limited ability to implement international agreements where their subjects touch on provincial jurisdiction. Mexico's constitution, on the other hand, has provisions enabling the federal government to bring under its jurisdiction matters that are within the states' competence and also provides that the laws made by the Congress and provisions of treaties shall be the supreme law of the land. The Mexican Supreme Court of Justice recently ruled that there is a hierarchy of law in Mexico—the constitution, followed by international treaties that have been approved by a majority of the Senate, and finally laws made by the Congress (Rocher & DiGiacomo 2008: 200–01).

Central Bank Independence

Central banks play important roles in economic governance, including setting monetary policy, controlling the money supply, responding to economic and financial market conditions, regulating the banking system, and issuing the currency (Picker 2007: 5). When governments grant autonomy or independence to central banks, they abdicate control over important policy areas central to the management of the economy. The trend in the neoliberal globalization period was toward increasing levels of central bank independence from governments. The Cukierman Index of Central Bank Independence (CBI), 1989–2000 (Polillo & Guillén 2005), captures the extent to which the central bank is independent from governmental power, and it is also most widely used. The index is a continuous score ranging between zero and one, where one indicates maximum independence. It is obtained by aggregating 16 characteristics of central bank charters describing four aspects: procedures concerning the governor of the central bank (appointment, dismissal, and legal term of office); the relationship between the government and the bank, and the location of authority over monetary policies; objectives of the central bank; and the relationship between the government and the bank in terms of borrowing. For many countries in the current period there is an upward trajectory measured by this indicator of central bank independence—indeed, 54 of the 91 countries covered by the index showed increased levels of CBI, 36 remained unchanged, and in only one (Malta) did the central bank become less independent. Canada remained the same (0.45 on the index), as did the US (0.48), but the UK jumped from 0.27 to 0.47 in 1997–98, and Mexico increased from 0.34 to 0.56 in 1992–93. Germany represented the paradigmatic case at 0.92.

CONCLUSION

A considerable network of institutions of global economic governance exists. Some are informal and others more rigid. Taken collectively, they undermine or usurp national constitutions, and in the process create a two-tiered world of constitutional rights: rights for transnational corporations (TNCs) at the global or regional levels, but no general political or social rights at these levels. The more formal of these governance mechanisms include international trade and investment treaties, which, I have argued here, have a constitutional impact in that they prohibit certain state actions and condition states' economic behaviour.

The construction of this highly elaborate system of binding and enforceable legal framework has been pushed by internationally oriented capital and by leading states, especially the US. Its effect is to lock in neoliberal rules for global economic transactions by making these more difficult to change than would otherwise be the case.

The new constitution that is created is not complete, and there are certainly signs of resistance to it. These may be expected to intensify if the economic crisis is prolonged. Its impact on national policy capacity may be inversely related to level of development; that is, it has more impact on less developed countries. Its reach is thus hierarchical, and it can be seen as one instrument by which the developed countries dominate the less developed. Like any constitution it operates to influence, but does not absolutely determine, the plans of regulators and other decision makers. Their outputs influence the world economy and are subject to challenge and sanction if they are found to violate the terms of the economic agreements. And this influence has also been felt in the developed world as one element in a system of power that strives to maintain and advance neoliberal hegemony.

NOTES

1　The author gratefully acknowledges funding from the Social Sciences and Humanities Research Council of Canada (Standard Grant 410–2006–1184) and is grateful for the valuable research assistance of Heather Whiteside.

2　Social structures of accumulation (SSA) theory shares some features with regulation theory, but comparison need not detain us as the SSA approach here is being used in a heuristic fashion to highlight the correspondence between an emerging institutional structure and the needs of capital accumulation.

3　For more on the private authority issue see the chapter by Cutler in this volume (Chapter 3).

4　For useful overviews see Lee (2002) on the IMF and Griffin (2006) on the World Bank.

5　The Bank for International Settlements (BIS) was originally established in 1930 to deal with German war-reparation payments, and shortly thereafter adopted the role of a "central bank for central banks" (depositing and investing official reserves and providing some small short-term loans to central banks). It is also now involved with "conduct[ing] its own research in financial and monetary economics and contribut[ing] to the collection, compilation, and dissemination of economic and financial statistics" (Pelaez & Pelaez 2005).

6　International development banks, such as the World Bank Group (the International Bank for Reconstruction and Development, the International Finance Corporation, and the International Development Association) and the regional development banks (e.g., Asian Development Bank, Inter-American Development Bank, the European Bank for Reconstruction and Development), not only provide credit and loans for projects, but also provide funds for financial crisis bailouts, implement conditionality, and provide technical advice and monitoring. The World Bank also collaborates with the IMF in the Financial Sector Assistance Program, which evaluates the financial sectors of countries (Pelaez & Pelaez 2005).

7　The US had been the leading force in successive rounds of trade negotiations. Its role is based on the perception that real economic gains to the US result from trade liberalization. For one view of this see Bradford, Grieco, and Hufbauer (2006).

REFERENCES

Akyuz, Yilmaz. 2000. "The Debate on the International Financial Architecture: Reforming the Reformers." United Nations Conference on Trade and Development. No. 148, April.

Auernheimer, Leonardo. 2003. *International Financial Markets: The Challenge of Globalization*. Chicago: University of Chicago Press.

Blackwood, Elizabeth, and Stephen McBride. 2006. "Investment as the Achilles Heel of Globalization?: The Ongoing Conflict between the Rights of Capital and the Rights of States." *Policy and Society* 25(3): 43–67.

Bowles, Paul, Ray Broomhill, Theresa Guttierez-Haces, and Stephen McBride (eds.). 2008. *International Trade and Neoliberalism: Towards Reperipheralisation in Australia, Canada and Mexico?* London: Routledge.

Bradford, Scott C., Paul L. Grieco, and Gary Clyde Hufbauer. 2006. "The Payoff to America from Globalisation." *The World Economy* 29(7): 893–916.

Canada. 1991. *Shaping Canada's Future Together: Proposals.* Ottawa: Government of Canada.

Cass, D.Z. 2001. "The 'Constitutionalization' of International Trade Law: Judicial Norm-Generation as the Engine of Constitutional Development in International Trade." *European Journal of International Law* 12(1): 39–75.

Clarkson, Stephen. 1993. "Constitutionalizing the Canadian-American Relationship." In Duncan Cameron and Mel Watkins (eds.), *Canada Under Free Trade.* Toronto: Lorimer. 3–20.

Cohn, Theodore. 2000. *Global Political Economy: Theory and Practice.* New York: Longman.

Das, B.L. 1998. *An Introduction to the WTO Agreements.* Penang: Third World Network.

DeLuca, Dallas. 1994. "Trade-Related Investment Measures: U.S. Efforts to Shape a Pro-Business World Legal System." *Journal of International Affairs* 48(1): 251–76.

Fairris, David. 1999. "Social Structures of Accumulation." In Phillip Anthony O'Hara (ed.), *Encyclopedia of Political Economy.* New York and London: Routledge. 1065–68.

Frankel, Ken. 2008. "A Trade Deal is good for Colombian Human Rights." *Globe and Mail* 8 January: A13.

Gagné, Gilbert, and Jean-Frédéric Morin. 2006. "The Evolving American Policy on Investment Protection: Evidence from Recent FTAs and the 2004 Model BIT." *Journal of International Economic Law* 9(2): 357–82.

Gal-Or, Noemi. 1998. "Private Party Direct Access: A Comparison of NAFTA and the EU." *Boston College International and Comparative Law Review* 1(21): 1–40.

Gastle, Charles M. 1995. "Policy Alternatives for Reform of the Free Trade Agreement of the Americas: Dispute Settlement Mechanisms." *Law and Policy in International Business* 26: 735–823.

Gill, Stephen. 1992. "Economic Globalization and the Internationalization of Authority: Limits and Contradictions." *Geoforum* 23(3): 269–83.

Gill, Stephen, and David Law. 1989. "Global Hegemony and the Structural Power of Capital." *International Studies Quarterly* 33(4): 475–99.

Harmes, Adam. 2006. "Neoliberalism and Multilevel Governance." *Review of International Political Economy* 13(5): 725–49.

Harvey, David. 2003. *The New Imperialism.* Oxford: Oxford University Press.

——. 2005. *A Brief History of Neoliberalism.* Oxford: Oxford University Press.

———. 2006. *The Limits to Capital*. London: Verso.

Hirschl, Ran. 2004. "The Political Origins of the New Constitutionalism." *Indiana Journal of Global Legal Studies* 11: 71–108.

Kelsey, Jane. 1999. "Global Economic Policy-Making: A New Constitutionalism?" *Otago Law Review* 9: 535–55.

Kenen, Peter B. 2001. *The International Financial Architecture: What's New? What's Missing?* Washington, DC: Peterson Institute for International Economics.

Kotz, David M. 1994. "Interpreting the Social Structure of Accumulation Theory." In David M. Kotz, Terrence McDonough, and Michael Reich (eds.), *Social Structures of Accumulation: The Political Economy of Growth and Crisis*. Cambridge: Cambridge University Press. 50–71.

Kotz, David M., Terrence McDonough, and Michael Reich (eds.). 1994. *Social Structures of Accumulation: The Political Economy of Growth and Crisis*. Cambridge: Cambridge University Press.

Lee, Marc. 2001. *Inside the Fortress: What's Going on at the FTAA Negotiations*. Ottawa: Canadian Centre for Policy Alternatives.

Macrory, Patrick. 2002. *NAFTA Chapter 19: A Successful Experiment in International Trade Dispute Resolution*. C.D. Howe Institute Commentary, No. 168, September. <http://www.worldtradelaw.net/articles/macrorychapter19.pdf>.

McBride, Stephen. 2006. "Reconfiguring Sovereignty: NAFTA Chapter 11 Dispute Settlement Procedures and the Issue of Public-Private Authority." *Canadian Journal of Political Science* 39(4): 755–75.

———. 2005. *Paradigm Shift: Globalization and the Canadian State*. 2nd ed. Halifax: Fernwood.

———. 2003. "Quiet Constitutionalism in Canada: The International Political Economy of Domestic Institutional Change." *Canadian Journal of Political Science* 36(2): 251–73.

———. 1993. "Renewed Federalism as an Instrument of Competitiveness: Liberal Political Economy and the Canadian Constitution." *International Journal of Canadian Studies* 7–8: 187–205.

McDonough, Terrence. 1994. "Social Structures of Accumulation, Contingent History and Stages of Capitalism." In David M. Kotz, Terrence McDonough, and Michael Reich (eds.), *Social Structures of Accumulation: The Political Economy of Growth and Crisis*. Cambridge: Cambridge University Press. 72–85.

Ocampo, José Antonio. 1999. *Reforming the International Financial Architecture: Consensus and Divergence*. Santiago: United Nations.

O'Hara, Phillip Anthony. 2006. *Growth and Development in the Global Political Economy: Social Structures of Accumulation and Modes of Regulation*. London and New York: Routledge.

Ortiz Mena, Antonio. 2002. "Dispute Settlement Under NAFTA." In Edward J. Chambers and Peter H. Smith (eds.), *NAFTA in the New Millennium*. Edmonton: University of Alberta Press. 425–46.

Pelaez, Carlos M., and Carlos A. Pelaez. 2005. *International Financial Architecture*. Basingstoke: Macmillan.

Picciotto, Sol. 2003. "Private Rights vs Public Standards in the WTO." *Review of International Political Economy* 10(3): 377–405.

Picker, Anne D. 2007. *International Economic Indicators and Central Banks*. Hoboken, NJ: Wiley.

Polillo, Simone, and Mauro F. Guillén. 2005. "Globalization Pressures and the State: The Global Spread of Central Bank Independence." *American Journal of Sociology* 110(6): 1764–1802.

Rocher, François, and Gordon DiGiacomo. 2008. "National Institutions in North America: US, Canadian and Mexican Federalism." In Yasmeen Abu-Laban, Radha Jhhappan, and François Rocher (eds.), *Politics in North America: Redefining Continental Relations*. Peterborough, ON: Broadview Press. 195–220.

Schloemann, Hannes L., and Stefan Ohlhoff. 1999. "'Constitutionalization' and Dispute Settlement in the WTO: National Security as an Issue of Competence." *American Journal of International Law* 93(2): 424–51.

Schneiderman, David. 2004. "Canadian Constitutionalism, the Rule of Law and Economic Globalization." In P. Hughes and P.A. Molinari (eds.), *Participatory Justice in a Global Economy: The New Rule of Law?* Montreal: Les éditions Themis. 65–85.

——. 2000. "Investment Rules and the New Constitutionalism: Interlinkages and Disciplinary Effects." *Law and Social Inquiry* 25(3): 757–87.

Shadlen, Kenneth C. 2005. "Exchanging Development for Market Access? Deep Integration and Industrial Policy under Multilateral and Regional-bilateral Trade Agreements." *Review of International Political Economy* 12(5): 750–75.

Shaffer, Gregory. 2003. *Defending Interests: Public-Private Partnerships in WTO Litigation*. Washington, DC: Brookings Institution Press.

Shrybman, Steven. 1999. *Citizen's Guide to the World Trade Organization*. Toronto: Lorimer.

Smythe, Elizabeth. 1998. "Your Place or Mine? States, International Organizations and the Negotiation of Investment Rules." *Transnational Corporations* 7(3): 85–120.

Sornarajah, M. 2004. *The International Law on Foreign Investment*. 2nd ed. Cambridge and New York: Cambridge University Press.

Stiglitz, Joseph. 2002. *Globalization and its Discontents*. New York: Norton.

Story, Jonathan. 2003. "Reform of the International Financial Architecture: What Has Been Written?" In Geoffrey R.D. Underhill and Xiaoke Zhang (eds.), *International Financial Governance Under Stress*. Cambridge: Cambridge University Press. 21–40.

Thomas, Chantal. 2000. "Constitutional Change and International Government." *Hastings Law Journal* 52(1): 1–46.

Underhill, Geoffrey R.D., and Xiaoke Zhang (eds.). 2003. *International Financial Governance Under Stress.* Cambridge: Cambridge University Press.

United States. Department of State. 2003. US Trade Representative Robert B. Zoellick, US Secretary of Agriculture Ann Veneman, Final Press Conference, WTO Fifth Ministerial Meeting, Cancun, Mexico. September 14. <http://www.usinfo.state.gov/topical/econ/wto/03091403.htm>. Accessed 18 January 2004.

Valihora, Michael S. 1998. "Chapter 19 or the WTO's Dispute Settlement Body: A Hobson's Choice for Canada?" *Case Western Reserve Journal of International Law* 39(2/3): 447–88.

Van Harten, Gus 2005. "Private Authority and Transnational Governance: The Contours of the International System of Investor Protection." *Review of International Political Economy* 12(4): 600–23.

Wolfe, Robert. 1996. "Global Trade as a Single Undertaking: The Role of Ministers in the WTO." *International Journal* 51(4): 690–709.

Zhang, Daowei. 2007. *The Softwood Lumber War: Politics, Economics and the Long US-Canadian Trade Dispute.* Washington, DC: Resources for the Future.

3

The Privatization of Authority in the Global Political Economy

A. CLAIRE CUTLER

The idea of private global authority is deeply problematic and gives rise to considerable intellectual anxiety about the nature and role of theory in international relations. This anxiety underscores the pressing need to rethink or "unthink" international theory in the form of what is elsewhere described as a radical political economy critique of transnational economic law (Cutler 2008a). In this chapter I articulate the reasons for this anxiety by identifying a few central conceptual, theoretical, and normative challenges raised by the notion of private global authority. There are major deficiencies in contemporary, popular theorizations of transformations in the global political economy that are commonly associated with privatization and the post-Fordist de- or re-regulation of state authority. My goal here is to set the stage for a more fruitful approach that views private authority through the lenses of critical and transformative social and political theory. Before discussing the intellectual problems with this concept, it is necessary to provide a sense of the origin and empirical richness of proliferating studies of private modes of governance and regulation in the global political economy. The chapter will begin with a brief overview of research on private authority before considering analytical, theoretical, and normative problems with this work and proposing a more fruitful approach through a radical political economy critique.

PRIVATE AUTHORITY AND GOVERNANCE

For some time now, students of international affairs have been record-
ing what many believe to be major transformations in state power and
authority in the world. It is possibly the global political economists, or
international political economists as they were initially called, who first
articulated the expansion of private, non-state power in the world economy. This had been anticipated in studies that explored the relationships between states and corporations (Vernon 1971), by theorists of
transnational relations who were concerned with capturing the significance of transnational business corporations and other non-state actors
in world affairs (Keohane & Nye 1972), in the works of Susan Strange
and others on the changing balance between states, firms, and markets
(Strange 1988, 1996; Stopford & Strange 1991), and more recently in
a growing literature on corporate power (May 2006; Porter and Ronit
2008).[1] These concerns have reflected dissatisfaction with dominant
state-centric understandings of international affairs and began a challenge to conventional analytical and theoretical analyses that is gener-
ating important research (Kobrin 2008).

The beginning of analytical and conceptual concerns with the significance of non-state authority is thus intimately linked to the evolution of international relations theory and to the origins of the subfield
of the international or global political economy. Just as the subfield of
international political economy introduced a new set of actors or agents
and processes for study to the field of international relations, so too did
the field expand to embrace a wider range of problematics, including a
greater diversity of actors and processes. This is not to suggest that the
proper domain and problematic of international relations or international political economy were clearly defined, for there was and remains
considerable contestation over both. The field tended to harden into two
solitudes, with predominantly state-centric and neo-realist analysis of
international political economy occupying one, and studies of the global
political economy inspired by various critical approaches and focusing on a more heterogeneous set of actors and processes occupying the
other. Notwithstanding such contestation, the subfield grew, developing
a self-consciousness that mirrored dominant understanding in the related
fields of political economy, international law, and international organization. This self-consciousness may be summed up as reflecting, at least
amongst mainstream scholars, a faith in neoliberal political economy,
self-regulating markets, and soft law as the templates for governance
and regulation. With the emergence of neoconservative governments in
the UK, US, Canada, and elsewhere, this ethos developed a synergy with

developing beliefs in public-sector management and the overwhelming value of scientific, rational management as the *grundnorms,* or first principles, for organizing the world.

Stephen Gill (2003) has perceptively coined the terms "neoliberal market discipline" and "market civilization" to capture the way in which this ethos worked to reconfigure state–society relations, subordinating localities and societies to the discipline of global and, increasingly, transnational capitalism. Institutions and rules of a private nature proliferated in attempts to regulate greater areas of human activity, while the development and deepening of global and regional trade, investment, monetary, and financial regimes locked private disciplines in by preventing governments from passing local laws or regulations that might in any way impair or restrict the mobility and security of foreign finance, trade, investment, or services (Cutler 2003).

The first publication in international relations of a systematic overview of private global authority (Cutler, Haufler & Porter 1999) focused specifically on the under-researched role of private-sector, corporate non-state actors that are an integral part of global governance.[2] The volume articulated "private authority" as the analytical optic, rejecting ~~wer notions of private international regimes. It provided a typol-~~ ~~authority, identifying informal industry norms and prac-~~ ~~rvice forms, production alliances and subcontractor~~ relationships, business associations, and private international regimes as institutional variations in private authority. Since then, public–private partnerships (PPPs) have been added to the typology (see Börzel & Risse 2005). *Private Authority and International Affairs* also reviewed various explanations for the emergence of private authority, including rationalist, efficiency-based considerations, power-based explanations, and more historically informed trends and systemic developments. It contained chapters on the expansion of private regulation governing online commerce, international trade, communication and information technology, finance, intellectual property, insurance, and maritime transport. The edited volume by Rodney Hall and Thomas Biersteker (2002) followed and further elaborated the idea of private authority, containing chapters on the privatization of authority over electronic commerce, global finance, and the corporate regulation of labour, human rights, and environmental relations. Other works appeared that focused more on non-state actors (see Higgott, Underhill & Bieler 2000; Josselin & Wallace 2001; Ronit & Schneider 2000). These works and other more recent ones reveal that the focus on private authority has been predominantly in economic areas (Graz & Nölke 2008). Possibly the most heavily studied economic areas to date include the governance of finance, accounting and auditing (Porter 1993, 2005a, 2005b; Mügge 2006, 2008; Botzem & Quack 2006), central bank independence (Tsingou 2008), insurance and risk management (Haufler 1997), international commercial arbitration (Cutler 1995; Mattli 2001), intellectual property rights (Sell 2003), international services (Cutler 2008a), global standards (Mattli 2003), forestry management (Cashore, Auld & Newson 2003), secured transactions (Cohen 2007), competition law and policy (Djelic & Kleiner 2006), coordination service firms and bond-rating agencies (Sinclair 2004), the Internet and online commerce (Knill & Lehmkul 2002), investor protection and the global investment regime (Van Harten 2005; Schneiderman 2001), and corporate social responsibility (Cutler 2008b; Haufler 2001; Ougaard 2006). In these areas market mechanisms dominate regulatory efforts, and in some cases there has been increasing heterogeneity in the expansion of hybrid authority in the form of public–private partnerships (Börzel & Risse 2005).

Very little attention has strayed beyond the economic domain, although the Hall and Biersteker (2002) volume contains studies of the moral authority of markets and of non-state religious movements, as well as the illicit private authority of mercenaries and the mafia. Since then, there has been a burgeoning literature on the privatization of security and warfare (Avant 2005; Mandel 2002; Singer 2003), particularly in light of the prevalence of private security firms operating in Iraq, Afghanistan, and elsewhere. Notable as well, are efforts to sharpen the analytical understanding of the conditions under which corporations adopt security responsibilities in zones of conflict (Wolf, Deitelhoff & Engert 2007) and innovative theorizations of the political economy of private security provision (Krahmann 2008) and the role of private security firms in constituting a culture of security and insecurity (Leander 2006). Notwithstanding these novel approaches, the predominant emphasis appears to be on the legal and public policy dimensions of privatized security rather than on theory development (Kinsey 2005; Kontos 2005). Indeed, while growing empirically rich in case studies, the analytical, theoretical, and normative challenges posed by privatized authority, particularly in the security domain, remain fully unexplored (but see Cutler 2010).

ANALYTICAL, THEORETICAL, AND NORMATIVE PROBLEMS

The analysis will now turn to the intellectual anxiety to which the conception of private global authority gives rise. The analytical, theoretical, and normative problems will be approached from two vantage points. The first concerns the failure of studies of private authority to develop social theory that addresses the central analytical and theoretical concerns that the expansion of the authority of private institutions, actors, and processes in the world have for the study of international relations and the global political economy. The second relates to the pressing need to develop a normative agenda that focuses on the political legitimacy and accountability of private authority.

The Need for Social Theory

Social theory "seeks to understand society as a whole (as opposed to particular political forms) ..., distinguishes between and makes generalizations about different kinds of society; and ... is concerned in particular to analyze modernity, the forms of social life which have come to prevail first in the West and increasingly in the rest of the world ..." (Callinicos 1999: 2). Historically, the intellectual focus has been on three main dimensions of social power: the political economy, the ideology justifying power, and the patterns of domination (1). The great social theorists, such as Karl Marx, Emile Durkheim, and Max Weber, analyzed and theorized how these elements of social power interrelated in the constitution of modernity. Their concern, of course, was "indispensible to anyone seeking to make sense of, or to improve [the] world" (1).

In the context of the contemporary global political economy, there is great conceptual and analytical uncertainty with private authority and its relation to more general processes associated with globalization. Indeed, studies of private authority developed alongside studies of globalization, and it is instructive to consider their intersection. Studies of private authority in the regulation or governance of the global political economy share with globalization studies an assumption that there is a profound transformation occurring in the way in which social relations are regulated in the world, although there is a disagreement as to whether the state has been eclipsed or is undergoing a reconstitution. Both studies, however, reflect the recognition that a certain amount of authority to make decisions that matter is being disembedded from national and state controls and is relocating globally or transnationally (Albert 2007: 169; Djelic & Sahlin-Andersson 2006). Some globalization studies focus on the extent to which this transformation is occurring through legalization and juridification (Abbott et al. 2000), others regard it as contingent on transformations in and the compression of spatial-temporal relations (Giddens 1990; Harvey 1990; Robertson 1992), others see the transformation as the unfolding of world history (Gills & Thompson 2006), and yet others regard it as involving the emergence of a global world society (Scholte 2000). However, there is no agreed-upon theory of globalization as "*the* central process driving contemporary social change" (Albert 2005: 171). To put this criticism another way, there is no theoretical agreement about the crucial reference point concerning that which is being globalized. There is general agreement that we are talking about something analytically different from international-ization, but beyond that there is no sense of the social system or order that frames and gives rise to globalization or marks a globalized world as a distinctive social system from a pre-globalized world.

With regard to the privatization of authority in the global political economy, there is similarly no general theory that adequately accounts for the emergence, nature, operation, and political implications of pri-vate authority. Is private authority the phenomenon to be explained (the *explanandum*), or is private authority the explanation (the *explanans*)? What differentiates private authority from private power? How does private authority relate to globalization? Is private authority a cause or a result of the globalization of political economies and societies? Is pri-vate authority comparable to state authority or do we need a different sort of social theory to understand private authority? This is a more gen-eral problem with globalization studies, which Justin Rosenberg (2005) has so ably identified in his *post mortem* on the subject. Rosenberg argues that globalization theories fail to address central questions of social theory or to adequately assess the general applicability of exist-ing social and political theories to developments that are posited to move beyond the Westphalian structures that gave rise to the existing theories in the first place. This criticism should be qualified by noting that not all students are equally guilty of the uncritical application of social theories developed with national societies in mind to the global-ized world. Gramscian scholars, for example (Bieler & Morton 2006), debate the extent to which analytical concepts such as hegemony, civil society, and historical bloc, which were developed by Antonio Gramsci (1971) in the context of the Italian state, in fact travel analytically and theoretically to international relations so that we may speak of a global or transnational civil society in the absence of a world state. However, this is possibly the exception that proves the rule, and, in any case, this is hardly mainstream theory in international relations or in interna-tional political economy.

In response to this lack of reflexivity in globalization theory, some such as Mathias Albert (2007) have looked to classical social theo-rists, such as Auguste Comte, Herbert Spencer, Emile Durkheim, Talcott Parsons, and Niklas Luhmann for inspiration. Albert identifies "func-tional differentiation" as the central principle that operates in any social system, which he argues is already implicit in many accounts of inter-national relations. He illustrates this with the distinction between the international *political* and the international *economic* systems, which he regards as requiring no further legitimization (175). Albert also illustrates functional differentiation with his recognition of the ways in which power relations are mediated regionally and along functional lines of economy, security, and culture. The concept of functional differentiation "provides a useful vocabulary, which cuts across ... arguments about the role of the state in a globalized world ... and allows us ... to depict such structural change in terms of different and changing forms of differentiation," as in functional differentiation; spatial or temporal differentiation (compression of time and space); and stratificatory differentiation (as in global inequalities). These distinctions provide the foundation for developing theory about different forms of differentiation and their interplay and to "read the evolution of the global system as a process of varied and multilayered differentiation" (176).

This type of theorization is becoming increasingly influential in studies of private authority. It most likely can be traced to analyses in international relations that drew upon systems theory as developed by David Easton (1965), functional theories of international law and organization developed in the path-breaking works of David Mitrany (1976) and Ernst Haas (1964), and, more recently, the highly influential functional theory of international regimes developed by Robert Keohane (1984) and others. These theories attribute the emergence and nature of regulation and governance in international relations to institutions, processes, and actors that emerge to meet functional needs that are not met through interstate diplomacy. A variety of functional concerns relating to enhancing efficiency, cost reduction, market correction, and the provision of undersupplied public goods are identified as problematic in an international system characterized by formal anarchy, i.e., the absence of a government able to meet these systemic needs. Functional theory "implied analysing specific processes and institutions from the standpoint of their contribution to the overall well-being of the society in question" (Callinicos 1999: 123). These theories drew on evolutionary social theories that were articulated in the nineteenth century by Herbert Spencer (1894), among others. Evolutionary theory was heavily influenced by evolutionary biology and posited that society would evolve through a process of "progressive differentiation," "in the development of a more complex and internally articulated organization leading to increased efficiency" (Callinicos 1999: 109, citing Spencer). Emile Durkheim then recast evolutionary theory as a "science," attributing to social life a facticity that exists quite apart from the individuals comprising society and that could be studied through objective, positivist scientific methods.

Examples of functional analysis may be found in a collection of essays about the "reconstitution" of political authority in the world (Grande & Pauly 2005: 5). They focus on a "redistribution of responsibilities for the production of common goods among public and private actors, the emergence of new forms of private interest government (i.e., the private production of public goods), and new modes of cooperation between public and private actors (e.g., policy networks and public-private partnerships)." While the term "private authority" is not used in every chapter, the concern is clearly about the sorts of transformations with which students of private authority are concerned, including the privatization and the transnationalization of authority, which are argued to give rise to "transnational sovereignty" (13–14).[3] Unfortunately, there is no sustained theorization of these concepts. More problematically, many of the chapters reflect a functional determinism that is incompatible with even the most modest claim to social theory. Indeed, the introductory chapter characterizes the "redefinition of public functions" from privatization, liberalization, and de- and re-regulation as a "functional reconstitution of public authority." However, no theory is offered to explain this characterization. The chapters on the dynamics of institutional and normative reflexivity in changing perceptions of transnational or global risk (Beck 2005), world systems theory as a tool for analyzing transformations in governance (Albert 2005), and functional adaptations to changes in public-management thinking (Peters 2005: 74) invoke functional analysis but give no sense of the underlying causes or driving forces. They do not address the political economy underlying changes in the balance between governance through public and private mechanisms, the contested ideology justifying these changes,[4] or the relations of dominance in which they are imbricated, all of which constitute the very essence of social theory as we have defined it.[5] Alex Callinicos (1999: 5) reminds us that social theory "is an irredeemably political form of thought." However, these studies reflect *apolitical* social theory at its best, or worst, depending upon one's point of view!

Notions of "networks" and pluralistic "multilevel governance" emerge as the analytical solutions to the problem of governance without government that stems from the governance role adopted by private actors, which is argued to be driven by functional needs created by gaps in national governance (Eberlein & Grande 2005: 149). This putative pluralism in governance tends to create the appearance of equality amongst the diverse participants and obscures the political conflict and contestation over the terms of governance. There is no sense of the political economy of private governance or the "who gets what" out of this transformation in authority.

This tendency to apolitical, functional determinism is also evident in international legal studies of the "new constitutionalism" that is apparently sweeping the globe through the legalization and juridification of increasing dimensions of the life form; in other words, all life is being subjected to legal discipline.[6] This trend owes a great deal to the influence of the systems theory of Niklas Luhmann (1983) and a more recent reformulation in the legal theory of Gunther Teubner (1993), who imputes both autonomy and automaticity to private global legal ordering. Such analyses tend to verge on a form of legal determinism. Indeed, the move to functional analysis has profound consequences for our understanding of private authority by obscuring the political foundations of private rule-making. Albert argues that "[i]f the global system is primarily differentiated functionally, this implies that there is no hierarchy between functionally differentiated social systems with the political system occupying the top position—its function (to provide capacities for collectively binding decisions) does not translate into a privileged position (i.e., a form of stratified differentiation)" (2007: 176). Thus self-regulatory mechanisms, characteristic of private authority such as market mechanisms, are accorded the same legitimacy that is accorded other regulatory mechanisms, such as public or governmental institutions, through the principle of functional differentiation. Simply put, the politics of private authority drops out of the picture as functionality prevails. Functional analysis thus neutralizes the political and distributive dimensions and consequences of private authority. Private authority in turn is equalized with public authority and naturalized as just another mode of governance in a pluralistic, diversified system.

This flattening out of the distinction between public and private authority becomes even more alarming when the principle of functional differentiation is combined with the principle of rationalization, which posits that global institutions evolve rationally and are giving rise to a world culture through rationalizing (read Westernizing) processes and scripts (Lechner & Boli 2005). Private authority thus emerges not only as functionally inevitable, but also as efficient and therefore rational and good. This is then bolstered with appeals to the virtue of self-regulating markets (Djelic 2006) and to science (Drori & Meyer 2006).

In addition to becoming economically functional and practical, private authority becomes a form of rationality as an ideology and a political aspiration, but one that appears in a fetishized form as neutral and devoid of politics. The principle of functional differentiation performs an equalizing role between the public and private spheres by emptying the public domain of its privileged position in governance. Paradoxically, the anarchy problematic is reproduced as politics remain inside the state, while, on the outside, the apolitical or perhaps post-political world of functional rationality prevails. But one must pause and ask these questions: For whom is it functional and rational? Whom does private authority serve? Indeed, a common central finding in many studies of private authority in governance is that it raises acute problems of democratic accountability and legitimacy. For example, private authority in the constitution and management of the regime governing global trade and intellectual property rights serves powerful business corporations and under-represents the interests of developing states or of those on the periphery of international legality (Sell 2003; Higgott & Weber 2005; Shaffer 2004). The private authority exercised by corporations under the global investment regime effectively freezes out democratic participation (Sneiderman 2006), while private authority in regulating accounting standards favours Anglo-Saxon financiers (Nölke & Perry 2007) and privileges secured creditors over borrowers in the regulation of secured transactions (Van Harten 2005). These defects in private governance raise concerns over its legitimacy and accountability as a mode of governance, highlighting the importance of developing a more critical understanding of privatized global governance.

PUTTING POLITICS BACK INTO GOVERNANCE

We might begin by considering the crucial affirmation that "[t]heory is always *for* someone and *for* some purpose" (Cox 1996 [1981]: 87; emphasis in original). The sort of social theory we need must shift its optic to look at the underlying interests and purposes that are served by private authority. This implies engaging in the development of a radical political economy critique of private authority in the form of histori-cal-materialist analysis.[7] Historical materialism is a method of critical analysis and a philosophy of praxis. Analytically, historical materialism conceptualizes world order as an historical bloc comprised of material, ideological, and institutional forces that embody both traces of the past and seeds of the future (Cox 1996 [1981]). As critical theory, histori-cal materialism is inherently and unavoidably transformative: it entails "practices of critical scholarship ... [that] aim at de-reifying the apparent natural, universal, and politically neutral appearances of capitalist social reality" in order to "re-situate those abstract appearances in relation to the social processes and power relations implicated in their production ... to enable their transformation by human and social agents ..." (Rupert & Smith 2002: 1). Moreover, as a form of immanent critique, historical materialism is also a philosophy of praxis that directs attention to identifying and transforming the social forces that create and sustain a world characterized by increasing inequality and material dispossession. This involves unmasking privatized regimes that are posited to function neutrally and rationally in the efficient management of the world economy. It also requires disrupting the distinctions between economics and politics and between the private and the public spheres that proponents of functional analysis find unproblematic. It is necessary to reveal how these forms of "functional differentiation" are in fact ideological moves to depoliticize and naturalize activities that are inherently political (Wood 1995; Cutler 1997).

Private authority is best regarded as a mode of regulation that is specific to the global political economy under conditions of late capitalism and postmodernity. Late capitalist regulation is reflected in the increasing recourse to legal forms to facilitate the displacement of welfare states by competition states through liberalization, deregulation, and privatization; in the intensification and expansion of disciplines facilitating the global expansion of capitalism through flexible accumulation; and in the soft re-regulation of labour relations, consumer protection, environmental practices, and corporate ethics (Harvey 1990). Late capitalism, in turn, gives rise to a specifically postmodern form of regulation (Santos 2002), which reflects the global expansion and deepening of the logic of the market at the level of culture, collapsing distinctions between economy and culture and giving rise to a multiplicity of overlapping and intersecting regulatory orders, linking local and global political economies and societies.

Late capitalist and postmodern regulation is hegemonic in constituting privatized regimes of accumulation, which secure the interests of an increasingly transnational capitalist class (Cutler 2003; Robinson 2004; Sklair 2001). The transnational economic order constitutionalizes neoliberal market discipline, artificial understandings of authority, and exclusionary regimes and institutions that marginalize large populations of the world. Private authority in the regulation of trade in services, intellectual property rights, investment, international commercial arbitration, dispute settlement under the World Trade Organization and under regional associations including the North America Free Trade Agreement, financial and accounting services, banking, insurance, and the soft regulation of corporate social responsibility—all these must be examined as regimes that legitimate private capitalist accumulation and dispossession (Harvey 2005). For example, the General Agreement on Trade in Services (GATS), negotiated as part of the WTO Uruguay Round of Multilateral Trade Negotiations that succeeded the General Agreement on Tariffs and Trade (GATT), is advancing a highly privatized order that is creating new mechanisms of dispossession and exclusion. It redefines how governments conceptualize services, "their roles in society, and the objectives and principles according to which they should be governed" (Drake & Nicolaïdes 1992: 38). GATS extends GATT-like discipline to the provision of services provision, flattening out distinctions between trade in goods and trade in services and treating services as tradable commodities. This imports into the service relationship related liberal political economy assumptions about the efficiency and functionality of free trade in services. Thus GATT-like discipline and technical language that operationalizes state commitments to progressive liberalization and non-discrimination govern service delivery. However, in equalizing trade in goods and services, GATS obscures the distinctive nature of service provision as a relationship rooted in everyday life and "personal relationships that extend beyond the immediate parties to the transaction into families, communities and societies" and that "serve purposes that are intrinsically social, as well as environmental, cultural, and economic" (Kelsey 2003: 267). But the non-economic dimension of service provision disappears as the service relationship is commodified, privatized, and disembedded from local social and political controls.

Similarly, the emerging regime governing corporate social responsibility is best analyzed as a "transnational private legitimacy regime" whose purpose is the "*legitimation* of globalised private accumulation strategies" (Haslam 2007: 270; emphasis in original). Self-regulating corporate social-responsibility initiatives claim legitimacy through the efficient provision of collective goods concerning the environment, labour relations, and human rights. However, a critical analysis of the ontology and political economy of the business corporation contradicts the collective nature of the goods that they are said to supply or the public interests that they claim to represent (Cutler 2008b). Ontologically, private business corporations as self-regarding entities whose duties lie with their shareholders are ill suited for public governance. Furthermore, liberal political economy indicates that public goods tend to be undersupplied by private actors due to the problem of free-riding, i.e., the incentive for private actors to take advantage of public goods without contributing to their provision. As a consequence, the intervention of a public authority is regarded as necessary to fulfill required public functions and to provide public goods.

These problems with private authority suggest that there is an urgent need to critically analyze the distributional consequences and the democratic legitimacy of the expansion in private governance of the global political economy. In this regard, the role of international relations theory becomes a central concern. More specifically, apolitical theories of functional differentiation must not be allowed to neutralize and legitimate global regimes that dispossess and exclude all but the most powerful in the global political economy.

NOTES

1 Notable, as well, in the field of international relations are Rosenau and Czempiel (1992) and Rosenau (1997), and in international business, Hollingsworth and Boyer (1997) and Braithwaite and Drahos (2000).

2 Each of the authors had previously published on various dimensions of privatized authority (see Cutler 1995, 1997; Haufler 1993, 1997; Porter 1993).

3 The chapters by Porter, Börzel, and Risse clearly adopt the language of private authority.

4 But see Porter's (2005a) contribution, which focuses on the role of norms in private governance of finance.

5 Another example of appeals to functional differentiation as an explanation of private authority is offered by Tony Porter (2005b) in the analysis of the significance of the private authority exercised by experts in the globalization of accounting standards. Porter draws on the work of Niklas Luhmann (1983), arguing that technical authority operates alongside public and private authority as a distinct form of governance, reflecting a process of "politicized functional differentiation" of authority structures in the contemporary global system. Importantly, Porter attempts to incorporate the politics of private rule-making into his evolutionary model. See also Porter and Ronit (2006: 45) for an attempt to "identify evolutionary patterns common to all forms of self-regulation" in the study of private rule-making.

6 See also Black (1996), Streeck and Schmitter (1985), and Ayers and Braithwaite (1992) for the virtues of governance through the self-regulation of private actors.

7 For further elaboration of this topic, see Cutler (2005, 2008a).

REFERENCES

Abbott, K., R. Keohane, A. Moravcsik, A. Slaughter, and D. Snidal. 2000. "The Concept of Legalization." *International Organization* 54(3): 401–19.

Albert, M. 2007. "'Globalization Theory': Yesterday's Fad or More Lively Than Ever?" *International Political Sociology* 1(2): 165–82.

——. 2005. "Restructuring World Society: The Contribution of Modern Systems Theory." In E. Grande and L. Pauly (eds.), *Complex Sovereignty: Reconstituting Political Authority in the Twenty-first Century*. Toronto: University of Toronto Press. 48–67.

Avant, D. 2007. "The emerging market for private military services and the problems of regulation." In S. Chesterton and C. Lehnardt (eds.), *From Mercenaries to Market: The Rise and Regualation of Private Military Companies*. Oxford: Oxford University Press. 181–95.

Ayers, I., and J. Braithwaite (eds.). 1992. *Responsive Regulation: Transcending the Deregulation Debate*. Oxford: Oxford University Press.

Beck, U. 2005. "World Risk Society and the Changing Foundations of Transnational Politics." In E. Grande and L. Pauly (eds.), *Complex Sovereignty: Reconstituting Political Authority in the Twenty-first Century*. Toronto: University of Toronto Press. 22–47.

Bieler, A., and A. Morton. 2006. *Images of Gramsci: Connections and Contentions in Political Theory and International Relations*. London and New York: Routledge.

Black, J. 1996. "Constitutionalising Self-Regulation." *The Modern Law Review* 59(1): 24–55.

Börzel, T., and T. Risse. 2005. "Public-Private Partnerships: Effective and Legitimate Tools of Transnational Governance?" In E. Grande and L. Pauly (eds.), *Complex Sovereignty: Reconstituting Political Authority in the Twenty-first Century*. Toronto: University of Toronto Press. 195–216.

Botzem, S., and S. Quack. 2006. "Contested Rules and Shifting Boundaries: International Standard Setting in Accounting." In M. Djelic and K. Sahlin-Andersson (eds.), *Transnational Governance: Institutional Dynamics of Regulation*. Cambridge: Cambridge University Press. 266–86.

Braithwaite, J., and P. Drahos. 2000. *Global Business Regulation*. Cambridge: Cambridge University Press.

Callinicos, A. 1999. *Social Theory: A Historical Introduction*. New York: New York University Press.

Cashore, B., G. Auld, and D. Newsom. 2003. *Governing Through Markets: Forest Certification and the Emergence of Non-State Authority*. New Haven, CT: Yale University Press.

Cohen, E. 2007. "The Harmonization of Private Commercial Law: The Case of Secured Finance." In C. Brutsch and D. Lehmkuhl (eds.), *Law and Legalization in Transnational Relations*. London: Routledge. 58–80.

Cox, R. 1996 [1981]. "Social Forces, States, and World Orders: Beyond International Relations Theory." In R. Cox with T. Sinclair (eds.), *Approaches to World Order*. Cambridge: Cambridge University Press. 85–123.

Cutler, A.C. 2010. "The Legitimacy of Private Transnational Governance: Experts and the Transnational Market for Force." *Socio-Economic Review* 8(1): 157–85.

——. 2008a. "Toward a Radical Political Economy Critique of Transnational Economic Law." In S. Marks (ed.), *International Law on the Left: Revisiting Marxist Legacies*. Cambridge: Cambridge University Press. 199–219.

——. 2008b. "Problematizing Corporate Social Responsibility under Conditions of Late Capitalism and Postmodernity." In V. Rittberger and M. Nettesheim (eds.), *Authority in the Global Economy*. Houndmills: Palgrave Macmillan. 189–215.

——. 2005. "Gramsci, Law, and the Culture of Global Capitalism." *Critical Review of International Social and Political Philosophy* 8(4): 527–42.

————. 2003. *Private Power and Global Authority: Transnational Merchant Law in the Global Political Economy*. Cambridge: Cambridge University Press.

————. 1997. "Artifice, Ideology and Paradox: The Public/Private Distinction in International Law." *Review of International Political Economy* 4(2): 261–85.

————. 1995. "Global Capitalism and Liberal Myths: Dispute Settlement in Private International Trade Relations." *Millennium: Journal of International Studies* 24(3): 377–97.

Cutler, A.C., V. Haufler, and T. Porter (eds.). 1999. *Private Authority and International Affairs*. New York: State University of New York Press.

Djelic, M. 2006. "Marketization: From Intellectual Agenda to Global Policy-making." In M. Djelic and K. Sahlin-Andersson (eds.), *Transnational Governance: Institutional Dynamics of Regulation*. Cambridge: Cambridge University Press. 53–73.

Djelic, M., and T. Kleiner. (2006). "The International Competition Network: Moving towards Transnational Governance." In M. Djelic and K. Sahlin-Andersson (eds.), *Transnational Governance: Institutional Dynamics of Regulation*. Cambridge: Cambridge University Press. 287–307.

Djelic, M., and K. Sahlin-Andersson (eds.). 2006. *Transnational Governance: Institutional Dynamics of Regulation*. Cambridge: Cambridge University Press.

Drake, W., and C. Nicolaïdes. 1992. "Ideas, Interests and Institutionalization: 'Trade in Services' and the Uruguay Round." *International Organization* 46: 37–100.

Drori, G., and J. Meyer. 2006. "Scientization: Making a World Safe for Organizing." In M. Djelic and K. Sahlin-Andersson (eds.), *Transnational Governance: Institutional Dynamics of Regulation*. Cambridge: Cambridge University Press. 31–52.

Easton, D. 1965. *A Systems Analysis of Political Life*. New York: Wiley.

Eberlein, B., and E. Grande (eds.). 2005. "Reconstituting Political Authority in Europe: Transnational Regulatory Networks and the Informalization of Governance in the European Union." In E. Grande and L. Pauly (eds.), *Complex Sovereignty: Reconstituting Political Authority in the Twenty-first Century*. Toronto: University of Toronto Press. 146–67.

Giddens, A. 1990. *The Consequences of Modernity*. Cambridge: Polity.

Gill, S. 2003. *Power and Resistance in the New World Order*. Houndmills: Palgrave Macmillan.

Gills, B., and W.R. Thompson. 2006. *Globalization and Global History*. London: Routledge.

Gramsci, A. 1971. *Selections from the Prison Notebooks of Antonio Gramsci*. Ed. Q. Hoare and G. Smith. New York: International Publishers.

Grande, E., and L. Pauly (eds.). 2005. *Complex Sovereignty: Reconstituting Political Authority in the Twenty-first Century*. Toronto: University of Toronto Press.

Graz, J.C., and A. Nölke (eds.). 2008. *Transnational Private Governance and Its Limits*. London and New York: Routledge.

Haas, E. 1964. *Beyond the Nation State: Functionalism in International Organization*. Stanford, CA: Stanford University Press.

Hall, R., with T. Biersteker (eds.). 2002. *The Emergence of Private Authority in Global Governance*. Cambridge: Cambridge University Press.

Harvey, D. 2005. *The New Imperialism*. Oxford: Oxford University Press.

——. 1990. *The Condition of Postmodernity: An Enquiry into the Origins of Cultural Change*. Oxford: Blackwell.

Haslam, P. 2007. "Is Corporate Social Responsibility a Constructivist Regime? Evidence from Latin America." *Global Society* 21(2): 269–96.

Haufler, V. 2001. *A Public Role for the Private Sector: Industry Self-Regulation in a Global Economy*. Washington, DC: Carnegie Endowment for International Peace.

——. 1997. *Dangerous Commerce: Insurance and the Management of International Risk*. Ithaca, NY: Cornell University Press.

——. 1993. "Crossing the Boundary Between Public and Private: International Regimes and Non-State Actors." In V. Rittberger (ed.), *Regime Theory and International Relations*. Oxford: Clarendon. 94–111.

Higgott, R., G. Underhill, and A. Bieler (eds.). 2000. *Non-State Actors in the Global System*. London: Routledge.

Higgott, R., and H. Weber. 2005. "GATS in Context: Development, an Evolving *lex mercatoria* and the Doha Agenda." *Review of International Political Economy* 12(3): 434–55.

Hollingsworth, J.R., and R. Boyer (eds.). 1997. *Contemporary Capitalism: The Embeddedness of Institutions*. Cambridge: Cambridge University Press.

Josselin, D., and W. Wallace (eds.). 2001. *Non-State Actors in World Politics*. Basingstoke: Palgrave.

Kelsey, J. 2003. "Legal Fetishism and the Contradictions of the GATS." *Globalisation, Societies, and Education* 1(3): 267–80.

Keohane, R. 1984. *After Hegemony: Cooperation and Discord in the World Political Economy*. Princeton, NJ: Princeton University Press.

Keohane, R., and J. Nye. 1972. *Transnational Relations and World Politics*. Cambridge, MA: Harvard University Press.

Kinsey, C. 2005. "Regulation and Control of Private Military Companies: The Legislative Dimension." *Contemporary Security Policy* 26(1): 84–102.

Knill, C., and D. Lehmkuhl. 2002. "Private Actors and the State: Internationalization and Changing Patterns of Governance." *Governance: An International Journal of Policy, Administration and Institutions* 15(1): 41–63.

Kobrin, S. 2008. "Globalization, Transnational Corporations and the Future of Global Governance." In *Handbook of Research on Global Corporate Citizenship*. Cheltenham, UK, and Northampton, MA: Edward Elgar.

Kontos, A. 2004. "Privatized Security Guards: Privatized Force and State Responsibility Under International Human Rights Law." *Non-State Actors and International Law* 4(3): 199–238.

Krahmann, E. 2008. "Security: Collective Good or Commodity?" *European Journal of International Relations* 14(3): 379–404.

Leander, A. 2005. "The Power to Construct International Security: On the Significance of Private Military Companies." *Millennium: Journal of International Studies* 33(3): 803–26.

Lechner, F., and J. Boli. 2005. *World Culture: Origins and Consequences.* Oxford: Blackwell.

Luhmann, N. 1983. *The Differentiation of Society.* New York: Columbia University Press.

Mandel, R. 2002. *Armies Without States: The Privatization of Security.* Boulder, CO: Lynne Rienner Publishers.

Mattli, W. 2003. "Public and Private Governance in Setting International Standards." In M. Kahler and D. Lake (eds.), *Governance in a Global Economy: Political Authority in Transition.* Princeton: Princeton University Press. 199–225.

———. 2001. "Private Justice in a Global Economy: From Litigation to Arbitration." *International Organization* 55(4): 919–47.

May, C. (ed.). 2006. *Global Corporate Power.* Boulder, CO: Lynne Rienner Publishers.

Mitrany, D. 1976. *The Functional Theory of Politics.* New York: St. Martin's Press.

Mügge, D. 2008. "Keeping Competitors Out: Industry Structure and Transnational Private Governance in Global Finance." In J.C. Graz and A. Nölke (eds.), *Transnational Private Governance and Its Limits.* London and New York: Routledge. 29–43.

———. 2006. "Private-Public Puzzles: Inter-firm Competition and Transnational Private Regulation." *New Political Economy* 11(2): 177–200.

Nölke, A., and J. Perry. 2007. "The Power of Transnational Private Governance: Financialization and the IASB." *Business and Politics* 9(3): 1–25.

Ougaard, M. 2006. "Instituting the Power to Do Good?" in C. May (ed.), *Global Corporate Power.* Boulder, CO: Lynne Rienner Publishers. 227–48.

Peters, G. 2005. "Governance: A Garbage Can Perspective." In E. Grande and L. Pauly (eds.), *Complex Sovereignty: Reconstituting Political Authority in the Twenty-first Century.* Toronto: University of Toronto Press. 68–92.

Porter, T. 2005a. "The Private Production of Public Goods: Private and Public Norms in Global Governance." In E. Grande and L. Pauly (eds.), *Complex Sovereignty: Reconstituting Political Authority in the Twenty-first Century.* Toronto: University of Toronto Press. 217–37.

———. 2005b. "Private Authority, Technical Authority, and the Globalization of Accounting Standards." *Business and Politics* 7(3): article 2, 1–30.

——. 1993. *States, Markets, and Regimes in Global Finance*. New York: St. Martin's Press.

Porter, T., and K. Ronit (eds.). 2010. *The Challenges of Global Business Authority: Democratic Renewal, Stalemate or Decay?* Albany: State University of New York Press.

——. 2006. "Self-Regulation as Policy-Process: The Multiple and Criss-Crossing Stages of Private Rule-Making." *Policy Sciences* 39(1): 41–72.

Robertson, R. 1992. *Globalization: Social Theory and Global Culture*. London: Sage.

Robinson, W. 2004. *A Theory of Global Capitalism: Production, Class, and State in a Transnational World*. Baltimore and London: Johns Hopkins University Press.

Ronit, K., and V. Schneider (eds.). 2000. *Private Organizations in Global Politics*. London and New York: Routledge.

Rosenau, J. 1997. *Along the Domestic-Foreign Frontier: Exploring Governance in a Turbulent World*. Cambridge: Cambridge University Press.

Rosenau, J., and O. Czempiel (eds.). 1992. *Governance without Government: Order and Change in World Politics*. Cambridge: Cambridge University Press.

Rosenberg, J. 2005. "Globalization Theory: A Post Mortem." *International Politics* 42(1): 2–74.

Rupert, M., and H. Smith (eds.). 2002. *Historical Materialism and Globalization*. New York and London: Routledge.

Santos, B. 2002. *Toward a New Legal Common Sense: Law, Globalization, and Emancipation*. 2nd ed. London: Butterworths.

Schneiderman, D. 2006. "Transnational Legality and the Immobilization of Local Agency." *Annual Review of Law and Social Science* 2: 387–408.

——. 2001. "Investment Rules and the Rule of Law." *Constellations* 8(4): 521–37.

Scholte, J. 2000. *Globalization: A Critical Introduction*. Basingstoke: Macmillan.

Sell, S. 2003. *Private Power, Public Law: The Globalization of Intellectual Property Rights*. Cambridge: Cambridge University Press.

Shaffer, G. 2004. "Recognizing Public Goods in WTO Dispute Settlement: Who participates? Who decides? The Case of TRIPS and Pharmaceutical Protection." *Journal of International Economic Law* 7(2): 459–82.

Sinclair, T. 2005. *The New Masters of Capital: American Bond Rating Agencies and the Global Economy*. Ithaca, NY: Cornell University Press.

Singer, P. 2003. *Corporate Warriors: The Rise of the Privatized Military Industry*. Ithaca, NY: Cornell University Press.

Sklair, L. 2001. *The Transnational Capitalist Class*. Oxford: Basil Blackwell.

Spencer, H. 1961 [1894]. *The Study of Sociology*. Ann Arbor: University of Michigan Press.

Stopford, J., and S. Strange with J.S. Henley. 1991. *Rival States, Rival Firms, Competition for World Market Shares*. Cambridge: Cambridge University Press.

Strange, S. 1996. *The Retreat of the State: The Diffusion of Power in the World Economy*. Cambridge: Cambridge University Press.

———. 1988. *States and Markets: An Introduction to International Political Economy*. Oxford and New York: Basil Blackwell.

Streeck, W., and P.C. Schmitter (eds.). 1985. *Private Interest Government: Beyond Market and State*. London: Sage.

Teubner, G. 1993. *Law as an Autopoietic System*. Oxford: Blackwell.

Tsingou, E. 2008. "Transnational Private Governance and the Basel Process: Banking Regulation and Supervision, Private Interests and Basel II." In J.C. Graz and A. Nölke (eds.), *Transnational Private Governance and Its Limits*. London and New York: Routledge. 58–68.

Van Harten, G. 2005. "Private Authority and Transnational Governance: The Contours of the International System of Investment Protection." *Review of International Political Economy* 12(4): 600–23.

Vernon, R. 1971. *Sovereignty at Bay: The Multinational Spread of U.S. Enterprises*. New York: Basic Books.

Wolf, K., N. Deitelhoff, and S. Engert. 2007. "Corporate Security Responsibility: Towards a Conceptual Framework for a Comparative Research Agenda." *Cooperation and Conflict* 42(3): 294–319.

Wood, E.M. 1995. *Democracy Against Capitalism: Renewing Historical Materialism*. Cambridge: Cambridge University Press.

4

Corporate Accountability
Is Self-Regulation the Answer?

KAVALJIT SINGH

The financial crisis—which erupted in the aftermath of the subprime mortgage crisis in the US in mid-2007—has adversely affected most countries through trade and financial channels. At the policy level, the crisis has debunked several myths and purported benefits of deregulation, free markets, and the Anglo-Saxon capitalist model based on self-regulation. The neoliberal ideology, which has dominated global policy-making since the 1980s, is facing a backlash. Neoliberal policies have already lost credibility in many developing countries, particularly in Latin America, over the last decade.

Because of the meltdown in the global financial markets, the intellectual climate is changing, and consequently state intervention in the economy and greater regulation and supervision of financial markets are likely to return to the global policy agenda. For researchers, civil society, labour, and social and political movements, there is much to learn about, and contribute to, alternative policy proposals at this crucial juncture. The crisis has opened up new spaces and opportunities for social and political action that did not exist in the past. Questions central to the operation of transnational corporations (TNCs), namely, corporate codes of conduct and the principles of self-regulation that have been promoted by global corporations, now call for analysis.

THE EMERGENCE OF CODES OF CONDUCT

The globalization of trade and investment flows has been paralleled by the emergence of codes of conduct. Although the first corporate code of conduct was created by the International Chamber of Commerce (ICC) in 1949, the 1990s witnessed a plethora of voluntary codes and corporate social responsibility (CSR) guidelines. However, there is no consensus on the precise definition of a code of conduct. Codes can range from one-page broad statements to detailed benchmarks and guidelines on how to conduct business practices globally. Voluntary approaches are based either on a self-regulation model or on a co-regulation model between firms, citizen groups, and governments. Yet it is important to underscore that voluntary approaches did not emerge in a vacuum. Their emergence has more to do with a change in the paradigm of how global capital should be governed. Voluntary approaches, such as the OECD Guidelines on Multinational Corporations (see below), were a direct response to UN initiatives in the 1970s to regulate the activities of TNCs. However, unlike the UN initiatives, the OECD Guidelines were aimed not at protecting national sovereignty or addressing developmental concerns of the host countries, but rather at circumventing the UN initiatives themselves.

The deregulation and "free-market" environment of the 1980s gave greater legitimacy to the self-regulation model embedded in the Anglo-Saxon business tradition. Many developed countries, particularly the US, encouraged TNCs to adopt voluntary measures rather than enacting and enforcing strict laws governing their activities and behaviour. The argument against regulation was based on the belief that TNCs would undertake greater social and environmental responsibilities through voluntary measures.

In the late 1980s, campaigns launched by NGOs and consumer groups brought significant changes in the public perception of corporate behaviour, which in turn facilitated the further proliferation of voluntary initiatives. Campaigns in the developed countries focusing on popular consumer brands such as Nike and Levi's brought to public notice some of the appalling working and environmental conditions in some of these companies' overseas production sites. Realizing that bad publicity could seriously damage corporate and brand reputations and that their products could face consumer boycotts, many corporations suddenly started adopting codes of conduct and other CSR measures. Since the early 1990s, the majority of voluntary measures have been undertaken by individual corporations. US-based corporations were the first to introduce codes of conduct, with jeans manufacturer Levi's adopting one in 1991.[1] Pressures generated by the "ethical" investor community and other shareholders also contributed to the proliferation of voluntary measures.

Given that there is often a considerable discrepancy between a corporation's undertaking to follow a voluntary code and its actual business conduct, many critics argue that CSR measures have become corporate public relations tools used to create a positive corporate image. In today's competitive world, a positive image as a responsible company adds significant value to a company's business and reputation and helps it manage various risks. Therefore, the growing popularity of voluntary measures in recent years has not ended debates on the efficacy of such codes in regulating TNC corporate behaviour (Sethi 2002, 2003).

TYPES OF CODES

Over the years, a variety of codes of conduct governing whole corporate sectors have emerged. Some of those to emerge from international organizations include the International Labor Organization's (ILO) Tripartite Declaration of Principles Concerning Multinational Enterprises and Social Policy; the OECD Guidelines on Multinational Enterprises; the United Nations Conference on Trade and Development's (UNCTAD) Set of Multilaterally Agreed Equitable Principles and Rules for the Control of Restrictive Business Practices; the Food and Agriculture Organization's Code on the Distribution and Use of Pesticides; and the World Health Organization/UNICEF Code of Marketing Breast Milk Substitutes. Business associations have also drawn up codes, such as the US Chemical Manufacturers Association's Responsible Care Program and the International Chamber of Commerce's Business Charter for Sustainable Development. A diverse range of players have been involved in the development of voluntary codes of conduct. These include corporations, business associations, NGOs, labour unions, shareholders, investors, consumers, consultancy firms, governments, and international organizations.

Broadly speaking, codes of conduct can be divided into five main types: specific company codes (for example, those adopted by Nike and Levi's); business association codes (for instance, the International Chamber of Commerce's [ICC] Business Charter for Sustainable Development); multi-stakeholder codes (such as the Ethical Trading Initiative[2]); inter-governmental codes (for example, the OECD Guidelines); and international framework agreements (such as the International Metalworkers Federation agreement with DaimlerChrysler).

Despite their diversity, the majority of codes of conduct are concerned with working conditions and environmental issues. They tend to be concentrated in a few business sectors. Codes related to labour issues, for instance, are generally found in sectors where consumer brand image is paramount, such as footwear, apparel, sports goods, toys, and retail outlets. Environmental codes are usually found in the chemicals, forestry, oil, and mining sectors. In addition, codes vary considerably in both their scope and application. Very few of them accept the core labour standards, considering the ILO's prescriptions too comprehensive and restrictive. Although codes increasingly cover the company's main suppliers, they tend not to include every link in the supply chain. Codes, for instance, rarely encompass workers in the informal sector even though they may well form a critical link in these chains. In terms of ensuring compliance, moreover, only a small proportion of codes include provisions for independent monitoring.

It is interesting to note that various types of code have gradually evolved in response to developments in the governance of TNCs. When the limits of self-regulatory voluntary codes adopted by companies became apparent in the late 1990s, the focus shifted to co-regulation in the form of multi-stakeholder initiatives (MSIs) under which corporations, non-governmental organizations (NGOs), labour unions, and even governments draft and monitor codes. Unlike company codes, MSIs address a vast range of issues, provide independent monitoring mechanisms, and, therefore, are increasingly viewed as a credible alternative to company codes. MSIs are set up as non-profit organizations consisting of coalitions of companies, labour unions, and NGOs that develop specific standards. Some MSIs (such as Social Accountability International) have developed elaborate guidelines under which they certify that a company complies with the standards. Initiatives such as the Ethical Trading Initiative and the Clean Clothes Campaign are increasingly seen as progressive MSI models by both corporations and NGOs.[3]

International framework agreements also emerged in the late 1990s. More than 30 have been signed since 1999 in a variety of sectors, including mining, retailing, telecommunications, and manufacturing. The framework agreement signed between the International Federation of Building and Wood Workers (IFBWW) and Swedish retailing giant IKEA in 2001 is an example. Such an agreement is negotiated between a transnational company and the trade unions of its workforce at the global level. It is a global instrument with the purpose of ensuring fundamental workers' rights in all of the TNC's locations, as well as those of its suppliers. A framework agreement includes special reference to international labour standards and follows a similar structure and monitoring procedures to those of MSIs. Since they are negotiated on a global level and require the participation of trade unions, international framework agreements are considered preferential instruments for dealing with the issues raised by the globalization of investment flows by many social movements.

INTERNATIONAL CODES: THREE CASE STUDIES

Given their wider coverage, scope, and applicability, key features of three important international codes are discussed below.

OECD Guidelines on Multinational Enterprises[4]
In 1976, the OECD adopted a declaration on International Investment and Multinational Enterprises under which certain guidelines were included. Although legally non-binding, the guidelines have been adopted by the 30 member countries of the OECD and eight non-member countries (Argentina, Brazil, Chile, Estonia, Israel, Latvia, Lithuania, and Slovenia). Therefore, the coverage of the guidelines is vast, and most big TNCs fall under their remit. Addressed to businesses, the guidelines provide voluntary principles and standards to encourage companies to follow responsible business practices. The stated objectives of the guidelines are to ensure that TNCs operate in harmony with the policies of host countries and make positive contributions to them. Compared with company codes, the issues covered under the guidelines are wide-ranging: they include employment and labour relations, the environment, information disclosure, combating bribery, consumer interest, science and technology, competition, and taxation.

The guidelines have been reviewed and revised five times (in 1979, 1982, 1984, 1991, and 2000). After the 1991 review, a new chapter on environmental protection was added, while implementation procedures and supply-chain responsibilities on TNCs were included after the most recent review in 2000.

Even though the OECD does not provide any independent monitoring and verification processes for the guidelines, it does mandate signatory countries to set up a National Contact Point (NCP) to deal with the promotion, management, interpretation, and dispute settlement of the guidelines. Since 2000, more than 70 complaints regarding violations of the OECD guidelines have been filed by several labour unions and NGOs at various NCPs. But very few complaints have succeeded to date, indicating the inherent weakness of this institutional mechanism. A number of reports by NGOs and labour unions have highlighted the technical and administrative ineffectiveness and inability of NCPs to handle complaints against TNCs. The guidelines' confidentiality clauses and lack of transparency further restrict their use in creating public awareness on complaint cases.

Some NGOs consider the guidelines a potentially powerful tool to put pressure on TNCs that they believe are violating social and environmental norms. There is no denying that, compared to individual company or business association codes, OECD guidelines have better value because of governmental involvement, but they are still voluntary and non-binding in nature. They do not confer any rights on citizens in the signatory countries to take legal action against TNCs for not implementing them. In the long run, a strategy exclusively based on filing complaint cases will not be sufficient to hold TNCs accountable to the general public for their actions.

The ILO Tripartite Declaration of Principles Concerning Multinational Enterprises and Social Policy[5]

The policy measures implementing the ILO's labour principles for TNCs are mainly contained in the Tripartite Declaration of Principles concerning Multinational Enterprises and Social Policy. Adopted in 1977, the declaration is voluntary in nature, despite efforts made by labour unions to make it legally binding. Concerned with employment policy, job security, and health and safety issues, the declaration calls upon governments, employers, labour unions, and TNCs to work toward the realization of economic and social development. It calls for formulating appropriate national laws and policies and recommends the principles to be implemented by all concerned parties. It seeks to promote consistent standards for both domestic and international corporations. In addition, the declaration makes specific reference to the United Nations Universal Declaration of Human Rights, international covenants adopted by the UN, and the Constitution of the ILO.

The ILO has established a bureaucratic system to implement the declaration. Investigations are carried out by the ILO secretariat, which sends a questionnaire to governments to complete in cooperation with employers and employees. The secretariat then compiles various national reports that it presents to the Board of Directors of the Committee on Multinational Enterprises. The national reports are usually vague, with no reference to any specific TNC. Attempts made by labour unions for strict implementation procedures of the declaration have not yielded any results so far.

In addition to the Tripartite Declaration, several other conventions and labour standards adopted by ILO have a direct bearing on the operations of TNCs. For instance, the Declaration on Fundamental Principles and Rights at Work, adopted in 2000, seeks the contributions of TNCs to achieve basic labour rights, including freedom of association and the right to collective bargaining.

The UN Global Compact[6]

Launched in 2000, the Global Compact is a recent initiative by the UN aimed at engaging TNCs to support and implement ten principles covering human rights, labour, environmental protection, and anti-corruption. These principles are derived from the UN Universal Declaration on Human Rights, the ILO's Declaration on Fundamental Principles of Rights at Work, the Rio Declaration on Environment and Development, and the United Nations Convention Against Corruption. The stated goal of the Global Compact is to create "corporate citizenship" so that business can become part of the solution to the challenges of globalization.

To date, nearly 1,200 companies (both domestic and transnational) have indicated their support for the Global Compact, in addition to some international business associations, labour union bodies, and NGOs. The Global Compact runs a small secretariat, liaising with other UN agencies. Companies join this initiative by sending a letter of commitment to the UN Secretary General. Each year, the company is expected to publish in its annual report a description of the methods through which it is supporting the principles of the Global Compact.

While some NGOs have welcomed the Global Compact as a forum to engage with the corporate world, critics have expressed their apprehensions that it would be largely used as a public-relations tool by TNCs. Some of their concerns cannot be overlooked. First, no one can deny that the Global Compact is a purely voluntary initiative. Second, there are few effective mechanisms in place to ensure that companies comply with its ten principles. In other words, monitoring and accountability mechanisms are lacking. Third, it is for the company to decide which principles they wish to abide by in which of their activities. Fourth, there is no procedure to screen the companies that sign on: several TNCs that have long been charged with environmental and human-rights abuses in host countries have joined the Global Compact (such as Nike, Royal Dutch Shell, and Rio Tinto).

Critics also fear that initiatives like the Global Compact would further increase corporate influence within the UN system in terms of policy advice. It is little wonder that many critics see the initiative as more of an image-building exercise ("blue-washing," after the blue of the UN logo) than an attempt to improve social and environmental standards on the ground.

THE LIMITS OF VOLUNTARY APPROACHES

Voluntary approaches have several inherent weaknesses and operational difficulties, some of which are summarized here. First, as discussed above, corporate codes are purely voluntary, non-binding instruments. No corporation can be held legally accountable for violating them. The responsibility to implement the code rests entirely on the corporation. At best, corporations can be forced to implement codes only through moral persuasion and public pressure. Second, despite the fact that such codes have been in existence for many years, the number of companies adopting them is still relatively small. Moreover, corporate codes are limited to a few sectors, particularly those in which brand names are important in corporate sales, such as garments, footwear, consumer goods, and retailing businesses. Many other sectors remain outside the purview of corporate codes.

Third, many codes are still not universally binding on all the operations of a company, including its contractors, subsidiaries, suppliers, agents, and franchisees. Codes rarely encompass the workers in the informal sector, who could well be an important part of a company's supply chain. Further, a company may implement only one type of code, for instance, an environmental one, while neglecting other important codes related to labour protection and health and safety, for example. Fourth, corporate codes are limited in scope and often set standards that are lower than existing national regulations. For instance, labour codes recognize the right to freedom of association but do not guarantee the right to strike, whereas, in many countries such as India, the right to strike is a legally recognized instrument, an indication of the significance of state regulation.

Fifth, the mushrooming of voluntary codes in an era of deregulated business raises serious doubts about their efficacy. There is an increasing concern that corporate codes are being misused to deflect public criticism of corporate activities and to reduce the demand for state regulation of corporations. In some cases, codes have actually worsened working conditions and the bargaining power of labour unions. Moreover, increasing numbers of NGO–business partnerships established through corporate codes and CSR measures have created and widened divisions within the NGO community and sharpened differences between NGOs and labour unions. Voluntary codes of conduct can never substitute for mandatory regulations, whether at the state or the global, quasi-state level. Nor can they substitute for labour and community rights. At best, voluntary codes can complement binding state or global regulations and provide an opportunity to raise environmental, health, labour, and other public-interest issues.

IMPLEMENTATION ISSUES

Despite the recent proliferation of codes, their actual implementation and monitoring remain problematic. For example, information about codes is generally not available to workers and consumers; labour codes have often been introduced in companies without the prior knowledge or consent of the workers for whom they are intended. A key issue regarding the implementation process is the independence of the monitoring body. Since large auditing and consultancy firms usually carry out the monitoring of company codes with little transparency or public participation, whether the codes are actually being implemented remains a closely guarded secret. Besides, auditing firms may not reveal damaging information since they get paid by the company being audited.

Recent voluntary initiatives, such as MSIs, are considered more credible because NGOs and labour unions are involved as external monitors. But the authenticity of such monitoring cannot be guaranteed by the mere involvement of NGOs and civil society. Researchers have found that the development of standards by some MSIs has taken place in a top-down manner without the involvement of workers at the grassroots level (Shaw & Hale 2002: 104). For instance, concerns of workers in India and Bangladesh were not taken into account in the standards created by MSIs, such as the Ethical Trading Initiative and Social Accountability International (Utting 2002: 96–97).

If recent experience is any guide, the struggle to implement codes can be frustrating, time-consuming, and ultimately futile. It dissipates any enthusiasm to struggle for regulatory controls on TNCs. This was evident in the case of the decade-long campaign in India to develop a national code to promote breastfeeding and restrict the marketing of baby food by TNCs along the lines of World Health Organization (WHO) codes (Singh & Greer 1996: 39–43). Therefore, voluntary codes require serious rethinking on the part of those who consider them as a cure-all to problems posed by TNCs. The unveiling of corporate scandals, most famously Enron, Worldcom, and Parmalat underline the important role of strong regulatory measures.[7] One cannot ignore the fact that all these corporations were signatories to several international codes, while some of them (for instance, Enron) had developed their own codes.

WHY STATE REGULATION?

The proponents of neoliberal ideology argue that states should abdicate their legislative and enforcement responsibilities by handing them over to NGOs and civil-society organizations, which should in turn develop voluntary measures in collaboration with business. Without undermining the relevance of such voluntary approaches, it cannot be denied that the primary responsibility of regulating the corporate behaviour of TNCs remains with national states. It is difficult to envisage the regulation of TNCs without the active involvement of states. State regulations remain the primary vehicle for local and national government and international institutions to implement public policies. National governments have the primary responsibility of protecting and improving the social and economic conditions of all citizens, particularly the poorer and more vulnerable ones.

It is clear that not all states are democratic and that supervisory mechanisms are often weak, particularly in developing countries. Despite these shortcomings, however, states remain formally accountable to their citizens, whereas corporations are accountable only to their shareholders, and most international institutions derive their mandates from the states that create them. National regulatory measures are thus also necessary to implement international frameworks. The additional advantage of national regulatory measures is that they would be applicable to all companies, domestic or transnational, operating under a country's jurisdiction, thereby potentially maximizing welfare gains.

The national regulatory framework is very important, and it will not wither away under the influence of globalization. On its own, transnational capital lacks the necessary power and ability to mould the world economy in its favour. Rather, it strives for the support of nation-states and inter-state institutions to shape the contemporary world economy. State policies are vital for the advancement and sustenance of transnational capital on a world scale. Investment decisions by TNCs are not always influenced by the degree of national liberalization but are also governed by state regulations in areas as diverse as taxation, trade, investment, currency, property rights, and labour.

A stable economic and political environment is also an important determinant. Transnational capital looks upon legislative, judicial, and executive institutions not merely to protect and enforce property rights and contract laws, but also to provide social, political, and macroeconomic stability. In the absence of such a policy framework, contemporary globalization would not have taken place. Social and political conflicts are also resolved primarily through state mechanisms. The fact that a strong and stable state is a prerequisite for the development and sustenance of the market economy is evident from the failure of economic reforms in many developing countries. In addition, state intervention is also necessary to prevent and correct market failures. There are innumerable instances of market failures with huge economic, social, and environmental costs throughout the world, with pollution and monopoly power being the most popular examples of market failure; however, the government can introduce pollution taxes and regulate monopolies to correct the distortions created by such market failure. Besides, the government is expected to provide public goods and services (for example, schools, hospitals, and highways) to all citizens because the market has failed to do so.

In the context of global capitalism, national states provide the legal framework within which all markets operate. The notion of a "free market" is a myth, because all markets are governed by regulations, though the nature and degree of regulation may vary from market to market. Even the much-acclaimed self-regulation or co-regulation model would lack legitimacy if it were not backed by a government decree. In fact, it is impossible to conceive of contemporary neoliberal globalization without laws, which for the most part exist within the realm of nation-states. Even the global rules on trade enforced by international institutions (for instance, the WTO) are not completely independent of national states.

WHITHER THE REGULATORY FRAMEWORK?

The first step toward regulating TNC behaviour, I argue, begins at the national level. To accomplish this goal, host countries in particular need to adopt appropriate regulatory measures on transparency, labour, environmental, and taxation matters. At the same time, these countries could follow the US example—in such legislation as the Foreign Corrupt Practices Act, which penalizes US-based corporations for bribery and corrupt practices in foreign countries—and put in place regulations to ensure that the same standards are followed by their TNCs, irrespective of where they operate in the world. National regulatory measures could be supplemented by new forms of regulatory cooperation and coordination between states at regional and international levels. By providing the overall framework and guiding principles, regional and international efforts would enhance the policy space and powers to regulate TNCs and foreign investment in order to meet national developmental objectives.

At the domestic level, the political climate in many developing countries has drastically changed in the past two decades. Neoliberal policies now frame almost every political process and go unchallenged even among some ranks of the left. There is a strong lobby in many developing countries (for instance, India) consisting of big business, the upper middle classes, and the media, which supports the entry of foreign capital and demands fewer regulatory mechanisms. Some developing countries, such as India and China, are also witnessing the emergence of

"third-world TNCs" that are expanding their businesses in other countries. These developments make the task of regulating corporations still
more difficult. How can such countries demand greater regulation of
private capital flows? Besides, it fragments the coalitions of developing countries and weakens their collective-bargaining power in international economic policy arenas such as the WTO.

However, the global financial crisis that began in the US and
European countries in 2007 has put a serious question mark about the
efficacy of the self-regulation model, as many banks and financial institutions were "lightly" regulated, on the presumption that institutions
know what they are doing. As the crisis has clearly revealed, banks and
financial institutions, left to themselves, did not follow prudent corporate
governance norms. Many of them have had to be bailed out by national
authorities at a massive cost to the taxpayers. There is a growing consensus on greater and better regulation of banks and corporate entities.
It remains to be seen how the crisis unfolds in the coming years and if
it will bring back an agenda of greater regulation in the policy arena.

Nonetheless, even though the task of establishing the authority of
states over TNCs may be difficult, it would not be impossible as long as
efforts were backed by strong domestic political mobilization. Herein
the role of NGOs, labour unions, and other civil-society organizations
becomes important to strengthen domestic political processes.

It needs to be stressed here that a robust, transparent, and efficient
supervisory framework is also required to oversee the implementation of
national regulations. Otherwise, expected gains from a strong regulatory
framework would not materialize. India provides a classic example of
having a strong regulatory framework but poor supervisory structures.
In the present world, there is a need for greater international supervision of private investment flows based on cooperation between home
country and host country supervisors.

While acknowledging that voluntary approaches could be used as
tools for leverage on corporate behaviour, and therefore are worth testing, my discussion in this chapter underscores the need for enhancing
the state regulatory and supervisory frameworks. The preceding analysis of the problems with voluntary codes shows that strategies aimed
at privatizing regulation are unlikely to succeed; even the limited gains
made in the past through voluntary approaches always rested on governmental backing. Voluntary codes of conduct can never be a substitute for regulations, nor can they substitute for labour and community
rights. At best, voluntary codes can complement state regulations and
provide space for raising environmental, health, labour, and other public-interest issues. As pointed out by Rhys Jenkins, "[c]odes of conduct .

should be seen as an area of political contestation, rather than as a solution to the problems created by the globalization of economic activity" (2001: 70).

NOTES

1   "Global Sourcing and Operating Guidelines." <http://www1.umn.edu/humanrts//links/levicode.html>.

2   The Ethical Trading Initiative is an alliance of corporations, unions, and NGOs intended "to improve the working lives of people across the globe who make or grow consumer goods." <http://www.ethicaltrade.org/>.

3   See <http://www.cleanclothes.org/>.

4   See <http://www.oecd.org/document/18/0,3343,en_2649_34889_2397532_1_1_1_1,00.html>.

5   See <http://actrav.itcilo.org/actrav-english/telearn/global/ilo/guide/triparti.htm>.

6   See <http://www.unglobalcompact.org/aboutthegc/index.html>.

7   See Francesca Di Meglio, "Inside the Parmalat Scandal," <http://www.italian-srus.com/articles/ourpaesani/parmalat.htm>; "The Worldcom Story," <http://www.cbc.ca/news/background/worldcom/>; and "The Enron Scandal," <http://www.businessweek.com/magazine/toc/02_04/B3767enron.htm>.

REFERENCES

Jenkins, Rhys. 2001. *Corporate Codes of Conduct: Self-Regulation in a Global Economy*. Geneva: UNRISD.

Sethi, S. Prakash. 2003. *Setting Global Standards: Guidelines for Creating Codes of Conduct in Multinational Corporations*. New York: Wiley.

———. 2002. "Corporate Codes of Conduct and the Success of Globalization." *Ethics and International Affairs* 16(1): 89–107.

Shaw, Linda, and Angela Hale. 2002. "The Emperor's New Clothes: What Codes Mean for Workers in the Garment Industry." In Rhys Jenkins, R. Pearson, and G. Seyfang (eds.), *Corporate Responsibility and Labor Rights: Codes of Conduct in the Global Economy*. London: Earthscan. 101–12.

Singh, Kavaljit, and Jed Greer. 1996. *TNCs and India: A Citizen's Guide to Transnational Corporations*. New Delhi: Public Interest Research Group.

Utting, Peter. 2002. "Regulating Business via Multistakeholder Initiatives: A Preliminary Assessment." In *Voluntary Approaches to Corporate Responsibility: Readings and a Resource Guide*. Geneva: UN Non-Governmental Liaison Service Development Dossier.

5

Globalization and the Labour Process[1]

BOB RUSSELL

In this chapter I discuss how we conceptualize the labour process and changes to it in the era of capitalist globalization. Without wishing to be reductionist, I argue that changes in the way goods and services are produced, including where they are created, is central to the whole theme of globalization. So, just as the analysis of capitalist production commences with a study of the labour processes that define it (Marx 1971), returning to the labour process provides a fruitful way in to the subject matter of contemporary globalization. This chapter is mainly an opportunity for theoretical reflection, although where appropriate I provide empirical examples, drawn from fieldwork conducted both by myself and by other researchers, in order to highlight changes in the labour process and the contributions of such to globalization.

To begin with, the labour process can formally be defined as the way things, whether it be goods or services, are produced. Necessarily it entails the use of technologies that are applied to inputs, such as raw materials in the case of manufacturing, or to other people in the provision of services. Technologies are social creations, and their utilization assumes definite forms of organization. Therefore the labour process refers to the way in which working relationships are organized around the use of technologies to produce designated outcomes. The notion of job design in part captures the concept of the labour process under capitalism, in which relationships of domination and subordination inhere to the actual conduct of work, beginning when someone other than the worker does the designing. Such relationships imply a dialectic of control over the design, selection, and utilization of technologies, and in studies of the labour process it is essential to understand how such control is manifested. An examination of the labour process and globalization such as that undertaken here is therefore required in order to consider how control over work processes is changing.

In this chapter I see an intimate connection between changes in the labour process, how and where we produce, and globalization. In particular, three key developments that have taken hold over the last twenty years or so and that have fundamentally altered the nature of the labour process may be identified. These changes are centrally implicated in the new cycle of global accumulation that was unleashed during the 1990s and that followed the economically fraught period that lasted from approximately 1973 through to the early 1990s.[2] During that period of "creative destruction," the ground was prepared for the up-tick that would follow as new innovations were incorporated into work processes and old structures for regulating work relations were torn asunder and replaced by new managerial paradigms. The changes can be summarized under the following three headings:

- the information and communications technology revolution, with ICTs coming to constitute the principal new means of production in a global economy, which is increasingly based around flows of information;
- the birth of a new management paradigm, driven by the rise of human resource management but more commonly known as managerialism; and
- the spatial reconfiguration/dispersal of labour processes across the global economy.

These changes have had profound effects on both the technical division of labour—how people work—and the social division of labour—who does what where—and have triggered major upheavals along the way. In the remainder of this chapter, I will first discuss how each of these factors individually is altering the nature of work. I will then map out the main interconnections between technological innovation, managerialism, and spatial reconfiguration. In the process, I will point out how contemporary changes to the ways in which work is organized represent insufficient solutions to the contradictions that are posed by a regime of globalized accumulation.

In order to avoid confusion, and perhaps at the risk of stating the obvious, I should make it clear that this chapter is about the capitalist labour process and the changes that it is undergoing. These changes are both a cause and a consequence of globalization. In this account, and to use the helpful language of the regulationists (Boyer 1990), I investigate some of the elements of a new regime of production, namely those that are occurring around the organization of work. These are structural changes to the ways in which people work in jobs, but in capitalism such changes are usually manifested through cyclical crises that are both more prolonged and deeper than average, as was the case for the period that lasted from 1973 to 1993. Such changes are usually first observed in those leading economic sectors that set their stamp upon an age, while some of the empirical examples that are cited in this chapter are drawn from these work environments.

UNDOING THE DIVISIONS OF LABOUR: THE IMPACT OF ICTS

Personal computers (PCs) began to enter the workplace in the 1980s in both the manufacturing industry and the service sector (Baran & Teegarden 1987; Castells 2001; Greenbaum 1995; Zuboff 1988). This had profound, although disputed effects on the way work is carried out internally within organizations. Consider, for a moment, the following two ethnographic descriptions culled from a pulp and paper mill and a bakery, respectively.

> You need a new learning capability, because when you operate with the computer, you can't see what is happening. There is a difference in the mental and conceptual capabilities you need—you have to do things in your mind....
>
> You have to know what is happening when something is wrong by being able to relate the data you see to the actual process as you can envision it. (Zuboff 1988: 71, 86)

> Though simple to use, the dough-kneading machine was complex in design; its computer operating system was opaque ... we sat for two hours waiting for the service saviors to arrive from the firm which had designed the machines.... The waiting workers were morose and upset.... The bakers felt this impulse to cope but were flummoxed by the technology....
>
> Bread had become a screen representation. As a result of working in this way, the bakers now no longer actually know how to bake bread. (Sennett 1998: 68, 72–73)

In the first quotation, taken from Zuboff's *In the Age of the Smart Machine*, a worker is reporting upon the effects that computerization is having upon his work in a pulp-and-paper mill. These observations suggest fundamental changes to the way in which work is carried out in a contemporary manufacturing environment. From the gestation of political economy in Adam Smith's pin factory, it has been common to point to the growth in the technical division of labour in work. This refers to the ever finer subdivision of *jobs* into discrete *tasks* that are assigned to individual workers, a tendency of capitalist industry that was given full discursive expression in the principles of scientific management as enunciated by Frederick Taylor (Braverman 1974). Key to Taylor's system is the notion that "As far as possible the workmen ... should be entirely relieved of the work of planning and of all work which is more or less clerical in its nature. All possible brain work should be removed from the shop and centered in the planning or laying-out department" (Taylor 1972: 98–99). The work of planning, or what would later become known as job design, was ceded over to managerial prerogative. Non-managerial staff were to carry out whatever instructions they received, while unions would later come to bargain over the terms and conditions attached to each task (Jacoby 1991).

The paper-mill operative whom Zuboff cites suggests that this is no longer an accurate description of his job. He specifically alludes to a reintegration of the mental and manual aspects of his work, or, more accurately, it is the former that now seems to dominate his description. He attributes this to working with a computer, where a piece of information technology has become the principal means of production in the labour process being described. The computer in this scenario empowers the worker. It offers the user a broader overview of the operation and what it does. Work is mainly preoccupied with the interpretation of information upon which further operational decisions are taken. Large production facilities with a skeletal staff that spends most of its time off the production floor area in a "control" room is a common characteristic of such workplaces; indeed, anyone who has ever had the opportunity to visit the site of a highly automated process industry—whether it be an oil refinery, a metal-smelting operation, a steel mill, or a brewery—will recognize these features.[3] Meanwhile, more and more activity aims to replicate the main features that are exhibited in such highly automated, continuous-flow labour processes.

As implied in the preceding description, information technologies have made possible the recombination of tasks into larger job bundles. In such cases, workers are expected to take responsibility for a larger span of control in the processes they oversee. This might include a blurring of the boundaries between maintenance and production work, or between managerial and non-managerial work, as when supervisors are rostered off during unsociable hours (e.g., night shifts) and operations remain the responsibility of designated work teams. Indeed, much of the so-called de-layering of middle-management ranks in industry has been made possible as a result of the wider responsibilities assumed by those who have remained in employment (Grey 1999).

The same trends of reassembling work can be observed in labour processes where the principal output is information. For example, back-office work such as data entry and analysis is increasingly combined with customer-service work, which is itself more likely to be merged with marketing (e.g., up-selling). Job-holders interact with the public to produce and provide information, but in the process also input and possibly analyze data while maintaining organizational archives. Instead of a subdivision of work between receptionists, investigators, software navigators, and data file clerks, a new occupational title—the customer service representative (CSR)—is responsible for each of the above functions, some of which are undertaken with near simultaneity (Russell 2006). In addition, more and more lines of inquiry are run through general queues, where the workers who staff them are expected to provide "one-stop service" for a wide range of public demands. This logic is very much at work in the growth of contact centres, or what I have elsewhere termed info-service work (Russell 2009). In banking centres, for example, it is now common for workers to be "multi-skilled" in order to deal with and alternate between different product areas such as insurance and mortgage lending. Meanwhile, governments have recently taken to providing public services through single telephone-entry contact centres that cover all departments within a given jurisdiction under one telephone number. For example, at the local government level, workers are trained to be able to answer and act on queries dealing with property taxes, recreational and social services, public housing, and a range of other public amenities. In these work places, employees are expected to be able to cope with and resolve all manner of public inquiry rather than passing callers on to specific departments in an extended division of labour.

While information technologies have been critical in these developments, there should be no mistaking the fact that the more efficient use of labour (i.e., economizing on labour) has been a prime driver in these trends. One of the first examples of job amalgamation to come to mind can be found in the Japanese automotive industry, where the notion of one worker/one machine was discarded with the advent of continuous improvement and lean production systems that became synonymous with the industry (Womach, Jones & Roos 1990; Rinehart, Huxley &

Robertson 1997). Responsibility for different machines, as well as set-up, housekeeping, and some maintenance duties is simply part of the efficiencies that drive work in this post-Fordist environment. The same tendencies have been identified in other industries, such as steel and electronics manufacturing (Kenney & Florida 1993) and apparel manufacturing (Appelbaum et al. 2000), although some analyses have tended to mistakenly identify such trends with a "re-Taylorization" of the labour process on account of undeniably greater levels of work intensification that accompany such work systems (Baldry, Bain & Taylor 1998).

The advent of the customer contact centre and info-service labour is another case in point. Let us not forget that the rise of this type of work coincided with the closure of local branch offices and over-the-counter service in such sectors as banking, as well as in the provision of such public goods as telephone and utilities service (Bain and Taylor 2002; Ellis and Taylor 2006; Russell 2007). In other words, "bigger jobs" equated to greater rationalization in the use of labour, whether it be in the manufacturing industry or in the information and service sectors. Information technology has enabled such reconfigurations in the technical division of labour to take place, but of greater importance in driving such changes have been the magnified levels of domestic and global competition unleashed by the coordinated deregulation of the banking, transportation, and telecommunications sectors and, in the public sector, by the advent of competition policy and the new public sector management paradigm (du Gay 2007: chs. 5–7; Shields & Evans 1998).

While the application of *information* technologies has facilitated changes in the organization of work within units of production, the availability of new *communications* technologies has occasioned major shifts in the social division of labour between organizations as well as between regions of the world economy. Communications technologies refers mainly to the digitization of all forms of communication, including text, voice, and image. Global communication in its multifarious dimensions is now very cheap, while the infrastructure that has been constructed (primarily fibre-optic cable) is capable of carrying very heavy loads of traffic. While this has allowed for a flourishing of various types of much hyped e-business activity, more important are the effects that it has had on business-to-business relations. Here the movement has been in the opposite direction to that witnessed around the technical division of labour where, to some degree, jobs are being reassembled. In this case, communication technologies have made possible the partial disaggregation of the vertically integrated firm. This has now become a mantra in the business strategy texts through a focus on the identification of core capabilities and subsequent outsourcing opportunities while giving rise to considerable theoretical speculation on new organizational forms, including networks (Castells 1996, 2001), and reticulated organizations and rhizimorphous patterns of business operation (Boltanski & Chiapello 2007).[4] In a truly global system, outsourced activities may be placed anywhere where requisite skill pools and infrastructure can be found (or created); this takes us to the heart of globalization and its differences with previous forms of international integration, which remained comparatively shallow in retrospect (Dicken 2007).

In the next sections of the chapter I examine the extent to which the full potential of the new means of production are being undermined by the practices of managerialism and the search for competitive advantage on a global scale.

MANAGERIALISM, THE LABOUR PROCESS, AND HUMAN RESOURCE MANAGEMENT

Sennett's observations in the second quotation of the previous section raise issues that lead into the main theme of this segment. Although workers now have responsibility for whole processes, they are also distant from them in both literal and figurative senses. According to Sennett, today's workforce often lacks the deeper understandings that are necessary to cope with situations that deviate from smoothly flowing routines. Superficiality leads to a loss of identification with the work and all that goes with it. To this diagnosis it can be added that management does attempt to fill the void with measures of its own, and this has important implications for how the labour process is managed and for how workers are controlled.

Various factors have led to the growth of complexity in work processes. Just as ICTs have worked against the tyranny of distance at one level, more and more work takes place at a distance, both literally and metaphorically. Literally, although the notion of an "anywhere, anytime" production regime will always be a fanciful (dys)utopia,[5] the production of goods and services for global markets now takes place in a far greater number of places. Metaphorically, as the quotation taken from Sennett's *Corrosion of Character* above suggests, with the mediation of ICTs, workers are now more distant from the operations they oversee. Thus, while work processes may be more complex, this does not automatically equate to empowerment in the labour process. It does, however, pose new challenges for the management of work and the control of workers. As physical distance increases, trust may decrease, and this lessens the likelihood of self-management in the workplace (Batt, Doellgast & Kwon 2005). As metaphorical distance in the labour process increases, this may tax the ability and/or willingness of workers to take responsibility, as the example of Sennett's bakers and the incredible levels of product waste that he observes demonstrate. In both instances, the perceived need for managerial control becomes greater as work becomes more complex; part of this complexity is occasioned by computer-mediated distantiation.

These changes in the nature of the technical and social divisions of labour represent an important shift. While it used to be thought that more complex forms of work were more amenable to forms of responsible autonomy amongst workforces (Friedman 1977), today they have promoted the growth of managerialism. This currently popular term refers to ongoing efforts to render more transparent the work methods that constitute the object of its practice. This may be done by prescribing in ever greater detail how work should be conducted and by establishing ways of measuring conformance to established standards, without subdividing work into finer and finer individual tasks, as in classical Taylorism. Rather, as work becomes more complex—such as when it contains an aesthetic dimension, as much interactive service work does (Hochschild 1983)—or when elements of customization are present, such prescription is made much more challenging. There is always the danger that insistence upon conformity will undermine those very elements of the work that are especially valued (see Knights & McCabe 1997 and 2000, and Russell 2007, for illuminating examples). For these reasons, although managerialism is associated with standardization, it does not necessarily mean simplifying work, and it definitely does not occur through the task fragmentation of Taylorist systems of production. Recent attempts to label these new labour processes as exemplars of mass customized bureaucracies (Frenkel et al. 1998), as customer-oriented bureaucracies (Korczynski 2001, 2002), or as distinguishing between mass production, mass customization, and professional service work designs (Batt & Moynihan 2002) underscore these points of difference.

Given that the results of many work processes, especially in customer-service functions, are more opaque and defy strict standardization or modelling in their attainment, the managerialist impulse is directed toward the establishment of systems of documented accountability. In this case, increasing amounts of time are taken up by workers documenting just what they have accomplished, often in anticipation of having to defend actions that have been taken. As work has become more information-driven and consequently reflexive, its oversight by others (i.e., management) has consequently become more challenging. Attempts to standardize complexity and enforce documented accountability are two of the main managerialist responses to this situation. They often fall under the rubric of knowledge management, a discursive expression and perhaps a testimony to the ultimate futility in attempting to manage work that is high in informational content (Alvesson 2004). In short, as work is reassembled or compressed in time, and dispersed across space, concerns about the adequacy of documented processes and adherence to them are magnified. The nature of work moves in one direction that could signal greater empowerment for those who do it, while managerialism moves in another, bequeathing to labour responsibilities without power. This is a contradiction that is summed up in the notion of a dual movement observed in many workplaces, where more challenging work is met with tighter systems of control demanding ever more accountability. The growth of a quality-assurance "industry" in which vast amounts of time and other resources are dedicated to documenting that one does what one claims to be doing is one indicator of the managerial anxiety that is introduced with globalized labour processes. Another, the advent of human resource management, is also very much a part of this managerialist impulse.

Like the term globalization, human resource management (HRM) is a concept of recent vintage. Storey (2001) dates the rise of HRM from the early 1980s when it began to displace the older notion of personnel administration. In its broadest sense, HRM is claimed to portray the employment relationship in a different light and in a different relationship to the other dimensions of successful business practice. In the parlance of HRM, given the mobility of capital and the possibilities for technological transfer in a rapidly globalizing world, employees ought to be viewed as the most important competitive asset that organizations possess. While technologies can be copied, leased, or otherwise appropriated and capital can be raised on global financial markets, commitment on the part of employees is an input that cannot be superficially replicated. Performance is best viewed as a strategic organizational issue rather than the concern of a specialized department or function. With these as starting assumptions, HRM casts itself in the role of a driver rather than a passive attribute of contemporary business strategy.

The proponents of HRM argue that high and sustainable employee performance can come about only through the sort of commitment that constitutes the holy grail of successful HRM practice. Commitment in turn presumes both goal alignment between the parties to the employment relation and integration with an overarching business strategy (Guest 1987). A thoughtfully constructed HRM system should be capable of fulfilling both business needs and personal aspirations, at least according to proponents of the paradigm (e.g., Peters & Waterman 1988; for criticisms, see Guest 1990 and Legge 1995: ch. 3), in a new form of employment unilateralism (Fox 1974). As conveyed in the images of "best practice" and the currently fashionable "high performance work systems" approach (Appelbaum et al. 2000), HRM aims, in theory at least, at a holism that is directed at workers and their performance.

This begins with strategic recruitment and the selection of new employees, which often involves multi-stage interviewing and testing protocols and is followed up with systematic training and induction programs that typically carry on for weeks instead of days, involving certified trainers and classroom learning as well as on-the-job training (Callaghan & Thompson 2002). Many organizations, especially in info-service work, also dedicate a certain proportion of their operating budgets to ongoing training and development. In addition to providing workforces with continuous updates on new product and service options, such training may be used to develop more generic skills such as working in a team environment, group problem solving, and quality control (Smith 2001). Importantly, such ongoing development extends beyond narrow technical training, with the aim of instilling concerns for such matters as quality and business improvement in the workforce.

In this sense, contemporary HRM seeks to be more than a policy toolbox that blankets the employment relationship and seeks policy alignment from recruitment through to recognition, reward, and retention. In moving from compliance or even consent to commitment in workplace relations, there must also be shared beliefs both in the fairness and common-sense nature of work demands and in the goals that they espouse and serve. For this reason, such practices need to be situated within a broader field of subjective understandings or meanings about working for a specific organization. The object here is to provide an interpretive framework—a lens—through which organizational history, working relationships, and organizational choices may be decoded by group members in ways that make ethnomethodological sense. As Schoenberger (1997) reminds us, culture is very much about the exercise of power, the ability to have specific ways of defining and seeing accepted as natural and therefore legitimate (see also Kunda 1992); and contemporary managerialism is very strong on culture. In this schema HRM is not only a cultural practice but also one that works on culture through the values and policies that it enunciates and implements (Ezzamel & Willmott 1998; Willmott 1993). Thus, in addition to administering the employment relationship through recruitment, training, remuneration, etc., HRM is very much about operating on workplace culture in order to achieve the alignments that are sought for the globally competitive organization (Legge 1995: ch. 6).

Officially sanctioned cultures will try to influence commitment through operating on identity (Alvesson & Willmott 2002). HRM practices will attempt to establish strong identity ties between the worker and the meanings, codes, norms, rituals, and values that constitute the official face of the organization (Bolman & Deal 2003; Schein 1985). This is particularly important in face-to-face or voice-to-voice customer-centred work, where organizational identity ideally feeds into quality service delivery (Korczynski 2002). In other words, what is being suggested is that in work situations where direct control (Friedman 1977) through task simplification is rendered difficult because of the complexity, indeterminacy, or distance through which work is undertaken, cultural control may be lent a greater scope in the management of the labour process. Such control normalizes managerialism as a practice. Workers are expected to adhere to standards, service-level agreements, and contracts because they believe in their validity. Ideally, "who I work for," "what I do," and "how I do it" become part of "who I am," while considerable resources are invested in making certain that these aspects of work are treated as part of a natural order. In this scenario HRM assumes the mantle of cultural custodian, and normative control, that is control of the self, is turned into a principal component of managerialism.

To develop these points further, another comparison is instructive. Burawoy's (1979) analysis of machine-shop workers and the significance of the mental games they construct around the execution of their work represents an instructive point of difference with current circumstances in many labour processes. Burawoy locates the importance of such activity, beginning with the point that it is constructed by workers for their own individual edification. Such alternative mental constructs help people get through the working day, by producing satisfactions from the travails of bending and shaping metal. But just as important are some of the unintended consequences that emerge from such activity. Getting tacit agreement over the legitimacy of the game garners a broader consent for the social structures (i.e., employment relations) in which they are housed. As Burawoy states, "The game does not reflect an underlying harmony of interests; on the contrary, it is responsible for and generates that harmony.... The game becomes an end in itself" (1979: 82).

The game that is being referred to here is known among the social actors who construct it as "making out." Workers decide whether or not they will strive for the bonuses that are attached to producing above specific benchmark levels on individual jobs. Burawoy argues that the main incentive for "making out" is not monetary, but is rather the challenge, interest, wile, and camaraderie that such activity lends to participating in the labour process. Deciding whether or not to pick up the challenge of making out on any particular job constitutes an act of autonomy in its own right. Playing the game leads to acceptance into the informal work groups and status circles that populate the shop floor. Post-mortem narratives of making out dominate discussions among workers during meal breaks. Risk, uncertainty, and ultimately victory over recalcitrant materials construct new layers of meaning to the lived experience of work and in the process validates the self as a competent and skilled worker. In the end, even if production is not maximized—for there are well-understood ceilings to the amount of work that will be turned in at the end of every shift—it is enhanced. For this reason, shop-floor managers collude in the practices that workers initiate. These dynamics of "give and take" between workers and supervisors lend themselves to the production of a pluralistic culture that, although outwardly adversarial, also contains important elements of normative understanding around the rules of making out, and this contributes to the creation of consent.

Although this scenario of manufactured consent has several prerequisites (e.g., piece-rate wages paid to skilled metal workers producing in small batch lots), if we were to fast-forward 30 years, what changes might we detect? First, less seems to be left to chance in today's world of production. Burawoy describes in his account of consent the production of an organic culture rising up from the shop floor. In many workplaces it is no longer the case that workers informally agree among themselves upon an acceptable range of output, or negotiate such with line management. Rather, it is more likely that they will receive targets or be presented with benchmark KPIs (key performance indicators) to which adherence is expected following a period of induction and training (see, for example, the call-centre workplaces described in Knights & McCabe 1997 and Russell 2002). Such expectations are received as part of the organizational culture, which is likely to be codified in more general terms through the display of mission and values statements to which workers are invited to subscribe.

Nor are workers likely to have the option of choosing to meet such targets. Again, failure to attain KPIs may quickly escalate into a "performance management issue" for the worker, who will likely be offered "help" in the form of further training or perhaps one-on-one coaching with a team leader to get up to the prescribed benchmark or face dismissal. Also, more likely than not, today's workforce will be interacting directly with other human beings to provide a service, which may be fully or partially consumed in the act of its production. When this is the case, expectations are much more immediate. People are expected to be accountable for their actions in producing and delivering the service, and the tolerance for games, or even honest mistakes, on the part of the public is much less obvious. These points are continuously being emphasized in team meetings and training sessions. To the extent that fun and games are part of the job, they will be authored and led by management while workers are expected to join in with the same level of enthusiasm that they bring to other realms of their work (Collinson 2002; Kinnie, Hutchinson & Purcell 2000; Russell 2002).

While Burawoy problematized worker consent to capitalist labour processes, contemporary HRM alters this research agenda. Consent may be willingly extended, or it may at best be a begrudging affair, which suggests that it is conditional and subject to continuous reconsideration. Commitment suggests a stronger bond to one's work and the objectives that it embodies. It is said to be organized around a "psychological contract" (Rousseau 1995) between employer and worker—a telling term in its own right that reflects a preference for methodological individualism in the study of work (Guest 1999). Such "contracts" hold out the promise of joint gains forthcoming from mutually held expectations. Employer expectations are especially well defined in the age of managerialism. They are continuously being drilled home in the cultural mission that HRM has set for itself through the colonization of labour time, the spaces of globalized labouring activity, and self-identity. Note, however, that this theoretical assessment should not be assumed to prejudge the results of such endeavours; as other studies have demonstrated (see, for example, Scott 1994; Fleming & Spicer 2007), the acquisition of worker commitment remains a problematical quest. In lieu of the self-assured, "take it or leave it" mentality that emerges in Burawoy's study of metalworkers in mid-1970s America and that was to pose the challenge that HRM took up some thirty years on, Sennett introduces us to despondent bakers (1998) and depressed NHS nurses (2008). These groups seem to be quite removed from the highly energized, committed workforces that are the ultimate desideratum of HRM, an indication that the ambitions of managerialism as exhibited in HRM practice continue to reach beyond what is attainable and desirable. The promise that was inherent in a movement away from Taylorism has been undermined by new normative forms of control that are highlighted in contemporary managerialist practice and, as we see in the next section, by the uncertainties associated with the emergence of new social divisions of labour.

SPATIAL RE-MAPPINGS

I discussed what is commonly referred to as globalization when referring above to spatial shifts in the social division of labour that occurred in the wake of advances in information and communications technology.

The most visible expression of this is the outsourcing boom that is fundamentally redrawing the economic map of the world economy. China, which in 1980 accounted for less than one per cent of world manufacturing exports, presently supplies over seven per cent (Glyn 2006) and in the process has taken over the mantle, "workshop of the world" (Arrighi 2007). In US dollars this represents a growth of over 3000 per cent, with manufactured commodities especially in sectors such as electronic equipment, textiles/garments, and steel making up the bulk of such exports (China Statistical Information and Consultancy Service Centre 2005).[6]

To this paradigm of export-led industrialization, India has added an additional twist, in what we have dubbed an Export Led Services Provision (ELSP) model (Thite & Russell 2007). This refers to the growth in outsourced services of all types, including IT development and Information Technology Enabled Services (ITeS) that together form a suite of business process outsourcing (BPO) capabilities (Srivastava & Theodore 2006).[7] Some idea of the significance of such outsourcing can be ascertained simply by noting that over 400 of the Fortune 500 companies in the US, and 70 of the top FTSE 100 firms in the UK, currently outsource some of their work to India (Budhwar & Malhotra 2008). Employment growth in BPO has expanded from about 280,000 workers in 2002 to a projected 3.7 million in 2012, of whom the vast majority will be in long-distance customer service (Government of India 2003). As recently as 1995, gems, jewellery items, and textiles/apparel topped the list of Indian exports to the rest of the world. Today IT products (such as software) and ITeS services top the list; such have been the changes.

Whether it be the outsourcing of car-parts manufacturing to northern Mexico, computer assembly to Malaysia, apparel production to China, or call-centre service to India, these practices have had profound effects on how economic units are managed and on how labour is controlled. The development of new industries such as logistics, and new fields of management study such as supply-chain and inventory management, owe their existence to these trends (Bonacich & Wilson 2008). With outsourcing has come a greater focus on rationalizing what Marx termed the sphere of commodity circulation, given the growing importance of a new social division of labour in the world economy. Planning, tracking, and accounting for the movement of goods and services on a global scale has grown alongside the globalization of other labour processes.

Outsourcing amends the logic of economic relations in the world economy. *Comparative* advantage gives way to *competitive* advantage. The former refers to exchanges of different goods or services between national economies based upon natural (Ricardo 1973) or contrived (Emmanuel 1972; Amin 1974) advantages. The latter relates to the production of the same or related goods or services in different host economies in a true globalization of labour processes, which means that the same work or work requiring the same skills and qualifications is undertaken in the same way with comparable results, but in vastly different places (Russell & Thite 2008). For example, one could virtually "visit" call centres operated by a company one conducts business with and find workers at branches in Manchester, Mumbai, Montreal, and Melbourne doing exactly the same work. Extending the example, if one were to call the business, depending upon the time the call was placed one might be served by a worker in any of the above locations, with requests being met in identical ways and with indistinguishable results. This implies not only a globalization of productive functions with a consequential undoing of the old social division of labour between the "north" and the "south," but at the same time a globalization of the managerial practices that were detailed in the preceding section.

This type of deep economic integration comes about when firms are able to take advantage of the vastly different cost structures that prevail in different locations. This is especially consequential in more labour-intensive operations; hence the movement of apparel, footwear, computer assemblage, toy manufacturing, etc., to China, and call-centre and business services work to India. To continue with the example of the last paragraph, the worker at the Mumbai call centre continues to earn almost exactly 10 per cent of the salary of her counterpart in Melbourne. When productivity is more or less standardized across global space, differentials in labour costs of these startling proportions become very decisive indeed. And, when in the words of one highly successful Indian CEO "it is possible to outsource anything that can be put down a fibre-optic cable," the lure of wage arbitrage may become an irresistible fact in the absence of countervailing political regulation (Beck 2000). Under such conditions, new competitive pressures are placed squarely on labour as national systems of regulation are expected to adapt to new global benchmarks of performance.[8] This is undoubtedly one factor that accounts for the normalization, if not the success, of managerialism in today's workplaces.

CONCLUSION: CONNECTIONS AND CONTRADICTIONS

Connections between the three changes that we have been considering— the centrality of ICT usage in contemporary work processes, managerialism, and spatial disembedding—can now be considered in a more relational fashion. At the centre of these relationships lies the transnational corporation (TNC), the main organizing entity in a globalizing world. Although we are used to thinking of these as "western institutions," this no longer does justice to the realities of globalization and the growing presence of Chinese and Indian TNCs on the world stage, including their foreign investments in western host markets. ICTs constitute the chief means of production in global economic activity in the sense that they make possible the production and transmission of the information that are necessary for coordinating the work activity and production cycles that are carried out on a global scale. Furthermore, ICT development is not only an enabler of globalization; it has been subject to the same dynamics of globalization as other industry sectors. Thus, software programs written in India power computers that are manufactured in China and offered for sale in Canada.

The deployment of ICTs has had contradictory effects on the management of work. As previously suggested, there has been something of an undoing of the classical division of labour in the labour process as a result of ICT usage, and this has led to a certain amount of re-skilling. Broader jobs, which were once associated with systems of responsible autonomy, have instead spawned managerialism. This calls forth new forms of managerial regulation that place a greater onus on documented employee accountability, which may be enforced through a greater degree of direct monitoring and measurement. Such control is made possible by the adoption of information technologies or by a greater emphasis on the documentation of results by workers themselves. Therefore, whether the emphasis is on control through ICTs or through the construction of strong cultures, HRM is an effort to accommodate the new means of production in the labour process on management's terms. In so doing, the use of ICTs by HR departments is also critical. Thus, there is a reciprocal relationship between the adoption of information technologies and the rise of HRM as a distinct and influential paradigm. More frequent measurement of employee performance, enhanced capacities for surveillance, the mapping of training needs, and the creation of self-paced, computer-aided training modules are all examples of how HRM makes use of ICTs in the workplace.

While dedicated to the achievement and maintenance of international competitiveness, HRM is more than a "human technology" for getting the most out of workers. It is also a belief system or culture in its own right, which targets organizational culture as being of prime importance in the realization of its mission. As such, HRM has not only been driven by the search for competitive advantage that globalization has initiated; in undertaking such activities as the benchmarking of best practice, HRM is also an active contributor to the phenomenon of globalization and the diffusion of its culture and standards across global worksites. Like the relationship between technology and management, the connections between HRM and globalization are also mutual. So just as HRM represents one dimension of the globalization of labour processes through its advocacy of "best practice," it is also subject to the dynamics of globalization. Ironically, to an increasing extent HR functions for major corporations (e.g., payroll and benefits administration) are being outsourced to low-cost, overseas providers, with the rise of new transnational firms such as India's Accenture Corporation. In other words, HRM provision is becoming a service industry in its own right and one that is increasingly being globalized.

As I have sought to demonstrate in this chapter, the most important contradictions to emerge from the globalization of the labour process are centred on the relationships between technology, management, and location. While potentially empowering, ICTs are used through HRM to control and further micro-manage workers. While possibly leading to greater work satisfaction, the commitment that HRM seeks to instil comes up against the contingencies and insecurities generated by outsourcing and the search for momentary competitive advantage on a global plane. In these senses, capitalist labour processes continue to pose significant obstacles to full human development through dignified work in all regions of the globalizing world.

NOTES

1 Parts of this essay are excerpted from the first chapter of Russell (2009).

2 Useful economic histories of this period include Brenner (2002) and Glyn (2006).

3 Useful descriptions of such work sites may be found in Blauner (1964), Kenney and Florida (1993), Rankin (1992), and Russell (1999).

4 As noted by Boltanski and Chiapello (2007), "In a reticular world, social life is composed of a proliferation of encounters and temporary, but reactivatable connections with various groups, operated at potentially considerable social, professional, geographical and cultural distance. The *project* is the occasion and reason for the connection" (104). In the world of organizational life and business this translates into web-like constellations of subcontracting, outsourcing, and mutual cooperation on work that is organized in the form of "projects." "The rhizomorphous form ... is employed in particular to emphasize the autonomy and even the volition of the network, which is stronger than that of the beings immersed in it and whose properties are then described in the language of *self-organization, self-regulation* ..." (119; emphasis in original).

5 A utopia for managers who would like to have the flexible mobility of being able to produce anything, anywhere, any time; a dystopia for workers who

would see employment security as well as terms and conditions radically decline in such a scenario.

6   Electrical goods, including VCRs, DVDs, etc., accounted for 41.7 per cent of the value of Chinese exports in 2004, with textiles and garments making up another 15 per cent and steel products 7 per cent (China Statistical Information and Consultancy Service Centre 2005: Table 18–6).

7   The ITeS banner is taken to include back-office data entry, processing and analysis (e.g., market research), customer contact services (in-bound call centres, telemarketing, IT help desks), corporate support functions (HR administration, procurement, accounting and financial services). More recently some researchers have referred to KPO—knowledge process outsourcing— which includes such work as engineering design, content development, and new product design.

8   For a detailed example of the process of national labour-market adaptation in the face of global competitive anxiety, see Bowden and Russell (2000).

REFERENCES

Alvesson, M. 2004. *Knowledge Work and Knowledge-Intensive Firms*. Oxford: Oxford University Press.

Alvesson, M., and H. Willmott. 2002. "Identity Regulation as Organizational Control: Producing the Appropriate Individual." *Journal of Management Studies* 39: 619–44.

Amin, S. 1974. *Accumulation on a World Scale*. New York: Monthly Review Press.

Appelbaum, E., T. Bailey, P. Berg, and A. Kalleberg. 2000. *Manufacturing Advantage*. Ithaca, NY: Cornell University ILR Press.

Arrighi, G. 2007. *Adam Smith in Beijing: Lineages of the Twenty-First Century*. London: Verso.

Bain, P., and P. Taylor. 2002. "Ringing the Changes? Union Recognition and Organisation in Call Centres in the UK Finance Sector." *Industrial Relations Journal* 33(3): 246–61.

Baldry, C., P. Bain, and P. Taylor. 1998. "'Bright Satanic Offices': Intensification, Control and Team Taylorism." In P. Thompson and C. Warhurst (eds.), *Workplaces of the Future*. Houndmills: Palgrave. 163–83.

Baran, B., and S. Teegarden. 1987. "Women's Labor in the Office of the Future: A Case Study of the Insurance Industry." In L. Beneria and C. Stimpson (eds.), *Women, Households and the Economy*. New Brunswick, NJ: Rutgers University Press. 201–44.

Batt, R., V. Doellgast, and H. Kwon. 2006. "Service Management and Employment Systems in U.S. and Indian Call Centres." In S. Collins and L. Brainard (eds.), *Offshoring White-Collar Work*. Washington, DC: Brookings Press. 335–72.

Batt, R., and L. Moynihan. 2002. "The Viability of Alternative Call Centre Production Models." *Human Resource Management Journal* 12(4): 14–34.

Beck, U. 2000. *What is Globalization?* Cambridge: Polity.

Blauner, R. 1964. *Alienation and Freedom.* Chicago: University of Chicago Press.

Bolman, L., and T. Deal. 2003. *Reframing Organizations.* San Francisco: Jossey-Bass.

Boltanski, L., and E. Chiapello. 2007. *The New Spirit of Capitalism.* London: Verso.

Bonacich, E., and J. Wilson. 2008. *Getting the Goods: Ports, Labor and the Logistics Revolution.* Ithaca, NY: Cornell University Press.

Bowden, B., and B. Russell. 2000. "Benchmarking, Global Best Practice and Production Renorming in the Australian Coal Industry: The Impact of Globalization." In S. McBride and J. Wiseman (eds.), *Globalisation and its Discontents.* Basingstoke: Macmillan Press. 97–110.

Boyer, R. 1990. *The Regulation School: A Critical Introduction.* New York: Columbia University Press.

Braverman, H. 1974. *Labor and Monopoly Capital.* New York: Monthly Review Press.

Brenner, R. 2002. *The Boom and the Bubble.* London: Verso.

Budhwar, P., N. Malhotra, and V. Singh. 2009. "Work Processes and Emerging Problems in Indian Call Centres." In M. Thite and B. Russell (eds.), *The Next Available Operator: Managing Human Resources in Indian Business Process Outsourcing Industry.* Delhi: Sage. 59–82.

Burawoy, M. 1979. *Manufacturing Consent.* Chicago: University of Chicago Press.

Callaghan, G., and P. Thompson. 2002. "'We Recruit Attitude': The Selection and Shaping of Routine Call Centre Labour." *Journal of Management Studies* 39: 233–56.

Castells, M. 2001. *The Internet Galaxy.* Oxford: Oxford University Press.

——. 1996. *The Rise of the Network Society.* Oxford: Blackwell.

China Statistical Information and Consultancy Service Centre. 2005. *China Statistical Yearbook.* Beijing.

Collinson, D. 2002. "Managing Humour." *Journal of Management Studies* 39(3): 269–88.

Dicken, P. 2007. *Global Shift.* 5th ed. London: Sage Publications.

Du Gay, P. 2007. *Organizing Identity.* London: Sage Publications.

Ellis, V., and P. Taylor. 2006. "'You don't know what you've got till it's gone': Re-contextualising the Origins, Development and Impact of the Call Centre." *New Technology, Work and Employment* 21: 107–22.

Emmanuel, A. 1972. *Unequal Exchange.* New York: Monthly Review Press.

Ezzamel, M., and H. Willmott. 1998. "Accounting for Teamwork: A Critical Study of Group-based Systems of Organizational Control." *Administrative Science Quarterly* 43: 358–96.

Fleming, P., and A. Spicer. 2007. *Contesting the Corporation: Struggle, Power and Resistance in Organizations.* Cambridge: Cambridge University Press.

Fox, A. 1974. *Beyond Contract: Work, Power and Trust Relations*. London: Faber and Faber.

Frenkel, S., M. Tam, M. Korczynski, and K. Shire. 1998. "Beyond Bureaucracy? Work Organization in Call Centres." *The International Journal of Human Resource Management* 9(6): 957–79.

Friedman, A. 1977. *Industry and Labour*. London: Macmillan.

Glyn, A. 2006. *Capitalism Unleashed: Finance, Globalization and Welfare*. Oxford: Oxford University Press.

Government of India. 2003. *Task Force on Meeting the Human Resources Challenge for IT and IT Enabled Services: Report and Recommendations*. Delhi: Department of Information Technology.

Greenbaum, J. 1995. *Windows on the Workplace*. New York: Monthly Review Press.

Grey, C. 1999. "'We are all managers now'; 'We always were': On the Development and Demise of Management." *Journal of Management Studies* 36(5): 561–85.

Guest, D. 1999. "Human Resource Management—the Workers' Verdict." *Human Resource Management Journal* 9(3): 5–25.

——. 1990. "Human Resource Management: Its Implications for Industrial Relations and Trade Unions." In J. Storey (ed.), *New Perspectives on Human Resource Management*. London: Routledge. 41–55.

——. 1987. "Human Resource Management and Industrial Relations." *Journal of Management Studies* 24(5): 503–21.

Hochschild, A. 1983. *The Managed Heart*. Berkeley: University of California Press.

Jacoby, S. 1991. *Employing Bureaucracy*. New York: Columbia University Press.

Kenney, M., and R. Florida. 1993. *Beyond Mass Production*. New York: Oxford University Press.

Kinnie, N., S. Hutchinson, and J. Purcell. 2000. "'Fun and Surveillance': The Paradox of High Commitment Management in Call Centres." *International Journal of Human Resource Management* 11(5): 967–85.

Knights, D., and D. McCabe. 2000. "'Ain't Misbehavin'?' Opportunities for Resistance under New Forms of 'Quality' Management." *Sociology* 34(3): 421–36.

——. 1997. "'How would you measure something like that?': Quality in a Retail Bank." *Journal of Management Studies* 34(3): 371–88.

Korczynski, M. 2002. *Human Resource Management in Service Work*. Houndmills: Palgrave.

——. 2001. "The Contradictions of Service Work: The Call Centre as Customer-oriented Bureaucracy." In A. Sturdy, I. Grugulis, and H. Willmott (eds.), *Customer Service: Empowerment and Entrapment*. Houndmills: Palgrave. 79–102.

Kunda, G. 1992. *Engineering Culture: Control and Commitment in a High-Tech Corporation*. Philadelphia: Temple University Press.

Legge, K. 1995. *Human Resource Management: Rhetorics and Realities*. London: Macmillan.

Marx, K. 1971. *Capital*. Vol. 1. Moscow: Progress Publishers.

Peters, T., and R. Waterman. 1988. *In Search of Excellence*. Sydney: Harper and Row.

Rankin, T. 1992. *New Forms of Work Organization: The Challenge for North American Unions*. Toronto: University of Toronto Press.

Ricardo, D. 1973 [1817]. *The Principles of Political Economy and Taxation*. London: Dent.

Rinehart, J., C. Huxley, and D. Robertson. 1997. *Just Another Car Factory?* Ithaca, NY: Cornell University Press.

Rousseau, D. 1995. *Psychological Contracts in Organizations*. Thousand Oaks, CA: Sage Publications.

Russell, B. 2009. *Smiling Down the Line: Info-Service Work in the Global Economy*. Toronto: University of Toronto Press.

——. 2007. "'You gotta lie to it': Software Applications and the Management of Technological Change in a Call Centre." *New Technology, Work and Employment* 22(2): 132–45.

——. 2006. "Skill in Info-service Work: Australian Call Centres." In J. Burgess and J. Connell (eds.), *Developments in the Call Centre Industry: Analysis, Changes and Challenges*. London: Routledge. 92–116.

——. 2002. "The Talk Shop and Shop Talk: Employment and Work in a Call Centre." *Journal of Industrial Relations* 44(4): 467–90.

——. 1999. *More With Less*. Toronto: University of Toronto Press.

Russell, B., and M. Thite. 2008. "The Next Division of Labour: Work Skills in Australian and Indian Call Centres." *Work, Employment and Society* 22(4): 615–34.

Schein, E. 1985. "How Culture Forms, Develops and Changes." In R. Kilmann, M. Saxton, and R. Serpa (eds.), *Gaining Control of the Corporate Culture*. San Francisco: Jossey-Bass. 17–43.

Schoenberger, E. 1997. *The Cultural Crisis of the Firm*. Cambridge, MA: Blackwell.

Scott, A. 1994. *Willing Slaves? British Workers Under Human Resource Management*. Cambridge: Cambridge University Press.

Sennett, R. 2008. *The Craftsman*. New Haven, CT: Yale University Press.

——. 1998. *The Corrosion of Character*. New York: W.W. Norton.

Shields, J., and B. Evans. 1998. *Shrinking the State: Globalization and Public Administration "Reform"*. Halifax: Fernwood.

Smith, V. 2001. *Crossing the Great Divide: Worker Risk and Opportunity in the New Economy*. Ithaca, NY: Cornell University Press.

Srivastava, S., and N. Theodore. 2006. "Offshoring Call Centres: The View from Wall Street." In J. Burgess and J. Connell (eds.), *Developments in the Call Centre Industry: Analysis, Changes and Challenges*. London: Routledge. 19–35.

Storey, J. 2001. "Human Resource Management Today: An Assessment." In J. Storey (ed.), *Human Resource Management: A Critical Text*. London: Thompson. 3–20.

Taylor, F.W. 1972. *Scientific Management*. Westport, CT: Greenwood Press.

Thite, M., and B. Russell. 2007. "India and Business Process Outsourcing." In J. Burgess and J. Connell (eds.), *Globalisation and Work in Asia*. Oxford: Chandos Publishing. 67–92.

Willmott, H. 1993. "Strength is Ignorance; Slavery is Freedom: Managing Culture in Modern Organizations." *Journal of Management Studies* 30(4): 515–52.

Womach, J., D. Joncs, and D. Roos. 1990. *The Machine that Changed the World*. New York: Rawson Associates.

Zuboff, S. 1988. *In the Age of the Smart Machine*. New York: Basic Books.

6

Regulating Labour Standards in the Global Economy
Emerging Approaches to Global Governance

MARK THOMAS[1]

Concerns about the erosion of labour standards in both the global North and global South are frequently raised in critical analyses of the contemporary global political economy. Due to the power of transnational corporations, the fragmentation of production through global supply chains, and the spread of neoliberalism as an ideological framework for "globalization," the "race to the bottom" in wages, working conditions, and labour rights is a commonly heard refrain. In this context, international institutions such as the United Nations (UN) and the International Labour Organization (ILO) have identified the need to promote basic rights at work as a key challenge for the twenty-first century, and have sought to reframe established "core" labour standards as fundamental human rights. Moreover, unions and other civil-society organizations have pushed for new approaches to transnational labour-rights regulation, including calls for "social clauses" in international trade agreements, the formation of transnational labour-rights advocacy networks, and privatized forms of labour-standards regulation to either supplement or create an alternative to national and sub-national systems of labour law.

In this chapter, I assess emerging approaches to transnational labour-rights regulation, focusing on both those rooted in state-based systems of governance, as well as strategies developed by private actors.[2] I begin with an analysis of the ILO, outlining its efforts to define and promote "core" international labour standards, and then consider the labour-standards side agreement to NAFTA—the North American Agreement on Labour Cooperation (NAALC)—as a second example of transnational labour-rights regulation that occurs through nation-states. In the second half of the chapter I assess examples of privatized regulation, focusing first on corporate codes of conduct, and second on international framework agreements (IFAs) negotiated between transnational corporations (TNCs) and global unions. While I outline a range of different approaches to labour-rights regulation, several common questions run through the chapter. What are the labour-rights principles that frame the development of each example? More importantly, how are these principles implemented and enforced? And what are the capacities of each strategy to protect and advance workers' rights in the contemporary global political economy? I conclude by arguing that in order to implement truly effective mechanisms of transnational labour-rights regulation, labour-rights strategies must move beyond binary approaches to regulation rooted in state-based versus privatized methods.[3] Strategies are needed that more effectively combine emerging forms of transnational regulation with traditional methods of labour regulation, such as local labour laws and collective agreements, as a means to ensure the enforcement of international labour norms.

LABOUR STANDARDS AND THE GLOBAL POLITICAL ECONOMY

Efforts to re-regulate international labour standards have emerged in relation to the combined pressures created by the competitive dynamics of global production chains and the spread of neoliberal approaches to labour regulation. Underlying these processes is the ongoing transformation of the global political economy, a transformation characterized by "attempts to shift capitalist production to new spaces within the world economy—sites where means of production, labour, and credit can be mobilized in order to produce more profitability" (McNally 1999: 47–48). Transnational production chains with labour-intensive processes link Northern TNCs with suppliers in labour markets where labour costs are relatively low, enforcement of labour legislation is relatively weak, and workers' attempts to organize unions are often met with severe repression (Harrison 1994; Moody 1997; Ross 2004).

Neoliberalism provides the ideological framework to legitimate and advance these processes. Neoliberal principles underpin key institutional arrangements that codify the rules of the global political economy. Multilateral trade agreements facilitate the transnational expansion of production chains and enhance the power of transnational capital (Broad 2000; Chambers & Smith 2002; Clarkson 2002). International financial institutions such as the World Bank and the International Monetary Fund promote free-market practices in the economies of the global South through structural adjustment programs that commodify natural resources and privatize national industries (Leiva 2006; Yaghmaian 2002).

These processes are connected to the "race to the bottom" in labour standards in several ways. Decentralized and just-in-time production processes in transnational supply chains intensify the competitive dynamics of the global political economy, with pressure on suppliers to minimize labour costs being a key competitive factor.[4] This competitive pressure has a political dimension as well, as jurisdictions compete to retain or attract investment by either reducing or failing to enforce minimum labour standards, particularly in those sectors and occupations that are the most susceptible to global competition, such as the global garment industry (Miller 2004; Wells 2004). Finally, the regulation of labour standards has been sidelined in the negotiation of free trade agreements due to opposition from corporate interests, neoliberal governments in the North, and states in the South concerned about Northern protectionism (Elliot & Freeman 2003; Haworth & Hughes 1997; Seidman 2004; Sengenberger & Wilkinson 1995).

In the context of the ongoing transformation of the global political economy that includes the processes described above, calls for new forms of global governance and labour-rights regulation have also emerged (Adams 2002; Fung, O'Rourke & Sabel 2001). In what follows, I examine four leading examples of emerging approaches to the regulation of international labour standards, focusing on their capacities to counter the tendencies of the "race to the bottom" by defining, defending, and advancing transnational labour rights.

THE INTERNATIONAL LABOUR ORGANIZATION

International labour standards are generally recognized as beginning with the principles established by the International Labour Organization, a tripartite organization composed of representatives from government, business, and labour. Based in Geneva, Switzerland, the ILO has over 170 country members and has drafted labour-standards conventions in areas including forced labour, child labour, discrimination in employment, freedom of association, health and safety, social security, working time, and rights for migrant workers.[5] While the ILO establishes international standards, these standards are not meant to replace existing national or sub-national labour laws with a system of transnational governance. Rather, the ILO operates within the traditional framework of state-based labour law, encouraging member states to adopt its international standards and assisting in their implementation. The ILO's role is thus largely promotional and educational, as it does not hold the legal capacity to ensure that its standards are actually implemented or enforced.

The ILO was founded in 1919 on the following principles: (a) that "labour is not a commodity"; (b) that "freedom of expression and of association are essential to sustained progress"; (c) that "poverty anywhere constitutes a danger to prosperity everywhere"; and (d) that "the war against want requires to be carried on with unrelenting vigour within each nation" (ILO 1994: 22). At its first meeting, the ILO adopted the following as international labour standards: the right of association, a "reasonable living wage," the eight-hour day or 48-hour week, a weekly rest period of at least twenty-four hours, the abolition of child labour, and the principle of equal pay for work of equal value for male and female workers. Following World War II, the ILO committed itself to a role in constructing the postwar global economy by promoting America's New Deal approach to the international stage. Specifically, through its Declaration of Philadelphia, the ILO called for full employment and rising living standards; a just distribution of wages, hours, and other benefits; decent working conditions and a minimum living wage; the right of collective bargaining; and safe and healthy work environments.[6]

In response to transformations in global political economy outlined in this chapter, the ILO has recently sought to focus international attention on what it has articulated as "core" labour standards (ILO 1994: 22). In 1998, the ILO issued a *Declaration on Fundamental Principles and Rights at Work*, defining these fundamental rights to be freedom of association and the effective recognition of the right to collective bargaining, the elimination of all forms of forced or compulsory labour, the effective abolition of child labour, and the elimination of discrimination in respect of employment and occupation. Member states are expected to respect, promote, and realize these fundamental rights, even if they have not ratified the respective ILO conventions that codify these principles. These core labour standards form the basis of the emerging international consensus that has developed in response to concerns about the "race to the bottom." Building on this framework, the ILO has also sought to promote the broader goal of creating "decent work": jobs that provide income and employment security, equity, and human dignity (ILO 2002).

While the ILO plays a key role in defining the content of international labour standards, its role is normative rather than legislative. Member states are expected to present ILO conventions to their legislatures for consideration; yet, as mentioned, the ILO is not able to compel member states to adopt these conventions. This limits the ILO's capacity to advance international labour standards through a common international platform.[7] Further, even for those states that choose to ratify ILO conventions, effective implementation is not guaranteed. While the ILO may issue condemnations of member governments that have not respected its international labour standards, governments are not bound by such pronouncements, as the institution has no enforcement mechanism (Reed & Yates 2004).[8] With no sanctions-based system to enforce its standards, it must rely on education, training, and moral persuasion to promote labour standards.

Recent tendencies toward neoliberal principles further undermine the ILO's mission to promote the decommodification of labour (Thomas 2009). For example, in its 2004–05 *World Employment Report*, the ILO promotes productivity-based strategies as solutions to poverty (ILO 2005). While the goals of employment creation and poverty reduction are presented through its established "decent work" framework, the report prioritizes the need to connect poverty reduction to productivity-enhancing strategies. The report asserts that it is unproductive employment, rather than unemployment or substandard remuneration, that is the problem to be addressed. This neoliberal turn further compromises the ILO's limited labour-rights framework in that it deflects attention away from the connections between poverty and the need for living wages and social security, for example, priorities that had been previously established by key ILO conventions.

In summary, the ILO's core labour standards are a clear articulation of important principles that, if effectively implemented, could constitute a cornerstone in the struggle for better working conditions in the global economy. Further, as a prominent international institution, the ILO provides workers and unions with a yardstick against which to measure standards in their respective national boundaries. The 1998 *Declaration on Fundamental Principles and Rights at Work* attempts to construct and promote a new global consensus regarding "core labour standards" and, as will be seen in what follows, these core standards anchor other emerging approaches to transnational labour-rights regulation. Yet, in contemporary global political economy, a normative approach that is dependent on the political will of member states to adopt and enforce its conventions is a fundamental weakness that limits the capacities of the ILO to effectively advance this labour-rights consensus.

NORTH AMERICAN AGREEMENT ON LABOUR COOPERATION

While the ILO develops labour-rights norms at the international level, the North American Agreement on Labour Cooperation is designed to regulate labour standards in the North American economic region. The NAALC is a side agreement to NAFTA that was negotiated in response to public pressure stemming from fears that free trade would lead to an erosion of labour standards within North America. The agreement includes a commitment to promote guiding principles in the area of labour standards that are built from key ILO standards. Specifically, the NAALC principles include freedom of association and the right to organize; the right to bargain collectively; the right to strike; prohibition of forced labour; labour protections for children and young persons; minimum employment standards, including minimum wages and over-time pay; elimination of employment discrimination on such grounds as race, religion, age, or sex; equal pay for women and men; prevention of occupational injuries and illnesses; compensation in cases of occu-pational injuries and illnesses; and equal treatment in working condi-tions for migrant workers.

Like the ILO, while the NAALC defines transnational labour-rights principles, it relies on individual nation-states to implement those prin-ciples. Specifically, rather than establish common labour standards for the NAFTA countries, the NAALC requires that the NAFTA countries comply with their respective labour laws in the areas covered by the NAALC principles. And, also like the ILO, the agreement provides very limited power to ensure compliance, with no enforcement mechanisms for most of the principles. Sanctions can be levied only in cases involv-ing child labour, health and safety, or minimum wages, and cannot be levied against private companies (Carr 1999). The investigations pro-cess is lengthy and time-consuming and is of questionable indepen-dence, with investigations conducted by National Administrative Offices established by each national government (Clarkson 2002). Finally, the effectiveness of the NAALC is further compromised through the devo-lution of labour laws to sub-national levels of government, as is the case in Canada where labour standards for most workers are regu-lated through provincial legislation. Without ratification by each prov-ince, the NAALC has little bearing on the regulation of Canada's labour standards, except for those that fall under the jurisdiction of the fed-eral government. Over a decade after its ratification, only four provinces (Alberta, Manitoba, Quebec, and Prince Edward Island) have ratified the NAALC (Finbow 2006).

Assessing the results of the NAALC complaints process demonstrate that its capacity to effectively regulate labour standards is severely limited (Thomas 2009). Between 1994 and 2004, 28 complaints were laid through the NAALC: 18 regarding conditions in Mexico, 9 in the United States, and 2 in Canada.[9] Twenty-one complaints included issues related to unionization (freedom of association, the right to organize, the right to bargain collectively, the right to strike). Three were subsequently withdrawn, and five were not accepted for review. Fifteen complaints resulted in ministerial consultations, with follow-up activities that included seminars, public forums, studies and reports, and government-to-government meetings, but no real sanctions.

A well-documented case regarding pregnancy screening further illustrates these trends. In 1995, Human Rights Watch (HRW), a New York-based NGO, launched a campaign against pregnancy-screening practices that were taking place in the manufacturing plants along the Mexico-US border. The campaign was initiated in response to employers firing or refusing to hire pregnant women, a practice common in the border industries as a means to avoid payment of the three months of maternity leave required by Mexican labour law. After gathering testimony from hundreds of women affected by this practice, Human Rights Watch filed a complaint against Mexico under the NAALC. Yet, while this complaint produced ministerial consultations and outreach sessions, these had little concrete impact at the workplace level, and practices of pregnancy screening continued (Hertel 2006).

Overall, while the NAALC attempts to promote a model of labour-rights regulation at the transnational level, like the ILO it nonetheless works through existing systems of nationally based labour law and fails to provide enforcement mechanisms to improve or even protect existing standards.

CORPORATE CODES OF CONDUCT

Corporate codes of conduct—company policies that establish labour-standards principles and practices for suppliers in transnational supply chains—are another strategy for regulating international labour standards that have emerged in recent years (Block et al. 2001; Wells 2006). Largely in response to pressure from labour movements and labour-rights NGOs, many companies with transnational supply chains have developed corporate codes as part of broader programs of Corporate Social Responsibility (CSR) (Rivoli 2003; Seidman 2005).[10] Since the mid-1990s, CSR departments have become widespread, as corporations develop social and environmental codes and advance the business case for sustainable economic practices (Kelly 2005). CSR reflects a wide range of company-driven practices regarding the social and environmental impacts of investment decisions, production methods, and supplier practices. As a result of environmental and labour-rights campaigns in particular, which have drawn attention to both environmental damage and labour-rights abuses resulting from growing corporate power and the transnational fragmentation of production systems, corporations have sought to present a public message that identifies the interests of the corporation with environmental and social awareness (Murray 2004). Within the business community, CSR is often taken to mean "a company's commitment to work in a socially and environmentally responsible manner while taking into account interests of stakeholders," or "to be responsive to civil society concerns."[11] With respect to labour rights, CSR involves practices and policies that include incorporating international labour norms into codes of conduct for suppliers in transnational production chains, developing internal monitoring and compliance programs to ensure that suppliers abide by such codes, and disclosing information about factory conditions to the general public.

There is wide variation in the scope, content, and regulatory practices embedded within corporate codes. The codes are voluntary, in that there is no legal body that compels TNCs to adopt a code of conduct. They are largely a privatized method of labour regulation in that they are not developed, implemented, or enforced by state agencies. They are also largely unilateral, in that they are developed by individual companies, at their own discretion. While privatized, the stronger examples of codes nonetheless build on ILO labour standards, particularly those regarding child and forced labour and no discrimination, and also often require suppliers to abide by local labour laws. And while unilateral, in recent years some TNCs have developed their codes in consultation with labour-rights NGOs and have developed monitoring practices that involve independent, third-party auditing agencies.[12]

In addition to outlining principles for labour standards, corporate codes include a range of practices for labour-standards regulation around information dissemination, grievance resolution, and worker representation. Table 6.1 outlines examples of these practices in corporate codes from nine major TNCs. The table illustrates common practices, as well as key differences amongst these major actors in the global political economy.

As CSR initiatives develop, it is increasingly common for corporations to provide some level of public-information disclosure regarding labour-standards practices, directed largely at Northern consumers. The amount of information ranges from providing statements of principle on company websites to making data from factory audits publicly available (ETAG 2005). Moving one step further, in 2005 Nike publicly disclosed the names and addresses of factories producing in its supply chain. Since that time, other companies—Levi Strauss and Timberland—have followed suit by publicly disclosing the locations of suppliers.[13] Mountain Equipment Co-op has also pledged to provide information about factory locations.[14] While public disclosure of factory locations in no way ensures compliance with labour-standards codes, it is considered by CSR proponents to be an important step in making visible production conditions in the global economy and thereby contributing to improvements in labour-standards practices (Doorey 2005).

Workplace auditing practices are a key aspect of most corporate codes. Monitoring practices are commonly done either through in-house inspections teams or in conjunction with third-party auditing agencies (Intertek Labtest and Independent Global Compliance Services), multistakeholder initiatives (Fair Labor Association, Social Accountability International, Global Reporting Initiative), and/or labour-rights NGOs (Verite). External auditors are chosen in order to lend greater credibility to the auditing process.[15] Auditors conduct factory inspections, review contracts and payroll documents, and conduct interviews with managers and workers. These monitoring practices are connected to the information dissemination practices to the extent that companies make auditing results publicly available. While individual companies and auditing firms develop their own standards and evaluate their application through their own criteria, some movement has been made toward standardizing factory audits by developing universal certification processes. For example, Social Accountability International has developed an auditing system—SA 8000—that sets in place a standardized method of evaluating social compliance with labour-rights norms and that can be adopted by auditors when conducting factory inspections.[16]

Most recently, some TNCs and NGOs have sought to further collaboration efforts in auditing practices, for example through information sharing between competitors with common suppliers.[17] This process is facilitated through participation in NGOs such as Fair Factories Clearinghouse, which collects and disseminates factory audit data to member companies. Sharing this type of information is meant to promote greater transparency, efficiency, and movement toward convergence in the auditing process.[18] A second form of collaboration occurs through participation in multi-stakeholder initiatives, which bring together companies, NGOs, and labour organizations to develop education and training strategies designed to improve conditions in suppliers where there are high levels of non-compliance.

TABLE 6.1 Corporate Codes of Conduct

COMPANY	SECTOR	INFORMATION DISSEMINATION	GRIEVANCE RESOLUTION	WORKER REPRESENTATION	WORKPLACE MONITORING
IKEA	Retail Home	Suppliers must "effectively communicate" standards to all sub-suppliers and co-workers	• Company has formed a global compliance and monitoring group • Suppliers in violation of the code require a plan of action to comply with the code within an acceptable timeframe or face termination of the business relationship	Freedom of Association	Internal: IKEA Trading Service Office and follow-up by a "global compliance and monitoring group"
H&M	Apparel Retail	No language	• Will "work with our suppliers to achieve workable solutions in each individual case" • Will terminate relationship with supplier if some conditions of the code (e.g., child labour) not followed	Freedom of Association	"Reserves right to visit factories and to allow company-approved third party inspections" by Fair Labor Association
Mountain Equipment Co-op	Apparel Retail	Have adopted Fair Labor Association Monitoring principles: "Ensure that all Company factories as well as contractors and suppliers inform their employees about the work-place standards"	Provide a worker "hotline" to report complaints	Freedom of Association	Partnership with third party monitors to regularly audit suppliers
Hudson's Bay Corporation	Retail Including Apparel	Training for Bay employees, factory suppliers and vendors	Internal Dispute Resolution Process	Freedom of Association	External: third party factory audits by Intertek Labtest & Global Compliance Services

[Table 6.1 continued]

COMPANY	SECTOR	INFORMATION DISSEMINATION	GRIEVANCE RESOLUTION	WORKER REPRESENTATION	WORKPLACE MONITORING
GAP	Apparel Retail	No language	Terminate the business relationship or require the factory to implement a corrective action plan if violations of the code are found	Freedom of Association	Internal: company "Vendor Compliance Officers" include 90 full-time employees worldwide
American Apparel	Apparel Retail	Company HR personnel provides info to workers and addresses their questions re: pay, benefits	HR department available to employees to address questions/ concerns	No language	No language
Levi's	Apparel Retail	• Education/training initiatives for factory management • In some cases, education provided to workers • Code available in English and local language	May withdraw production or require a contractor to implement a corrective action plan if violations of a code are found during auditing	Freedom of Association	External: third party factory audits by Verite
Nike	Retail Including Apparel	Contract factories directed to post the Code of Conduct in local languages	"Grievance Reporting Systems" (grievance box, hotline, access to labour union office, email addresses)	No language	External: third party factory audits by Fair Labor Association (FLA)
Wal-Mart	Retail Including Apparel	No Language	No language	Freedom of Association	Internal: company announced and unannounced audits

Corporate self-regulation through codes of conduct is presented by proponents as one of the primary alternatives to state-based labour-rights legislation in the contemporary global political economy. Their voluntary nature, the lack of consistency in content, and voluntary enforcement mechanisms constitute fundamental weaknesses in their approach to labour-standards regulation, however (Doane 2005). Corporate codes are supported by the assumption that a company is more likely to follow a code it developed itself, yet there are no sanctions if a company fails to enforce its own code, meaning that labour-rights violations may persist in a supply chain even if there is a code of conduct present (Ross 2004; Wells 2007). Companies may establish their own priorities in terms of which violations are to be addressed, and may design their own strategies for action in dealing with non-compliant vendors, ranging from severance of the relationship to forms of remediation and/or education. While NGO engagement has emerged in recent years as a means to increase corporate accountability and transparency (Esbenshade 2004; Rodriguez-Garavito 2005), NGO involvement in the monitoring process is often compromised, as TNCs retain high degrees of control over the terms of engagement (Wells 2007).

The lack of consistency between codes illustrates the inherent weakness in the voluntary approach (Pearson & Seyfang 2001). Without an external regulatory body, there is great variation in content and application, in the involvement of third-party auditors, and in the amount of information shared with employees, competitors, and/or the general public. The codes may not include provisions for supplier monitoring or define responsibilities with respect to sub-contractors. They may not guarantee full disclosure of audits of factories or workplaces. They may create enclaves of protected workers, while excluding others, for example, those outside the "first tier" of suppliers in a supply chain. While the CSR practices developed by some companies—for example GAP, Levi's, Nike—appear quite comprehensive, they are reflective of a small sample of very large companies. For many smaller companies with narrower profit margins, developing a supplier code of conduct is particularly challenging due to limited resources in a highly competitive business environment.[19] Even for large companies that purport to create brand images around corporate responsibility, violations of core labour rights embedded within corporate codes continue to surface, as evidenced by reports of child labour in GAP factories in 2007 (McDougall 2007). Overall, while including principles developed through the ILO is increasingly commonplace in CSR practices, due to their unilateral, voluntaristic, and privatized character, corporate codes cannot be considered as the basis for effective transnational labour-rights regulation in the global political economy.

INTERNATIONAL FRAMEWORK AGREEMENTS

In response to the unilateral character of corporate codes of conduct, some Global Union Federations (GUFs) have pressured TNCs to negotiate international framework agreements.[20] Like the corporate codes, IFAs are designed to regulate labour standards across transnational supply chains, are built upon the international labour standards of the ILO, and bind their signatories to local labour laws. Unlike the corporate codes, however, IFAs result from negotiation between TNCs and global unions, and are designed to establish an ongoing process of consultation and dialogue between the two parties (Miller 2004; Papadakis 2008; Riisgaard 2005; Stevis & Boswell 2007; Thomas 2010). Moreover, global unions that have pursued IFAs as a labour-rights strategy see the agreements not only as a way to regulate labour standards "from above," but more importantly as a way to promote unionization across a supply chain by pressuring suppliers to respect freedom of association rights. They do not invoke a process of mandatory certification across a supply chain, nor do they replace national and/or local-level negotiations between workers and companies; rather, they provide a framework through which local-level agreements may be negotiated and a minimum floor upon which they may build. By 2007, there were close to 50 IFAs negotiated with TNCs by six global union federations. The agreements cover approximately 4.3 million workers in transnational supply chains in natural resources, food, manufacturing, telecommunications, and retail sectors. The first agreement was negotiated between the food company Danone and the International Union of Foodworkers (IUF) in 1988. Through the 1990s and early twenty-first century, framework agreements were negotiated by the Building and Wood Workers International (BWI), the International Federation of Chemical, Energy, Mine and General Workers' Unions (ICEM), Union Network International (UNI), the International Metalworkers' Federation (IMF), and Public Services International (PSI).

As stated, IFAs build upon the labour-rights norms of the ILO. The ILO maintains a set of recommendations for the negotiation of standards in IFAs, and the content of the agreements generally begins with the four core labour standards pertaining to freedom of association, child labour, forced labour, and discrimination in employment. Beyond these core standards, the provisions of the agreements vary, as they are subject to negotiation between the TNCs and union federations.[21] Yet while they establish key labour-standards principles for a transnational supply chain, it is not these principles that differentiate IFAs from corporate codes, as many of the codes contain a similar normative framework. A key factor that sets IFAs apart from the unilateral codes is the ways in which they establish a process for monitoring and implementing the labour-standards principles. As an illustration of these practices, Table 6.2 provides examples of processes regarding information dissemination, workplace monitoring, and dispute resolution taken from a sample of ten framework agreements that cover workers in a wide range of sectors.

While they are not collective agreements that determine working conditions at the local level, like a collective agreement IFAs commonly require an employer to provide written notice of the agreement and its provisions to all covered employees and suppliers in the supply chain. In the area of workplace monitoring, joint-responsibility provisions in most framework agreements establish a process for regular meetings of monitoring groups composed of representatives of the TNC and global union. Monitoring groups review the application of agreement provisions in supplier factories.[22] Building on this process of joint review, dispute-resolution processes bring the TNC and the global union together to identify and resolve complaints and disputes in the implementation of the agreement across the supply chain.[23] At the level of the workplace, the framework agreements place individual workplace grievances under the jurisdiction of the local-level collective agreement, if one is present. When there is no local collective agreement, however, the dispute-resolution process becomes very individualized insofar as it places the onus on non-unionized employees to raise complaints. IFAs contain no localized grievance-resolution mechanisms on their own.[24]

The primary aim of negotiating an IFA—from the perspective of global unions—is to promote freedom of association across transnational supply chains, another key point of distinction between IFAs and corporate codes. All IFAs contain a statement committing the TNC and its suppliers to respecting the ILO convention on Freedom of Association and Collective Bargaining.[25] IFAs have been successfully used by some global unions to promote unionization in supply chains (Stevis & Boswell 2008). For example, affiliates of the BWI used framework agreements to organize IKEA suppliers in Poland and Malaysia and to elect independent worker representatives in China and Malaysia in the Faber Castell chain.[26] After an eight-week strike at a DaimlerChrysler supplier in Turkey, the IMF was able to use its framework agreement to pressure the supplier to negotiate a first collective agreement for the workers (Hammer 2005).[27] A framework agreement negotiated between the

International Union of Foodworkers-COLSIBA (a coalition of banana workers' unions) and Chiquita was used by banana workers' unions to support unionization efforts in both Honduras and Colombia, as it facilitated organizers getting access to worksites and workers (Riisgaard 2005).

Despite these examples of successful implementation, however, there remain limits in the approach to labour-standards regulation established by IFAs (Thomas 2010). First, they are voluntary agreements, whereby TNCs are under no legal obligation to enter into framework agreements with global union federations.[28] While some global unions have been successful in their negotiations with TNCs, many of the existing IFAs are in sectors with traditionally high levels of unionization, such as resource industries, construction, and industrial manufacturing, indicating that sectoral union density and sectoral union strength may be key elements in negotiating IFAs (Hammer 2005). For sectors with relatively low levels of unionization, such as the global garment industry, employer resistance may create a significant obstacle to negotiating a framework agreement, as has been the case with the International Textile, Garment and Leather Workers' Federation (Miller 2004).[29] Moreover, as they rely on the voluntary participation of a TNC and its suppliers, they may create potential for extending unionization across a supply chain; but they do not formally bind suppliers to a process of collective bargaining. The actual implementation of freedom of association across the chain depends on organizing drives at the workplace level at local production sites. Finally, even when an IFA is respected by suppliers, there is no assurance of uniform application and enforcement of the framework agreement across the supply chain. This was the case with the IUF-Chiquita agreement, which, while it was used to facilitate union organizing, was not evenly enforced by suppliers once implemented (Riisgaard 2005).

In summary, framework agreements establish processes for social dialogue between TNCs and global unions, including joint processes for resolving disputes over implementation and compliance. The effective implementation of IFAs must be accompanied by strong and localized workplace-based organizing and representation, however, as it remains the prerogative of the TNC and supplier companies to address union and worker concerns relating to the adoption of and compliance with the framework agreement. Thus, there is a twofold challenge in using IFAs to regulate international labour standards: first, to negotiate an agreement with a TNC; and second, to use the IFA to take on non-compliant suppliers at the level of the local worksite.[30] In other words, while the framework agreement may provide a stronger measure than codes of conduct for promoting corporate accountability across transnational

TABLE 6.2 International Framework Agreements

COMPANY/ GLOBAL UNION*	SECTOR/ INDUSTRY	INFORMATION DISSEMINATION	WORKPLACE MONITORING	GRIEVANCE RESOLUTION
IKEA/BWI	Furniture	Information on agreement provided to BWI affiliates and workers	• IKEA-established "compliance organization" called Trading Service Office • Company and union meet two times per year	In accordance with IKEAs Code of Conduct
Lafarge/ BWI	Building Materials	Company will provide info re: this agreement in written or verbal form in countries where applicable	Group of company reps and GUFs will meet once a year or when necessary to follow up and review the agreement	"Differences arising from the interpretation or implementation of the agreement examined jointly"
Chiquita/ IUF	Agriculture	Parties commit to publicizing agreement in all company's banana operations in Latin America	• "Chiquita will require its suppliers, contract growers and joint venture partners to provide reasonable evidence that they respect national legislation and the Minimum Labor Standards" • Joint committee to review implementation	Joint committee to review the implementation of the agreement and resolve disputes
Danone/IUF	Food Processing	BSN and IUF "undertake to encourage management and trade union to negotiate agreements ... and to publicize these ... to the workforce to the widest extent possible"	• BSN and the IUF undertake to "monitor proper compliance throughout all BSN subsidiaries with ILO Conventions 87, 98 and 135" • "the process of informing and educating trade union and worker representatives should develop within each BSN subsidiary with the goal of ensuring effective implementation"	Language regarding the commitment by BSN and IUF to encourage negotiations between companies and trade unions
Volkswagen/ IMF	Auto Industry	Employees are "informed about all provisions of this declaration" by both employee reps and management	VW "supports and expressly encourages its suppliers and contractors to take this declaration into account in their own respective corporate policy"	Joint administration through Global Works Council

[Table 6.2 continued]

COMPANY/ GLOBAL UNION*	SECTOR/ INDUSTRY	INFORMATION DISSEMINATION	WORKPLACE MONITORING	GRIEVANCE RESOLUTION
Chrysler/IMF	Auto Industry	Principles of the framework agreement "will be made available to all employees and their representatives in an appropriate form"	Corporate management "will regularly report to and consult with the international employee reps on implementation of standards"	Relies on complaints by partners, customers, employees to address any violations of the agreement
H&M/UNI	Garment Retail	No language	Joint responsibility for administration of the agreement	Joint responsibility for administration of the agreement
Telefónica/ UNI	Telecommunication	"Telefónica S.A. will provide information concerning this agreement to all companies of the Group"	Joint responsibility for administration of the agreement	· Joint responsibility for administration of the agreement · Joint committee for resolving disputes regarding the agreement
EDF/ ICEM-PSI	Energy Sector	Company will supply info on activities and results to labour and stakeholders	· Annual review of agreement implementation · Report presented to joint monitoring group	Consultation between employers and employee reps is "preferred" method for addressing issues or for the settling of disputes
LUKOIL/ ICEM	Energy/ Oil Sector	· "LUKOIL will notify its contractors, licensees and major suppliers of the existence of the Agreement and encourage them to comply with the standards and principles contained within it" · "ICEM will distribute copies of the Agreement to all its member unions"	· Company and ICEM meet annually to discuss "issues and actions" · General Secretary of ICEM and Lukoil President are "ultimately responsible" for the administration of the agreement	· Framework agreement to supplement local industrial relations processes · LUKOIL and ICEM will meet annually to review implementation

* IUF: International Union of Food, Agricultural, Hotel, Restaurant, Catering, Tobacco and Allied Workers' Association; ICEM: International Federation of Chemical, Energy, Mine and General Workers' Union; UNI: Union Network International; IMF: International Metalworkers' Federation; PSI: Public Services International; BWI: Building and Wood Workers International.
Source: Thomas (2010).

supply chains, it is no substitute for more traditional forms of workplace regulation such as local union organizing and collective bargaining. In the context of the contemporary global political economy, the framework agreement may be seen as an emerging means that could construct a bridge to a more traditional end.

CONCLUSION

In the contemporary global political economy, there is a need for forms of labour-standards regulation that respond to the challenges created by the transnational character of production. Yet, while there may be a growing consensus regarding the need to establish stronger international labour standards, this review of existing models of transnational regulation reveals that there remain many challenges to such a project. International institutions such as the ILO and the NAALC establish normative frameworks but lack the means to effectively implement or enforce the norms. Moreover, while these norms form the basis for emergent strategies such as corporate codes of conduct and international framework agreements, as this review has demonstrated, each of these strategies also needs to go further. Though Corporate Social Responsibility policies are becoming commonplace amongst TNCs, statements of principle will do little to address the conditions of the "race to the bottom" without effective measures of implementation and enforcement. As jointly implemented agreements, IFAs provide a stronger method of regulation than the unilateral corporate codes. Yet despite the key differences between corporate codes and IFAs, framework agreements create a top-down approach to labour-rights regulation that is ineffective without local union strength to ensure compliance with international labour standards.

Transnational labour-rights regulation must move beyond these tendencies by more effectively combining emerging transnational initiatives with traditional methods of workplace regulation such as labour laws and collective agreements. Bridging the gap between international norms and localized enforcement is a necessary next step in protecting, promoting, and advancing labour rights in the contemporary global political economy.

NOTES

1 I would like to thank Sarah Rogers for research assistance with this paper. I would also like to thank the anonymous reviewers for helpful comments in the revisions process. The research for this paper was funded by a York

University Faculty of Arts Research Grant and a SSHRC Standard Research Grant.

2 Key informant interviews referenced in this chapter are coded as follows: (i) representatives from Corporate Social Responsibility departments in companies with transnational supply chains (coded as CSR-#); (ii) representatives from non-governmental organizations engaged in labour-rights advocacy (coded as NGO-#); and (iii) representatives from global union federations (coded as GU-#). The interviews (n=15) were 60 to 90 minutes in length. Interviews were conducted in person with those participants located in Toronto, Canada, and by telephone with representatives from Europe and the United States. Follow-up requests for clarification and additional information were conducted by email.

3 I build on Trubeck, Mosher and Rothstein (2000) and Weil and Mallo (2007) in developing this argument.

4 Interview GU-3, December 2007.

5 Details of ILO conventions can be accessed at <http://www.ilo.org/ilolex/english/subjectE.htm>.

6 *The ILO: What It Is, What It Does.* Geneva: International Labour Office, <http://www.ilo.org>, accessed October 2007.

7 For example, while Canada is an active member of the organization, it had ratified only a small number of ILO standards, 30 out of over 180 ILO conventions by 2000 (Torobin 2000).

8 Interview GU-2, December 2007.

9 NAALC, Summary of Public Communications, <http://www.naalc.org/english/public.shtml>, accessed May 2010.

10 Interview NGO-1, July 2007.

11 Interviews NGO-2, NGO-3, July 2007.

12 Interview NGO-2, July 2007.

13 Factory lists can be found at: <http://www.itglwf.org/lang/en/documents/Levis_000.pdf >; <http://www.nikebiz.com/responsibility/documents/Nike_CRR_Factory_List_C.pdf>; <http://www.itglwf.org/lang/en/documents/Q3_2009_Factory_list_000.pdf>. All accessed May 2010.

14 Interview CSR-3, July 2007.

15 Interview CSR-1, June 2007.

16 Interview NGO-4, August 2007.

17 Interview NGO-6, September 2007.

18 Interview NGO-6, September 2007.

19 Interview CSR-5, August 2007.

20 Marion Hellmann, "Social Partnership at the Global Level: BWI Experiences with Global Company Agreements" (Geneva: Building Woodworkers International, n.d.); interview GU-2, December 2007.

21 Key provisions in the agreements may build upon ILO standards in the areas of wages, health and safety, and hours of work (Papadakis 2008).

22 Unlike corporate codes, framework agreements do not establish processes for third-party monitoring, though some companies that have signed an IFA,

like IKEA, may engage in third-party monitoring processes through their broader CSR programs. Interview GU-1, June 2007.

23 Interview GU-1, June 2007.

24 Interview GU-2, December 2007.

25 Some agreements go further to promote freedom of association. For example, the agreements negotiated by Union Network International (UNI) with both H&M and Telefónica also include the principles established by ILO Convention 135 on worker representation, stating that "[t]he company guarantees that workers [sic] representatives shall not be discriminated against and shall have access to all workplaces necessary to enable them to carry out their representation functions." UNI-Telefónica Code of Conduct, signed 12 March 2001; Agreement between H&M Hennes & Mauritz AB and Union Network International on Cooperation in order to secure and promote fundamental workers' rights at H&M's workplaces worldwide, signed 14 January 2004.

26 Hellman, "Social Partnership at the Global Level"; interview GU-1, June 2007.

27 International Metalworkers' Federation, "How the IMF Works: International Framework Agreements." Accessed at www.imfmetal.org/main/index.cfm?n=47&1 =2&c=8202, May 2010.

28 Interview GU-1, June 2007.

29 Interview GU-3, December 2007.

30 Interviews GU-1, June 2007 and GU-3, December 2007.

REFERENCES

Adams, R. 2002. "Implications of the International Human Rights Consensus for Canadian Labour and Management." *Canadian Labour and Employment Law Journal* 9: 119–39.

Block, R.N., K. Robert, C. Ozeki, and M.J. Roomkin. 2001. "Models of International Labor Standards." *Industrial Relations* 40(2): 258–91.

Broad, D. 2000. *Hollow Work, Hollow Society? Globalization and the Casual Labour Problem in Canada.* Halifax: Fernwood.

Carr, B. 1999. "Globalization from Below: Labour Internationalism Under NAFTA." *International Social Science Journal* 51(159): 49–59.

Chambers, E., and P. Smith. 2002. *NAFTA in the New Millennium.* La Jolla, CA: Center for U.S.-Mexican Studies.

Clarkson, S. 2002. *Uncle Sam and Us: Globalization, Neoconservatism, and the Canadian State.* Toronto: University of Toronto Press.

Doane, D. 2005. "Beyond Corporate Social Responsibility: Minnows, Mammoths and Markets." *Futures* 37: 215–29.

Doorey, D.J. 2005. "Who Made That? Influencing Foreign Labour Practices Through Reflexive Domestic Disclosure Regulation." *Osgoode Hall Law Journal* 43: 353–403.

Elliott, K.A., and R.B. Freeman. 2003. *Can Labor Standards Improve Under Globalization?* Washington: Peterson Institute for International Economics.

Esbenshade, J. 2004. "Codes of Conduct: Challenges and Opportunities for Workers' Rights." *Social Justice* 31(3): 40–59.

Ethical Trading Action Group (ETAG). 2005. *Coming Clean on the Clothes We Wear.* Toronto: ETAG.

Finbow, R. 2006. *The Limits of Regionalism: NAFTA's Labour Accord.* Aldershot: Ashgate.

Fung, A., D. O'Rourke, and C. Sabel. 2001. *Can We Put an End to Sweatshops?* Boston: Beacon Press.

Hammer, N. 2005. "International Framework Agreements: Global Industrial Relations Between Rights and Bargaining." *Transfer* 11(4): 511–30.

Harrison, B. 1994. *Lean and Mean: The Changing Landscape of Corporate Power in the Age of Flexibility.* New York: BasicBooks.

Haworth, N., and S. Hughes. 1997. "Trade and International Labour Standards: Issues and Debates Over a Social Clause." *Journal of Industrial Relations* 39(2): 179–95.

Hertel, S. 2006. *Unexpected Power: Conflict and Change among Transnational Activists.* Ithaca, NY: ILR Press.

International Labour Organization. 2005. *World Employment Report, 2004–05: Employment, Productivity and Poverty Reduction.* Geneva: International Labour Office.

——. 2002. "Towards a Policy Framework for Decent Work." *International Labour Review* 141: 161–74.

——. 1994. *Visions of the Future of Social Justice: Essays on the Occasion of the ILO's 75th Anniversary.* Geneva: International Labour Office.

Kelly, M. 2005. "Holy Grail Found." *Business Ethics Magazine.* February. <http://www.business-ethics.com>.

Leiva, F.I. 2006. "Neoliberal and Neostructuralist Perspectives on Labour Flexibility, Poverty and Inequality: A Critical Appraisal." *New Political Economy* 11(3): 337–59.

McDougall, D. 2007. "Child sweatshop shame threatens Gap's ethical image." *The Observer* 28 October.

McNally, D. 1999. "Turbulence in the World Economy." *Monthly Review* 51: 38–52.

Miller, D. 2004. "Preparing for the Long Haul: Negotiating International Framework Agreements in the Global Textile, Garment and Footwear Sector." *Global Social Policy* 4(2): 215–39.

Moody, K. 1997. *Workers in a Lean World: Unions in the International Economy.* London and New York: Verso.

Murray, J. 2004. "Corporate Social Responsibility Discussion Paper." *Global Social Policy* 4(2): 171–95.

Papadakis, K. (ed.). 2008. *Cross-Border Social Dialogue and Agreements: An Emerging Global Industrial Relations Framework?* Geneva: International Institute for Labour Studies.

Pearson, R., and G. Seyfang. 2001. "New Hope or False Dawn? Voluntary Codes of Conduct, Labour Regulation and Social Policy in a Globalizing World." *Global Social Policy* 1(1): 49–78.

Reed, A., and C. Yates. 2004. "The ILO Declaration on Fundamental Principles and Rights at Work: The Limitations to Global Labour Standards." In M. Irish (ed.), *The Auto Pact: Investment, Labour, and the WTO*. London: Kluwer Law International. 243–56.

Riisgaard, L. 2005. "International Framework Agreements: A New Model for Securing Workers Rights?" *Industrial Relations* 44(4): 707–36.

Rivoli, P. 2003. "Labor Standards in the Global Economy: Issues for Investors." *Journal of Business Ethics* 43(3): 223–32.

Rodriguez-Garavito, C.A. 2005. "Global Governance and Labor Rights: Codes of Conduct and Anti-Sweatshop Struggles in Global Apparel Factories in Mexico and Guatemala." *Politics and Society* 33(2): 203–33.

Ross, R. 2004. *Slaves to Fashion: Poverty and Abuse in the New Sweatshops*. Ann Arbor: University of Michigan Press.

Seidman, G. 2005. "'Stateless' Regulation and Consumer Pressure: Historical Experiences of Transnational Corporate Monitoring." *Research in Rural Sociology and Development* 11: 175–207.

———. 2004. "Deflated Citizenship: Labor Rights in a Global Era." In A. Brysk and G. Shafir (eds.), *People Out of Place: Globalization, Human Rights, and the Citizenship Gap*. New York and London: Routledge. 109–29.

Sengenberger, W., and F. Wilkinson. 1995. "Globalization and Labour Standards." In J. Mitchie and J. Grieve Smith (eds.), *Managing the Global Economy*. Oxford: Oxford University Press. 111–34.

Stevis, D., and T. Boswell. 2008. *Globalization and Labor: Democratizing Global Governance*. Lanham, MD: Rowman & Littlefield.

———. 2007. "International Framework Agreements: Opportunities and Challenges for Global Unionism." In K. Bronfenbrenner (ed.), *Global Unions: Challenging Transnational Capital through Cross-Border Campaigns*. Ithaca, NY: ILR Press. 174–94.

Thomas, M. 2009. *Regulating Flexibility: The Political Economy of Employment Standards*. Montreal and Kingston: McGill-Queen's University Press.

———. 2010 [forthcoming]. "Global Industrial Relations? Framework Agreements and the Regulation of International Labor Standards." *Labor Studies Journal*.

Torobin, A.J. 2000. "The Labour Program and the International Labour Organization: Looking Back, Looking Ahead." *Workplace Gazette: An Industrial Relations Quarterly* 3: 85–91.

Trubek, D.M., J. Mosher, and J.S. Rothstein. 2000. "Transnationalism in the Regulation of Labor Relations: International Regimes and Transnational Advocacy Networks." *Law and Social Inquiry* 25(4): 1187–1211.

Weil, D., and C. Mallo. 2007. "Regulating Labour Standards via Supply Chains: Combining Public/Private Interventions to Improve Workplace Compliance." *British Journal of Industrial Relations* 45(4): 791–814.

Wells, D. 2007. "Too Weak for the Job: Corporate Codes of Conduct, Non-Governmental Organizations and the Regulation of International Labour Standards." *Global Social Policy* 7(1): 51–74.

——. 2006. "'Best Practice' in the Regulation of International Labor Standards: Lessons of the U.S.-Cambodia Textile Agreement." *Comparative Labor Law and Policy* 27(3): 357–76.

——. 2004. "How Credible Are Corporate Labour Codes? Monitoring Global Production Chains." In J. Stanford and L.F. Vosko (eds.), *Challenging the Market: The Struggle to Regulate Work and Income.* Montreal and Kingston: McGill-Queen's University Press. 365–83.

Yaghmaian, B. 2002. "The Political Economy of Global Accumulation and Its Emerging Mode of Regulation." In B. Berberoglu (ed.), *Labor and Capital in the Age of Globalization.* Lanham, MD: Rowman & Littlefield. 125–44.

7

Global Health
A Political Economy of Historical Trends and Contemporary Inequalities[1]

DAVID COBURN

Most political economists of health focus on contemporary health inequalities within or among nations. Yet the ideal political economy of health would help us to understand not only historical and contemporary inequalities but also historical trends. Such an explanation also would have to cast light on why, in the early twenty-first century, there are so many instances of apparent indifference to the suffering of others. I have argued elsewhere that prominent contemporary social and health policies, including attitudes toward the less fortunate, can be understood as a consequence of the current prevalence of a particular fundamentalist capitalist way of viewing the world. Within this view, commonly called neoliberalism, human well-being is best left to the operation of markets and individuals (Coburn 2000, 2004; Navarro 1998, 2002).

But the task of creating an adequate political economy of global health is only at its beginnings. This chapter builds on the writings of Navarro and others (see, for example, Navarro et al. 2003; Raphael, Bryant & Rioux 2006; Hofrichter 2004) in arguing for a class-based political economy of health. Health is the fulcrum of many different disciplines, of which the main influential policy-oriented one today is economics. This review of political economy is therefore necessarily based on a critical analysis of the currently dominant economistic views of health.

The contemporary world is a capitalist one, so in comparing nations and regions I am contrasting various forms of capitalism rather than capitalist and non-capitalist types. I point out that some types of society are better for health than are others, and some types of development are better than others. My main criticisms are directed at the revival of nineteenth-century capitalist doctrines of the dominance of markets over society.

At its most basic level, neoliberalism asserts that free-enterprise policies produce economic growth, which in turn has been the basis for human well-being. Thus, free trade and free markets both within and among nations will improve human welfare because such policies, it is claimed, are the best, or perhaps the only, way of producing economic growth. Neoliberals contend that "free" markets are in the larger public interest, because any interference with markets produces distortions and consequent "inefficiencies" (for a critique of neoliberal doctrines, see Coburn 2000, 2004). The contrary view taken here is that there is and has been more than one path to economic growth. The currently developed nations historically did not economically advance in a neoliberal world, nor is economic development in the contemporary era brought about only by neoliberal national and international policies (Navarro & Schmitt 2005). Most of the recent evidence in fact indicates that the kind of neoliberalism advocated by the United States, the IMF, and, for much of its history until recently, the World Bank, has been an international failure insofar as economic growth is concerned (see, e.g., the former chief economist at the World Bank, J.E. Stiglitz 2003, 2007). I will not discuss that issue here but rather move on to argue against other elements of the neoliberal world view.

Historically, economic growth did not "automatically" bring improved human well-being. Nor does it do so in the contemporary world. Indeed, economic growth is only contingently related to better health. Particular *types* of social and economic development, as exemplified in the social democratic welfare states identified by Esping-Andersen (1990, 1999), are more effective in improving health and human well-being than are neoliberal forms. Rather than being directly related to improved human well-being, current free-enterprise politics and policies in fact tend to undermine the social bases of human well-being and, many now contend, the very social bases of economic growth itself.

GLOBALIZATION AND NEOLIBERALISM

Capitalism influences everything within a capitalist social formation—from the beliefs people have, to what they consider desirable, to prevalent ideas, to politics, to social life. Capitalism is also characterized by the predominant power of those who own and control the means of production. Ownership not only gives the power to make investments where, when, and with whom owners of capital want, but also to control those who work for them. This power, however, also extends outside of work and the economy to an influence on the media, on politics, on the state, and on the type of society we have generally. Capitalism fundamentally limits what is possible, though the boundaries of the possible may be fuzzier in some national or global contexts than in others.

Capitalism is characterized by contradiction, crises, and conflict. Consequently, many of the positive aspects of liberal democratic capitalism are not the result of the workings of capitalism itself but rather a manifestation of its internal contradictions. With the rise of capitalism have come immense struggles against capitalist markets to help realize universal suffrage, legal and human rights such as the right of workers to organize, a living wage, better working conditions, the eight-hour day, unemployment insurance and protection for workers, public pensions, and equity of access to health care. Many of these, as the social determinants of health literature attests (WHO Commission on the Social Determinants of Health 2008; Evans, Barer & Marmor 1994; Navarro 2002; Wilkinson & Marmot 2003), are directly or indirectly related to improved human health. The institutions we are most proud of were not freely bestowed nor did they simply "emerge" as a result of economic growth, but rather were the result of immense social struggles.

One way of viewing historical developments and contemporary variations is through the notion of historical phases of capitalism (Ross & Trachte 1990) and its contemporary "types"—in the developed world, the latter are often, but not exclusively, viewed in terms of types of welfare state (Esping-Andersen 1990, 1999; for capitalist types see also Coates 2005). Capitalism is seen as moving through mercantile, entrepreneurial, monopoly, and most recently global phases, but also as showing differing contemporary types. Historically, each of the phases and types of capitalism has its own set of class, economic, and political characteristics. Moreover, the expression of capitalist relations varies from nation to nation within any given phase.

In the most recent phase of capitalism, beginning in the 1970s, economic globalization, as a real force and as an ideology, brought the re-emergence of business on national and international levels to a dominant class position from the previous phase of a nationally focused monopoly capitalism in which capital and labour had arrived at various forms of accommodation. In other words, neoliberalism replaced Keynesianism. Within global capitalism, the reduced market power and fragmentation of labour, and the shredding of the welfare state, led to major increases in social inequality, poverty, income inequality, and social fragmentation (Teeple 2000; Stubbs & Underhill 2000). The relative autonomy of the state from business decreased; nationally based corporations and business interests now have newfound power. International treaties, supposedly simply about trade, are actually about much more: they are a way of entrenching corporate rights and neoliberal policies at the global and national level beyond the reach of democratic discussion.

The Anglo-American nations, and particularly the United States, have been instrumental in implementing neoliberal policies directly as well as through their influence on international organizations or institutions. The latter include the International Monetary Fund (IMF), the World Bank, the World Trade Organization (WTO), the G8, the United Nations, and numerous other semi-public and private groups, often including generally progressive organizations such as the World Health Organization (WHO). The United States has effective veto power within the IMF, and traditionally an American heads the World Bank and a European the IMF. The United States and other Anglo-American nations heavily shape the policies of emerging global organizations (Sridhar 2007; Stiglitz 2003, 2007; Thirkell-White 2003, 2007). While power within the WTO is skewed toward the richest nations in the world, the rise of China, India, and Brazil, and the drive of many of the poorer countries for more adequate representation, are leading to change in the WTO and even in the IMF.

As the single most powerful nation, the United States has ambiguous relationships with various international organizations. The US seeks to be heavily involved in powerful global institutions when these are useful to its own interests, or, conversely, ignores them when they are not useful. Even the nations expressing the most fervent attachment to neoliberalism do so mainly when convenient for themselves. Neoliberalism as a vehicle for US power or Anglo-American control has its boundaries and at times threatens the national interests even of its most ideologically committed disciples. Empire and neoliberal ideology and policies create avenues of conflict and change.

In the nineteenth and twentieth centuries there were national struggles between capitalists and an emerging working class. Today, conflict is emerging at the global level between dominant and subordinate classes just as it did within the developed nations earlier. In parts of the world such as Latin America and the former Communist bloc nations, the American economics profession has played an important role in reinforcing neoliberal hegemony and providing ideological support for the dominance of capital (Fourcade 2006).

Corporate-dominated globalization was differentially resisted by nations, with varying national class and institutional structures producing, in the developed world, contrasting national welfare states. Esping-Andersen (1990, 1999) notes three major types of welfare state: the social democratic (mainly Scandinavian) welfare states, which show the greatest level of decommodification (the extent to which citizens can live a decent life outside of market participation—for most people this means whether one can live a decent life outside of the labour market) and an emphasis on citizenship rights; the liberal welfare states (mainly Anglo-American), which are the most market-dependent and which emphasize means and income testing; and an intermediate group—the conservative, corporatist or familist welfare states (e.g., France, Germany, and Italy)—which are characterized by class- and status-based insurance schemes and a heavy reliance on the family to provide support. Some now argue that there is a fourth, "Latin" type as exemplified in Portugal, Spain, and Italy (for a review see, e.g., Bambra 2006b; for a more complex view of welfare states see Huo, Nelson & Stephens 2008).

In this chapter, I use welfare-state types as one way of approaching the categorization of the OECD (Organization for Economic Cooperation and Development) nations. These include the 30 or so richest nations in the world in terms of GDP (Gross Domestic Product) or GNI (Gross National Income) per capita.[2] The argument I make, however, is not wholly dependent on Esping-Andersen's particular conception of welfare-state types. In places I simply follow Navarro and Shi (2001) in examining the influence on health of having governments of a particular political stripe.[3]

A major explanation for differences in welfare regimes is a class or class-coalitional perspective. Greater working-class strength and organization and upper-class weakness produce stronger welfare regimes or help preserve benefits for workers in the face of attack (Hicks 1999; O'Connor & Olsen 1998; Teeple 2000). The strength of both working-class and right-wing parties needs to be taken into account, as globalization helped both to create and to reflect growing right-wing political mobilization (Brady & Leicht 2007).

Classes, class mobilization, and politics are important for health because particular types of political democracy may provide the most favourable basis for "the healthy society." Those democratic societies that are inclusive of working-class political movements are likely to be healthier. Progressive social and class movements and parties are the dynamic forces pushing for more widespread improvements in the human condition rather than simply more of everything for the rich. Business dominance leads to a skewing of economies toward the accumulation of wealth by a few rather than for the many. Ironically, this contradicts the "need" within market capitalism for mass markets for the goods and services produced. What is in the interests of individual capitalists or the capitalist class as a whole is not necessarily in the interests of the capitalist system.

The welfare state or "types of capitalism" literature, however, is directed mainly at the experience of the developed nations. As yet, little has been done to conceptualize the structure of the developing nations, at least as far as health is concerned, except perhaps as extensions of dependency theory, world system theory (see, for example, Moore 2006; Moore, Teixeira & Shiell 2006; Gough & Wood et al. 2004; Wood & Gough 2006), or ideas stemming from more traditional views of nineteenth- and twentieth-century imperialism and colonialism. Given the different political economies of the poorer nations, the class dynamics of such societies are likely to be very different from those in richer nations. Regarding globalization, the nature of class relations within nations is important because it is these relations, and national location in the world capitalist system, that determine whether nations are likely to be exploited by, or might even gain from, current global pressures toward the creation of "free enterprise" world markets.

THE SOCIAL DETERMINANTS OF HEALTH

The prevailing common-sense assumption about health, and about its historical improvement over time, has been that improved health is the product either of better health care or of growing economies. I will discuss the latter option below. Regarding health care, any study of health today begins with the premise that health is more a product of the way we live than it is of health care. This does not of course mean that health care is unimportant; the provision of simple primary health care, such as oral rehydration therapy for infants, public-health measures, and immunization, could radically improve the health of the least healthy nations of the world. Yet the idea that health is more a consequence of the way we live is an old one. It experienced a revival in the nineteenth century with such reformers and revolutionaries as Rudolf Virchow in Prussia, and Edwin Chadwick and Friedrich Engels in England. Virchow saw disease as produced by the social conditions under which populations live. Chadwick was one of the major English "sanitary reformers" of the nineteenth century who viewed the disgraceful conditions under which the labouring classes lived as the source of illness and disease. In the area of health, Engels is best known for his first major work, "The Condition of the Labouring Classes" (1987 [1845]), in which he described the horrific living conditions of the English working people and pointed out how these conditions produced the physical and mental stunting of the lower classes, whose lives he so dramatically described.

The social determinants approach rose to prominence again in the 1970s with such developments as the 1974 Lalonde Report in Canada, which emphasized that health was dependent on much more than simply access to health care. McKeown's (1976a, 1976b) analyses of the causes of population increase in the nineteenth and early twentieth centuries[4] had a major impact, as did the Black Report (Department of Health and Social Security 1980) in Great Britain. One consequence was the rise of the health promotion movement, and most recently a focus on population health (see Evans & Stoddart 1990), as opposed to individual illness and disease (for a brief recent history, see WHO 2005).

McKeown and others point out that historically most diseases were declining long before any medically efficacious drugs or technologies were applied. The factors that were deemed important for the health of populations included the material and psycho-social conditions of life, nutrition and improved living conditions, sanitary improvements, and, in the contemporary world of OECD nations, the influence of work, stress, and social supports. Recently, there has been an emphasis on the negative health effects of "the social gradient" or socio-economic status (SES) (see, e.g., Evans & Stoddart 1990; Evans, Barer & Marmor 1994; Poland et al. 1998). Canada was a leader in the fields of social determinants of health, health promotion, and population health. As I and others have noted, however, a focus on SES tends to neglect the social-structural determinants of SES or of income or social status hierarchies (Coburn 2000; Muntaner & Lynch 1999; Navarro 1998; Poland et al. 1998). A great deal of attention was paid to the pathways through which SES or income inequalities led to ill health, but little to what produced these inequalities in the first place. Yet placing SES inequalities themselves in a broader causal sequence led to a different, and more sociologically plausible, view of the way in which various societies produced varying average levels of health than did the focus on hierarchy *per se* (Coburn 2004).

While focusing on the social determinants of health was a necessary corrective to an assumption that more health care meant better health, it may be that health care is more or less important at various historical or developmental periods. Health care might have more of an influence on the health of populations after the change from the infectious to the chronic diseases as the major causes of death and illness (the epidemiological transition). The former are much more amenable to improvement from sanitary reform and advances in nutrition and pure water, for example, than are the latter. Moreover, practically speaking, most of the policy emphasis within nations is still on the financing and organization of health care as the most visible, and politically problematic, aspect of health.

Underlying the increasing emphasis on the social determinants of health is the conceptualization of disease in terms of host, pathogen, and environment interaction. The incidence or prevalence of disease is due to the susceptibility of humans to pathogenic substances, as well as the context within which pathogens interact with the human organism, and not only the presence of harmful toxins. For someone whose immune system is weakened by malnutrition, within an environment of great physical or psychological stress, even moderately toxic pathogens may result in sickness. With a more robust individual and/or a more supportive environment, the pathogen might have little or no effect, or, at least, would not result in death. This model supports the importance of adequate nutrition and water supplies and the social and psycho-social supports that enhance individual resistance to disease.

In this chapter, I view health as produced both by environmental (material, social, political, or psycho-social) factors and by health-care systems. Both of these broad areas are shaped or determined by the balance of national and international class forces.

MEASURES OF HEALTH

It might be assumed that increases in population are a measure of the health of the human species. If so, humans are now healthier than they have ever been. Two hundred years ago there were about 1 billion people on earth; one hundred years ago there were over 1.6 billion people. By 2007 there were over 6.5 billion people alive, and the total is projected to increase to 9.1 billion by 2050. Expanding populations, however, are more often perceived as a threat than an accomplishment. Population increase puts pressure on the earth's food, water, land, and other resources and strains the capacity of the world to absorb the pollutions produced by human civilizations. Population increase, therefore, is not an adequate measure of the health of the human species. There is an implicit ethical assumption that a mere physical existence is not enough. We all feel that to be fully human means the realization of at least some of our human capacities.

World population averages also conceal major national and regional differences. The richest nations are more or less stable in population, while parts of the less developed world are experiencing the huge population explosions associated with the demographic transition from a time of high birth and high death rates, to high birth and lower death rates (population increase), to the situation in the developed world characterized by low birth and low death rates. This demographic transition is also characterized by the "epidemiological transition" from a pattern of death from infectious diseases at younger ages to deaths from chronic diseases at older ages in the rich nations.

Though population growth is suspect as a measure of health, most of the ways we measure the health of populations rely on rates of infant mortality (IM) or of life expectancy (LE), both of which influence population increase. Infant mortality is assumed to more directly mirror current social conditions (e.g., those influencing the health of mothers) than does longevity (Chung & Muntaner 2006). Life expectancy, especially in the developed nations characterized by high chronic-disease rates, is likely to be a product of long-time exposure to various life-risk factors, and hence to reflect past as much as current conditions. Moreover, study of the life course indicates that health in later life is highly dependent on conditions during childhood, experienced many years earlier (Davey-Smith 2003). In addition, life-expectancy rates at birth may be highly influenced by the number of deaths during the first year of life—the two seemingly different measures of health are thus not actually independent. In this chapter I occasionally use as a measure of health the probability that 15-year-olds will die before age 60, a measure of adult health independent of IM.

Methodologically it is wise to remember that many health statistics, particularly those from the less developed nations, are often estimates rather than actual measures (see Deaton 2007). The differences between income and health averages and income and health distributions are also important, as are the contrasts between percentages and absolute numbers. The average GDP for the United States may be higher than that for Canada, but that does not mean that most Americans have higher incomes than most Canadians—rather that there are many more very rich Americans than very rich Canadians. In addition, a decline in, for example, the Swedish infant mortality rate (currently between 2 and 3 per 1,000 live births) of 33 per cent would mean that one more infant per thousand live births would survive to one year of age than presently survive. For Angola, on the other hand the same percentage decline would mean a change from an infant mortality rate of 154/1,000 to a rate of 103/1,000—in other words, 1 compared to 51 more children surviving for the same percentage decrease. The greatest possibilities for absolute health improvements would accrue, therefore, from improving the abysmal health of the less developed world.

GLOBAL HEALTH

Population increase aside, if we were to consider the earth as a single entity, then world health has generally improved over at least the past 100 years and, according to studies from the Western nations with the longest record keeping, England and Sweden, possibly since 1750 (see, for example, Riley 2001 and the Human Mortality Database). Although these are only estimates, life expectancy in 1820 was about 26 years, rising to 30 by 1890. The most rapid improvement took place in the twentieth century, with estimated life expectancy increasing from 33 in 1910 to nearly double that total by the end of the century. There was almost a 20-year increase in life expectancy between the middle and the end of that century. Similarly, world infant mortality was on average as high as 500/1,000 in the eighteenth century, declining to about 200–300/1,000 prior to 1900. The twentieth century saw dramatic decreases in infant mortality. In fact, much of the early rise in life expectancy was actually due to declines in infant mortality. At older ages the improvements were minuscule. For example, life expectancy amongst Finnish males in 1751–55 at age 65 was 11.3 years, a longevity measure that was not surpassed for over two hundred years, in 1956–60 (see Kannisto, Nieminen & Turpeinen 1999 and the Human Mortality Database).

More recently, since 1960 the mortality rate for those under five years old has been more than cut in half, from 198/1,000 live births in 1960 to 83 by the year 2000. Infant mortality rates have declined in both the poorer and the richer nations. Such declines have been striking within the OECD (OECD Health Data 2007); for example, for 28 nations of the OECD for which there are continuous data, average infant mortality was 30.4/1,000 live births in 1960 and 4.5 by 2004. Life expectancy during that time increased by about 16 years in the developing countries and six in the developed nations, resulting in some convergence between the rich and poor nations in life expectancy. For OECD countries the average life expectancy in 1960 was 69.6 (28 nations) and rose to 78.4 (30 nations) by 2003.

Possible future trends in longevity are in dispute. While some analysts have predicted a maximum lifespan, Oeppen and Vaupel (2002) point out that these predictions have always proven to be underestimates. Oeppen and Vaupel examined the highest life expectancy attained among a group of nations rather than the experience of individual countries, i.e., a form of life expectancy "best practice." Contrary to the idea that improvements in life expectancy are slowing, these analysts found that longevity amongst women has improved in a generally linear fashion, at a rate of three months per year for the past 160 years. Their conclusion

is that there are no signs of a slowdown in such improvements, so we
can expect continually rising life expectancies in the "best" countries in
the future (though not necessarily in any particular individual nation).

Still, a picture of improvements in average health, however encouraging, misses too much. In the first decade of the twenty-first century we
are confronted with a world in which there are simultaneous "epidemics" in human health across the globe: epidemics, in the richest countries,
of obesity; in the poorest nations, of undernutrition, disease, and death.
While the healthiest nations such as Sweden and Japan, show increasing life expectancy and extremely low infant mortality, other countries,
such as those of sub-Saharan Africa and the Russian Federation, display
shorter life spans than previously. Between 1989 and 2004, for example,
the life expectancy of Russian men declined by an astounding 13 years
to approximately 60 years—about the same longevity as men in India
(United Nations Human Development Report 2005). Life expectancy for
both males and females in Russia was lower in 2004 than it had been in
1970 (United Nations World Mortality Report 2005, 2006). Partly due
to the HIV/AIDS epidemic, many African nations also show declining
rates of life expectancy (United Nations World Mortality Report 2005,
2006), thus resulting in recent years in more divergence in life expectancy worldwide. In Swaziland, for instance, both male and female life
expectancy worsened by over 20 years between 1990–95 and 2000–05,
when the rate for men was 32.5 and for women, 33.4 (United Nations
World Mortality Report 2005, 2006). From the 1960s to the 1990s
there was some convergence between the developing and the developed
world, as the latter improved in infant mortality and life expectancy
more quickly than did the developed world. But, since 1990, "the convergence has ground to a halt" (UNHDR 2005: 25) similarly, there has
been a slowdown in the rate of improvement in child deaths, and the
divergence between rich and poor nations has been recently increasing.

In the early twenty-first century, the healthiest nations have longevity rates of about 80 years, while the unhealthiest nations show rates of
half that—around 40–45 years. A child in Swaziland is 30 times more
likely to die before the age of 5 than a child born in Sweden; a child in
Cambodia is 17 times more likely to die than a child in Canada. These
discrepancies are also evident in the adult years, even if someone escapes
the most vulnerable years of childhood. A 15-year-old female in Lesotho
is 18 times more likely to die by age 60 than a Japanese female of the
same age. A 15-year-old male in Zimbabwe has a 17-per-cent chance
of living to age 60, while a Swedish male has over a 90-per-cent chance
of reaching the same age. A male of the same age in Canada has five

times the chance of reaching 60 compared with a male in the Russian Federation (from the World Bank World Development Report 2006).

Within nations there are similar inequalities. In all nations of the world the rich and more powerful live longer, healthier lives than do the poor. Health inequalities within the OECD nations, for example, are now much greater than the average differences among these nations: "A baby boy from a family in the top 5% of the US income distribution will enjoy a life span 25% longer than a boy born in the bottom 5%" (UNHDR 2005: 58). Nor are the developing nations immune to the health effects of income and other social inequalities. The poorest 20 per cent of the population of Peru, for example, have over 40 per cent of all the child deaths in that country, eight times the rate of the richest 20 per cent.

While within nations the rich live longer lives than do the poor, it is not necessarily the case that richer nations, as opposed to classes or SES strata within nations, are always healthier than poorer nations (Wilkinson 1996; Wilkinson & Pickett 2007), the notoriously poor health of the wealthy (in average GNP/capita) United States relative to other OECD nations being a case in point. Indeed, the differences between and within nations provide interesting contrasts. For instance, the infant mortality rates in the poorest neighbourhoods in Canada in 1996 were better than the national rate of infant mortality in the US, yet the rates in the richest Canadian neighbourhoods were not much better than the national average rates in Sweden (Statistics Canada 2000). Health inequalities are now a focus of attention for the EU, which has recently commissioned special reports (Mackenbach 2005; Judge et al. 2005), and increasingly for the international community as a whole (the EU Special Group on Social Determinants and Health Inequalities and the WHO Commission on the Social Determinants of Health). Even the World Bank, once a central transmitter of the neoliberal mantra of free trade, small governments, and privatization, now focuses on poverty and inequalities, including inequalities in health. (The most recent example of a turn of direction is the World Bank's World Development Report from 2006.) However, the IMF and other influential international institutions remain mired in neoliberal ideology, despite its obvious failures (Labonte & Torgerson 2005; Labonte, Schrecker & Sen Gupta 2005; Stiglitz 2003, 2007; Thirkell-White 2003, 2007).

The health data thus show general improvements in health over the past 150 to 250 years, but continuing and perhaps growing disparities in health between and within nations. How have such trends and differences been explained? Unlike the monolithic neoliberal paradigm that advocates the same solution for many different issues at various times and places, more adequate analyses and policies will necessarily be more complex and context dependent. Yet, as I point out below, they are nevertheless broadly shaped by the dominant capitalist mode of production.

EXPLANATIONS FOR IMPROVEMENTS IN HEALTH

Some of the explanations for the general improvements in health over the past two centuries include the rising quality of and greater public access to medical services, innovations in medical technologies, the increasing numbers of doctors and other health-care providers, and more hospitals. Another seemingly obvious explanatory factor for health improvements is economic growth, because economies and improvements in health have grown in parallel. Some economists have seized on this correlation to argue that the only way to improve human well-being is through economic growth, and that the neoliberal way is the only way. But it appears that there are a number of different paths to economic growth, and not only the neoliberal version (see, for example, Navarro & Schmitt 2005). In what follows, however, I want to examine more closely the notion of economic growth as an explanation for health trends and inequalities, but most specifically to focus on the claim that neoliberalism has a unique role in producing improvements in human well-being.

There is no doubt that, historically, economic growth and health improvements show similar trends. Economies have grown and health has generally improved. And in today's world it is also clear that if we look at all nations cross-sectionally, their economic level (but not necessarily their rate of economic growth) shows a high correlation with their average levels of health. The Spearman's rank-order correlation of infant mortality with GNI/capita at purchasing power parity is 0.87 and shows a clear logarithmic relationship; i.e., improvements in infant mortality flatten out at higher GNI/capita levels (my calculations, from World Bank World Development Report 2006). Incidentally, the same shape of curve, although at lower economic and infant-mortality levels, was shown in various decades from 1900 to 2000 (Deaton 2007; Preston 1976). These data indicate that developing nations today have much better health than did the developed nations at similar economic levels many years ago. Quite clearly, improving health is not simply a function of higher GNP or GNI/capita. A major difficulty with the economic growth argument historically, however, is that many factors co-vary with, but are not necessarily dependent on, economic growth, particularly advancements in knowledge about health, ranging from insights into water and milk contamination to more recent innovations regarding the health influences of smoking and the effects of nutrition on health, as well as improvements in medical techniques and changes in class structure and socio-economic policies. Even the more econom-ically oriented are beginning to realize that economies are not separate from societies and that types of societal organization are crucial deter-minants of the well-being of nations and of citizens within nations, of economies, and of health.

Analyzing the contemporary relationship between GDP or GNI/capita and health, we find, as others have, that despite the high cor-relation of infant mortality or other measures of health with the loga-rithm of national income, the notion that "national wealth is related to national health" does not hold for the most advanced nations. That is, within the OECD, in the richest nations in the world—i.e., about the top quintile (30) of nations in income (of about 150 nations for whom there is income and health data)—higher GNI per capita at purchasing power parity (ppp) is unrelated to average national health (World Bank data). This fact, in conjunction with the universal finding that, within nations, the higher the wealth the higher the health, has led to a vari-ety of hypotheses trying to relate these two diverse findings. It has also led to the advanced nations being viewed separately from those of the developing nations because, for the latter, national level of wealth does seem to be correlated with health.

HEALTH IN THE WEALTHIEST NATIONS

There is a much more extensive literature on average health levels and inequalities within nations in the developed world than in less devel-oped nations. In addition, there is more discussion of contemporary health events than of health in historical perspective. The most prom-inent, but still contentious, contemporary hypothesis regarding health status and health differences focuses on income inequality (Wilkinson 1996, 2005; Kawachi, Kennedy & Wilkinson 1999). It is argued that the major determinant of the health of the developed nations, and hence of the average health differences between nations, is not GNP/capita, but rather the degree of income inequality itself, and its correlate or con-sequence: lowered social cohesion or trust (which itself contributes to poorer health). The distribution of income is more important than its average level because hierarchy (e.g., socio-economic status) is related, through bio-psychosocial mechanisms, to lowered self-esteem and sub-sequently to poorer health. These relationships would help to explain SES—health relationships within nations and the lack of a wealth/health correlation for the richer nations of the OECD.

Opponents of the income-inequality thesis contend that the relationships found by Wilkinson are artifactual and/or that income inequality is really a proxy for many other forms of social inequality that all influence health and that are consequences of different types of "welfare state" (Coburn 2000, 2004; Deaton 2003; Ellison 2002; Muntaner & Lynch 1999; Navarro 1998). Some writers have emphasized a "neo-materialist" interpretation of SES—health relationships, as opposed to what they view as Wilkinson's use of psycho-social factors to explain why SES or income inequality is related to health (Lynch et al. 2000). Placing SES within a broader causal sequence paints a picture of basic class-related structural factors that produce both elongated SES hierarchies and worse average levels of health, partly, but certainly not wholly, through income inequalities (Coburn 2000, 2004; Muntaner & Lynch 1999). Within this model, income inequalities may or may not be influential, depending on the national context. In fact, studies now suggest that income inequality may be important only in highly unequal nations such as the US and the UK (e.g., Ross et al. 2005).

Finally, a third hypothesis, not very well explicated, contends that national differences in health and within-nation health differences are due simply to the differential speed and spread of knowledge about health (Deaton 2003, 2007; Cutler, Deaton & Lleras-Muney 2006). Within nations, those higher in status and education are quicker to adopt healthy lifestyles, and have access to more health-promoting resources, than do those lower. At a national level, some nations may be more open to health knowledge and, as we will see, more socially competent at translating health knowledge from elsewhere to the benefit of their own populations. Earlier I mentioned the obesity epidemic in the richer nations. But this is not only a cross-national problem in which some nations show greater average levels of obesity, but also one within nations because it is the poorer strata, those lower in SES, who tend to be more obese—for many SES-related reasons. Similarly, there are historical changes in cross-national and within-nation differences in tobacco use: higher classes and wealthier nations once showed higher smoking rates, but the opposite is now generally true. Although the social mechanisms through which some nations spread knowledge or practices more quickly and extensively than do others has not been studied, education, public-health measures, and government actions regarding these are undoubtedly important.

INEQUALITIES AND HEALTH IN THE DEVELOPED NATIONS

Neoliberal governments and policies became dominant in the late 1970s and subsequent years, as exemplified by the Margaret Thatcher and Ronald Reagan regimes in the UK and the US, followed by similar regimes in other Anglo-American nations such as Canada, New Zealand, and Australia. These neoliberal regimes are viewed as replacing various strong or weak versions of Keynesian welfare states in which governments took some responsibility both for the operation and regulation of markets and for counterbalancing economic downturns through income supports and redistribution.

In fact, prior to the 1970s, the US and the UK showed declining inequalities. However, beginning in about 1968 in the US and 1977–78 in the UK, income inequality, for example, began a steep and rapid rise, with both nations reaching levels that had not been experienced in decades. There was a massive accumulation of wealth by the rich. This steep increase in inequality began in the UK under the Thatcher regime and was mostly halted, although not reversed, under subsequent Labour governments. A similar increase in income inequality was sustained in the United States during and after the Reagan regime. In the US the lowest 60 per cent of households actually experienced a *decrease* in after-tax income between 1977 and 1999. During the same period, incomes of the top 5 per cent of households grew by 56 per cent and the top 1 per cent mushroomed by 93 per cent (Bernstein, Mishel & Brocht 2000: 7). The increases in inequality in Britain were much greater even than in the United States (Atkinson 1999, 2005). Income inequality also increased in many, but not all, other OECD nations (Brandolini & Smeeding 2007).

Data from the OECD indicate that welfare regimes actually did what they were supposed to do: lessen poverty and inequality. Comparing nations, the US and the UK, but also Canada and Australia, show much higher income inequality than do such countries as Switzerland, Germany, or the Netherlands who, in turn, show higher inequality than do the Scandinavian countries (Gottschalk & Smeeding 2000; Kenworthy 1999; Korpi & Palme 1998; Luxembourg Income Studies Working Papers). In fact, despite being one of the richest nations on earth, in 1991 the United States had one of the highest rates of *absolute* (as well as relative) poverty[5] among the developed nations—of 15 countries only Italy, Ireland, Australia, and the UK had higher rates—the latter three all having neoliberal policies (Kenworthy 1999: 1125). At the end of the twentieth century, the neoliberal nations (Canada, Ireland, the UK, and the US) showed higher inequality than did the social democratic nations (including Austria, Denmark, Finland, Norway, and Sweden), with Gini's ranging from .30 to .37, as compared to the social demo-cratic nations' range from .22 to .25 (Brandolini & Smeeding 2007; the Gini is a measure of inequality in which 1 is total inequality and 0 is perfect equality).

Different welfare regimes and rising inequalities of various kinds have important implications for health inequalities within nations, since health inequalities are related to many different unequal social condi-tions. Thus, despite "expanding economies," health inequalities have increased. A study showed all-cause inequalities in mortality between low and high SES areas to have increased among adults in the US by 50 and 58 per cent (for males and females respectively) from 1969 to 1998 (Singh & Siahpush 2002, 2006). A commentator on Britain, a nation that experienced a prolonged period of neoliberal politics, noted that "[t]he inequalities in health between social classes are now the great-est yet recorded in British history" (Yamey 1999; see also Dorling 1997 and Shaw et al. 1999). Another British study shows an increasing gap "between social classes I [high] and V [low] [which] widened from 2.1:1 in 1970–72 ... to 3.3 in 1991–3" (Blane & Drever 1998). Even during an era of putatively "Labour" governments in Britain pledged to reduc-ing inequality, there remained persistent health inequalities.

Examining national levels of health by directly comparing the liberal with the social democratic nations amongst the more developed nations, the liberal nations show poorer average levels of infant mortality for all periods from the 1960s through to 2005. The liberal welfare-state regimes, including the US, the UK, Ireland, and Canada are not only absolutely worse off than the social democratic nations, but they also rank increasingly worse relative to other OECD nations regarding infant mortality rates between 1960 and 2005 (OECD Health Data 2007—see also Coburn 2010). A "league table" of infant mortality shows that in 1960, the UK, the US, and Canada were ranked 7th, 8th, and 9th, respectively, in infant mortality (of 18 nations, with first place indicating the lowest infant mortality rate). By 2005, these three nations ranked 16th (the UK), 17th (Canada), and 18th (the US). Comparing extreme cases, in 2005 if the US (IM 6.8/1,000) had had Sweden's infant mor-tality rate (2.4/1,000), about 20,000 more American babies would have reached their first birthday.

Using an ordinal index of decommodification (the degree to which individuals and families can live a reasonable life outside of being employed—one measure of welfare-state status), rather than the cat-egorical types of welfare state, shows the same results. Indices of de-commodification by nation are highly related to infant mortality (e.g., Bambra 2006b; Chung & Muntaner 2006; Navarro & Shi 2001). This relationship remains even when controlling for GDP/capita (Coburn 2004). Navarro and others have also shown that welfare measures, and health, are positively related to basic class/political institutions such as higher union membership and the number of years of left political party power (Navarro 1998; Navarro et al. 2003). Recent studies have also noted the negative influence on inequality and health of the rise to power of right-wing political parties (Brady & Leicht 2007). Thus, overall, the liberal welfare states show greater inequality, greater poverty, and poorer overall health status. There can be a "virtuous circle" in which economic growth is actually translated, through social policy, into lowered inequalities of many kinds, and (perhaps partially because of lowered inequalities), higher average levels of health and lessened health inequalities. In the case of the richer nations, however, national wealth is either only weakly, or not at all, related to national average levels of health.

Even within the category of neoliberal nations, the degree of market-orientation between them makes a difference. For example, studies comparing the United States and Canada, the latter having a slightly more developed social-welfare system than the former, indicate both a better health status for Canadians than Americans as well as less income inequality and less of a relationship between income inequality and health. A longitudinal analysis comparing the better health outcomes for Canada than for the United States over the second half of the twentieth century echoes the findings of a number of researchers comparing welfare-state types. This study concludes that "1) greater economic well-being and spending on health does not yield better health outcomes ... 2) public provision and income redistribution trump economic success where population health is concerned ... and 3) that the gradual development of public provision represents the build-up of social infrastructure which has long-lasting effects on health status" (Siddiqi & Hertzman 2006).

The World Health Organization publishes life tables, which show the proportions of people from an original cohort of 100,000 living to various ages, based on current age/sex-adjusted mortality rates. In 2006 the United States had an estimated 79,773 males and 87,264 females per 100,000 born still alive at age 65, the UK showed 84,355 and 90,055, while Sweden had 87,520 males and 91,774 females alive at age 65 (WHO Life Tables 2006). Again, Canada (85,714 males and 90,827 females) is closer to Sweden than to the US and has better survival rates than does the UK. Internationally, more people survive to age 65 in Costa Rica than in the United States. Cuba, a chronically underdeveloped nation suffering under a decades-long trade boycott by its neighbour, the United States, keeps about as many people alive until age 65 as does the US.

One seeming anomaly regarding overall average health status is the situation of Canada and Australia. Both these nations are classed as "liberal" (although there are some who argue with this classification), yet both nations show relatively good life-expectancy rates but poorer infant-mortality rates. One possible explanation for these discrepant findings is that these countries have very high levels of immigration, and therefore high percentages of foreign-born populations. Canada has about 20 per cent foreign born and Australia 22 per cent. There may be a "better health immigrant" effect, because immigrants are selected partly for their good health. On the other hand, Australia and Canada may be slightly different from some of the other liberal welfare state types. More case-study research on these nations, and other "anomalies" we shall point to in the less developed world, should prove informative.

If we are talking about particular types of society rather than simply a particular type of economy, it might be expected that health data would coincide with other measures of well-being (Wilkinson & Pickett 2007). I have hypothesized that the strong emphasis on markets within neoliberal societies, without corresponding protection against market failures, would particularly squeeze those lower in socio-economic hierarchies leading to more deviant behaviour of various kinds, including crime (Wacquant 2001). In addition, there seems to be a propensity among neoliberals to feel that crime is increasing, even when it is not. Neoliberal governments may or may not be smaller than other forms of government, but they are likely to be more authoritarian. Authority and coercion of various kinds are needed to force people to submit to the "discipline" of markets. Indeed, a preliminary look at relevant data does show that the neoliberal Anglo-American nations more than the social democratic nations are characterized not only by higher inequality and worse health but also by putting more people in prison and by longer working hours. Even in Tony Blair's Britain, supposedly an example of a "Third Way," prisons became so full that before more prisoners could be admitted, some had to be released (Travis 2007). Similar punitive policies are coming to the fore in Canada under the misleading heading of being "tough on crime." In view of the disparities between the developed and less developed world, I have already noted it is also interesting that the liberal welfare state types are only one-half to one-third as generous in official development aid as are the social democratic nations. Health is one measure of well-being—but certainly not the only one. The irony of the frequent use of the term "freedom" within market-authoritarian states is lost on neoliberals.

THE LESS-DEVELOPED WORLD

There are as yet no fully developed equivalents for poorer countries to Esping-Andersen's welfare state types, although Gough and colleagues have made a step in that direction (Gough et al. 2004; Wood & Gough 2006). Gough et al. argue that the less-developed world can be conceived in terms of differences between clientilist (social) security forms of state, in which one's well-being depends on personal relations with powerful persons, and more universalist security forms. A few analysts have applied models regarding core/periphery nations from world systems theory (Moore, Teixeira & Shiell 2006). Labonte and colleagues (Labonte & Torgerson 2005; Labonte, Schrecker & Sen Gupta 2005) have contextualized the poorer nations of the world within broader processes of economic globalization. However, the class relations within the developing nations can hardly be expected to be the same as those within OECD nations. The developing nations are much more diverse than the richer countries and show quite different political economies, particularly because many are either still mainly agrarian, peasant-like societies or have yet to experience the main waves of industrialization, while others are highly industrialized. The future for explaining national developments in the developing nations will involve the use of a more complex model involving the interaction between role in the world economy and type of national political economy (Huo, Nelson & Stephens 2008; Lee, Nielsen & Alderson 2007). For the moment, however, we are left with analyses by region or by national income as the usual official policy approaches. Here I will simply note specific national and within-nation health levels and disparities.

Life expectancy at birth in 2002 ranged from 78 years for women in developed countries to less than 46 years for men in sub-Saharan Africa. Japan has the highest HALE (health adjusted life expectancy) longevity in the world at 73.6 years (with Sweden close behind). By contrast, life expectancy in Angola was 28.7 years. I earlier mentioned huge differences in child mortality between the developing and the developed world. Some of these differences are increasing, particularly in sub-Saharan Africa. In 1980, child death rates in sub-Saharan Africa were 13 times higher than in rich countries; 25 years later they were 29 times higher (UNHDR 2005: ch. 1).

Average national health levels also ignore within-country inequalities. In a group of 22 low- or middle-income nations over a three- to six-year period in the late 1990s, 13 showed an increase in inequality in child (under age 5) deaths by income, with nine showing a decrease in income-related inequality (Wagstaff 2000). Moreover, this study showed no relationship between overall national levels of improvement in health and health inequalities, suggesting that policies to reduce inequalities need to be aimed specifically at the poor. There are similar inequalities in almost every nation. Within India, the death rates for children under five in Kerala (a state often mentioned as a jurisdiction having much better health than their wealth would suggest—and a state with an early communist government history) was 19/1,000, as opposed to 123 in Uttar Pradesh. Kerala also showed other positive health data, such as 80 per cent of children receiving vaccination, compared to 11 per cent in Behar (UNHDR 2005: 30). China has shown rapidly increasing economic growth in the past two decades, yet also a slowing of improvement in average health and rapidly increasing health inequalities. The death rate for those under five is 8/1,000 in Shanghai and Beijing, compared to 60 in Guizhou, the poorest province. The poorest 20 per cent in Bolivia show ten times the percentage of children severely under height for their age as do the richest 20 per cent (World Bank World Development Report 2006).

A number of analysts have pointed out that the Structural Adjustment Policies of the IMF and similar programs, aimed at market liberalization between and within nations, often created many more economic, social, and health problems than they solved (Labonte, Schrecker & Sen Gupta 2005; Stiglitz 2007). Extremely poor nations had little choice but to submit to lengthy lists of IMF prescriptions for smaller government, fewer subsidies, including for food or basic commodities, and moves toward markets, user fees or pay-as-you-go in health and health care. According to the IMF, free markets were apparently a universal panacea for the quite varied problems and issues showed by the less developed world. Furthermore, in terms of assistance, Labonte and others (Labonte, Schrecker & Sen Gupta 2005) have indicated the degree to which the G8 and similar organizations failed to live up to their promises of aid to the less-developed world. This lack of support occurred despite the fact that many of the African states now said to be "failed states" were the products of the imperialist and colonial policies of many of the G8 members themselves. As noted above, the question of exactly what a "failed state" entails is more complex than it might initially appear. Today, however, the IMF appears to be in both ideological and fiscal difficulties, as nations seek to escape from the dictates of IMF economists. Argentina is a pertinent example: although suffering under IMF proscriptions, it paid off its IMF loan specifically to become more independent, and began to flourish economically.

It is true that most of the unhealthiest nations are also the poorest. However, there are wide disparities in health for nations at similar levels of GNP/capita. Vietnam shows better infant mortality than Malaysia, which has over three times its income. Sri Lanka shows better infant and adult mortality than do Thailand and Indonesia, both of which have twice its income. Syria has better health than Saudi Arabia at over three times its income, and Ecuador has just as good health data as the twice-as-rich Brazil. Costa Rica and Cuba are medium- to very poor nations, yet both have better adult death ratios than does the United States, one of the richest nations in the world (my calculations from World Bank World Development Report 2006). There are sometimes startling comparisons even between the developed and the less-developed world. For example, the US white infant-mortality rate is worse than Malaysia's. The lesson is that even for the less-developed world, high GNP/capita is not a necessary condition for good average levels of health.

What differentiates those poorer nations with good health from their less healthy compatriots? The evidence suggests that nations that retain some control over their role in the world economy are both able to profit from processes of globalization in terms of economic growth and able to translate that growth into improved health. One study (Hopkins 2006) compared the policies and outcomes of Indonesia, Thailand, and Malaysia during the economic crises of the late 1990s. The former two nations followed World Bank prescriptions for adjustment, including cutbacks in government spending; the result was that they both experienced negative health outcomes. Malaysia, on the other hand, pursued its own independent policy, and the crisis had little impact on that country. Hopkins notes the "importance of social safety nets and the maintenance of government expenditures in minimizing the impact of economic shocks on health" (2006: 347). The IMF, the World Bank, and other international institutions today greatly emphasize the importance of "governance" in processes of national development. That is, there is much more emphasis on the politics of the developing nations than there was previously. However, for the IMF and the World Bank, governance seems to mean those institutional mechanisms that help develop or maintain capitalist (as opposed to personal) property rights. Still, it is a big step for some economists to admit non-economic factors as important regarding economic growth—a departure from their ideal-typical model of apparently "free standing" economies. There is a forced tacit admission of the embeddedness of economies within societies. The World Bank, and leading economists such as Jeffrey Sachs, now point to the possible role in development of many of the social factors pointed to earlier (Sachs 2001, 2008). Education, health, and various kinds of welfare measures may actually underpin well-functioning economies and are not simply consequences of them. These developments have come rather late, considering Marx's conception of "modes of production" in the nineteenth century and many years after Polanyi's (1944) non-Marxist theorization of the relation between economies and societies (see also Granovetter 1985; Sayer 2002; Adaman & Devine 2001). In this context it is interesting that the title of Esping-Andersen's second book on welfare states in 1999 was *The Social Foundations of Post-Industrial Economies*.

HEALTH-CARE SYSTEMS

Much of what I have noted about health applies not only to the social determinants of health but also to health-care systems. The health of nations is the result of both the conditions under which people live and the adequacy of health-care systems. The social determinants of health as well as health-care systems are themselves consequences of global and national socio-economic structures and actors (see, e.g., Starfield & Birn 2007).

Health-care systems everywhere are partly the product not only of broad political struggles, but also of the (class-structured) power of health-care providers—in most nations, the medical profession, and such powerful institutions as the drug industry—to shape health care in ways amenable to their interests. I have mentioned that neoliberal policies undermined the positive social determinants of health and also weakened those social factors that might have buffered the negative influence of weakened social structures on health. Health care can be classed in the "buffering category." Whether or not nations have national health systems, as in Britain, national health-insurance schemes, as in Canada, or mixtures of public and private systems (in fact no system is entirely public, or entirely private), as in the United States, all can be considered, as Navarro (1989) has argued, to reflect national differences in class power. Higher working-class and lower right-wing power produces more equitable and more publicly funded or organized health-care systems, leading to the ability to deliver a broader set of services to a wider and more diverse population than in market-oriented health-care systems.

Within a capitalist system, however, there are always, everywhere, pressures to re-commodify any goods or services that have been de-commodified. Hence, within Canada and in all other nations, there are persistent calls to privatize whatever is now produced in common or through government initiatives. In Canada, corporate enterprises and private individuals see fortunes to be made through the privatization of national health-insurance services. They are a continual source of pressure on governments to privatize the public commons in the health field.

Whereas neoliberal international organizations have pushed for the marketization of health, including user-pay systems, the experience in the developed world shows that public systems, and perhaps single-payer systems in general, are more efficient and more effective than private systems (Drache & Sullivan 1999). A prime comparison is, of course, between the national health system in Canada and the complex mixture of mostly private "non-systems" in the US. The latter is more expensive, spends more money on administration, and covers lower percentages of the population for a smaller number of procedures than does the Canadian system (the latter of course is not without faults, among them a degree of lack of responsiveness to patient concerns, needs, and wants). The lesson, that public systems are more effective and efficient than private systems, was ignored in the developing nations, although it has to be noted that health-care systems in many of the very poorest nations are primitive at best and the very poorest nations would benefit more from improved nutrition, water quality, and hygiene than from formal health care *per se*.

A NOTE ON ECONOMIC GROWTH AND HEALTH

The neoliberal stream within the global and national development literature implies that human well-being can be brought about only through economic growth and that free markets are the optimal path to this goal. A major difficulty with the economic growth argument historically, however, is that, though economic *level* and health are generally, but not universally, related, many factors co-vary with economic growth. There is a parallel between economic growth and advancements in knowledge about health, whether concerning nutrition, smoking, or new medical technologies. In an early paper, Preston (1976) argued that only a small percentage—less than 25 per cent and perhaps as low as 10 per cent of the massive international declines in mortality between the 1930s and the 1960s could be attributed to the effects of increasing income per capita, an estimate that Tapia Granados and Ionides contend "has not been seriously challenged" (2008: 546). In a study of 94 nations between 1962 and 1987, Jamison, Sandbu and Wang (2004) estimate that 66 per cent of improvements in infant mortality rates could be attributed to technical progress, 21 per cent to improvements in education, 7 per cent to income increases, and 7 per cent to the greater availability of doctors. As noted, nations today, with GNP/capita similar to those of the developed nations in the 1900s, nevertheless have much better health than did nations in the 1900s—diffusion of health knowledge and technologies obviously make a difference. Finally, in a recent direct test of the national income-growth hypothesis, health economist Angus Deaton (2007) found increases in national income unrelated to improvements in health for the period 1960–2000. He speculated that both of these are related to a so-far unnamed "third cause," for example, innovations in science and technology (see also Jamison, Sandbu & Wang 2004).

DISCUSSION

Historically, health levels show general improvement and particularly speedy progress was made in the twentieth century. Recently, however, health improvements have been slowing, and unacceptable health inequalities remain or are increasing.

With the rise of global neoliberalism, the common assumption has been that further progress in improving human well-being relies on economic growth and that "free markets" nationally and internationally are therefore the basis for health improvements. Yet, as I have pointed out, economic level or economic growth has only contingent or varying relationships with global or national health levels: some poor nations have much higher levels of health than their economic level would predict; in the rich OECD nations there is no relationship between GDP or GNI/capita and national levels of health; and economic growth *per se* is not related to improvements in health. In any event, economic growth requires particular social and institutional mechanisms in order to translate increasing average national income into improved health for the majority of the population. As the instances of Kerala, Costa Rica, and Cuba indicate, political factors vastly outweigh the influence of economic growth or economic level on health. Economic growth is not a prerequisite for improving the health of nations, although, at the level of the very poor nations, it would help. While, among the richer nations, high levels of economic growth may show positive or negative relationships with human well-being, the most important current issue for the less-developed world is not growth versus non-growth, but what *type* of economic growth. The neoliberal variety is more harmful than helpful as far as health and human well-being are concerned, in that it tends to undermine those social institutions that underwrite economic growth and that also help to promote human well-being generally.

Some societal forms are better able to convert economic growth into human well-being than are others. But such a statement tends to suggest that "economies" and "societies" are separate entities. The view taken here is that economies are "part of" society and the two are mutually constituted. I have argued that all facets of societal functioning in the modern world occur within national, and an increasingly international, capitalist mode of production which itself has particular trends, tendencies, contradictions, and effects on human well-being. A global political economy of health has to deal with current predominant biases toward neoliberal or market-oriented processes. Given the recent emphasis in the health literature on the importance of the diffusion of knowledge, the impact of an over-emphasis on markets is disturbing. Health knowledge itself, and indeed knowledge in general, is being commodified, that is, being made subject to payment in the market. The knowledge commons, often originating in universities, is being privatized, as the more developed nations and their corporations seek to profit from "intellectual property rights." The massive problems surrounding the issue of trying to obtain cheaper or generic drugs for AIDS/HIV patients in the less-developed world is a prime instance of the obstacles that such privatization poses for global health. Within markets the wants of the rich supersede the needs of the poor.

There are some small signs of movement toward a political economy of health rather than simply an economistic view. There is now more recognition than before of the importance of social organization in economic development and health. The IMF and World Bank, for instance, have explicitly recognized that "markets" have to be socially made and do not simply appear, nor can their preconditions be simply assumed. Jeffrey Sachs, a leading economist, now points to market deficiencies and argues for government actions (though his latest book is characterized by political and sociological naiveté regarding solutions—Sachs 2008). But the approach of international organizations is often contradictory. For example, the World Bank regularly publishes lists of countries that are "best for business." Countries are ranked on various criteria, ranging from the ease of opening a business to the ease of dismissing workers. The World Bank has been criticized not as much for publishing such criteria but for implicitly valuing and advocating them. At the same time, in such publications as the World Development Reports the World Bank evinces a growing concern with poverty and inequality. Strange bedfellows—nevertheless, both of these emphases contain an admission that economies cannot be considered outside of the context of which they are a part. The old idea of the economy somehow as an "engine" outside of the political and social environment within which it was developed and operates is now more or less moribund. Even mainstream economists now attack the notion that social-welfare spending is a drag on economic growth (Lindert 2004), and the whole fabric of neoliberal prescriptions as a universal panacea for development is fraying at the edges. The tendency now is to view economic development as contingent on extant institutions in the polity and in civil society. The ethical and practical barrenness of calls for humans to submit to markets is, within a world capitalist system, being replaced by questions about what kind of markets, in what context, and for what purpose.

These, however, are small steps when we are immediately confronted with such hugely unequal states of wealth and health as we face in the early twenty-first century. The divisions between those who have "too much" and those dying for the lack of the basic requirements for human biological existence do not have to be this way because of a lack of resources. There are ample resources in the world right now to ensure that everyone has enough to eat, as well as adequate housing and primary health care, education, and knowledge about health.

Any idea that we have responsibilities toward the less fortunate is not a popular topic for neoliberally oriented politics in the English-speaking world these days. Neoliberal ideology provides a pseudo-universalist cover for the interests of the powerful. It justifies ignoring the needs of the less fortunate because doing something about these, other than individual charity, would produce "economic distortions" harmful in the long run—a highly convenient doctrine for the wealthy. In a world of the immensely rich and immensely poor, the rich are all in favour of putting everything up for sale. Tommy Douglas, the social-democratic father of health insurance in Canada, had a saying for such occasions: "Everyone for themselves said the elephant dancing among the chickens."

Yet globalization broadly defined can produce positive orientations toward a "world community," the fact that we are all members of "spaceship earth." Globalization in wider perspective is stimulating collective human effort to solve mutual problems. There are now dozens of disparate groups with various aims and yet a common target: runaway neoliberalism. As Ratner (1997) put it, there is "one Goliath, many Davids" (271). At a time in world history when there are threats to the very existence of the human species, there are promising movements, yet tremendous resistance, toward a more humane form of human governance.

NOTES

1   I owe a great deal to Elaine Coburn for her ideas and suggestions and for co-authoring the paper on which this chapter is partially based (Coburn & Coburn 2007). Thank you also to Lesley Biggs, who spent valuable time editing and greatly improving this chapter, and to an anonymous referee for helpful comments.

2   GNI is a more inclusive measure of national income than is GDP.

3 While the theory of the welfare state has been criticized (Bambra 2006a; Scruggs & Allan 2006), it has also been buttressed by empirical cluster analyses of "types of economy" in the richer nations (Pryor 2004; Saint-Arnaud & Bernard 2003).

4 These findings are still much disputed. See, e.g., Szreter (1998, 2002), and the American Journal of Public Health 92.5 (2002).

5 In this instance, absolute poverty represented the US poverty rate in dollars or dollar equivalents applied to all nations. The relative poverty rate measured nationally specific poverty rates, that is, the percentage of households within each nation earning 40 per cent or below of the national average household income. See Kenworthy 1999.

REFERENCES

Adaman, F., and P. Devine. 2001. *Economy and Society: Money, Capitalism and Transition*. Montreal: Black Rose Books.

Atkinson, A.B. 2005. "Top Incomes in the UK over the 20th Century." *Journal of the Royal Statistical Society* 168(2): 325–43.

——. 1999. "Is Rising Income Inequality Inevitable? A Critique of the Transatlantic Consensus." WIDER Annual Lecture. United Nations University. Helsinki: World Institute for Development Economics Research.

Bambra, C. 2006a. "Decommodification and the World of Welfare Revisited." *Journal of European Social Policy* 16(1): 73–80.

Bambra, C. 2006b. "Health Status and the Worlds of Welfare." *Social Policy and Society* 5(1): 53–62.

Bernstein, J., L. Mishel, and C. Brocht. 2000. "Anyway You Cut It: Income Inequality on the Rise Regardless of How It's Measured." Economic Policy Institute. Briefing Paper No. 99. <http://www.epi.org/publications/entry/briefingpapers_inequality_inequality/>.

Blane, D., and F. Drever. 1998. "Inequality among Men in Standardized Years of Potential Life Lost 1970–93." *British Medical Journal* 317: 255–60.

Brady, D., and K. Leicht. 2007. "Party to Inequality: Right Party Power and Income Inequality in Affluent Western Democracies." Luxembourg Income Studies Working Paper 460. <http://www.lisproject.org/publications/liswps/460.pdf>.

Brandolini, A., and T.M. Smeeding. 2007. "Inequality Patterns in Western-type Democracies: Cross-country Differences and Time Changes." Luxembourg Income Studies Working Paper 458. <http://www.lisproject.org/publications/liswps/458.pdf>.

Chung, H., and C. Muntaner. 2006. "Political and Welfare State Determinants of Infant and Child Health Indicators: An Analysis of Wealthy Countries." *Social Science and Medicine* 63(3): 829–42.

Coates, D. (ed.). 2005. *Varieties of Capitalism, Varieties of Approaches*. London: Palgrave Macmillan.

Coburn, D. 2010. "Health and Health Care: A Political Economy Perspective." In T. Bryant, D. Raphael, and M. Rioux (eds.), *Staying Alive: Critical Perspectives on Health, Illness and Health Care*. 2nd ed. Toronto: Canadian Scholars', Press. 65–91.

———. 2004. "Beyond the Income Inequality Hypothesis: Globalization, Neoliberalism and Health Inequalities." *Social Science and Medicine* 58(1): 41–56.

———. 2000. "Income Inequality, Social Cohesion and the Health Status of Populations: The Role of Neoliberalism." *Social Science and Medicine* 51(1): 135–46.

Coburn, D., and E. Coburn. 2007. "Health and Health Inequalities in a Neo-liberal Global World." In Di McIntyre and G. Mooney (eds.), *The Economics of Health Equity*. Cambridge: Cambridge University Press. 13–35.

Cutler, D.M., A.S. Deaton, and A. Lleras-Muney. 2006. "The Determinants of Mortality." National Bureau of Economic Research, Working Paper no. 11963. <http:// www.nber.org/papers/w11963>.

Davey Smith, G. (ed.). 2003. *Health Inequalities: Lifecourse Approaches*. Bristol: The Policy Press.

Deaton, A. 2007. "Global Patterns of Income and Health: Facts, Interpretations and Policies." WIDER Annual Lecture. UN University World Institute for Development Economic Research, Helsinki.

———. 2003. "Health, Inequality and Economic Development." *Journal of Economic Literature* 41(1): 113–58.

Department of Health and Social Security, UK. 1980. *Inequalities in Health (The Black Report)*.

Dorling, D. 1997. *Death in Britain: How Local Mortality Rates Have Changed: 1950s to 1990s*. York: Joseph Rowntree Foundation.

Drache, D., and T. Sullivan (eds.). 1999. *Health Reform: Public Success, Private Failure*. London and New York: Routledge.

Ellison, G.T.H. 2002. "Letting the Gini out of the Bottle? Challenges Facing the Relative Income Hypothesis." *Social Science and Medicine* 54(4): 561–76.

Engels, F. 1987 [1845]. *Conditions of the Working Class in England*. Harmondsworth: Penguin.

Esping-Andersen, G. 1999. *Social Foundations of Postindustrial Economies*. Oxford: Oxford University Press.

———. 1990. *The Three Worlds of Welfare Capitalism*. Princeton, NJ: Princeton University Press.

Evans, R.G., M.L. Barer, and T.R. Marmor (eds.). 1994. *Why Are Some People Healthy and Others Not?* New York: Aldine de Gruyter.

Evans, R.G., and G.L. Stoddart. 1990. "Producing Health, Consuming Health Care." *Social Science and Medicine* 31(12): 1347–63.

Fourcade, M. 2006. "The Construction of a Global Profession: The Transnationalization of Economics." *American Journal of Sociology* 112(1): 145–94.

Gottschalk, P., and T.M. Smeeding. 2000. "Empirical Evidence of Income Inequality in Industrialized Countries." In A.B. Atkinson and F. Bourguignon (eds.), *The Handbook of Income Distribution*. Vol. 1. Amsterdam: Elsevier. 261–307.

Gough, I., and G. Wood, with A. Barrientos, P. Bevan, P. Davis, and G. Room. 2004. *Insecurity and Welfare Regimes in Asia, Africa and Latin America*. Cambridge: Cambridge University Press.

Granovetter, M. 1985. "Economic Action and Social Structure: The Problem of Embeddedness." *American Journal of Sociology* 91(3): 481–510.

Hicks, A. 1999. *Social Democracy and Welfare Capitalism*. Ithaca, NY, and London: Cornell University Press.

Hofrichter, R. (ed.). 2003. *Health and Social Justice*. San Francisco: Jossey-Bass.

Hopkins, S. 2006. "Economic Stability and Health Status: Evidence from East Asia Before and After the 1990s Economic Crisis." *Health Policy* 75(3): 347–57.

Human Mortality Database. n.d. University of California (USA), and Max Planck Institute for Demographic Research (Germany). Available at: <http://www.mortality.org>.

Huo, J., M. Nelson, and J.D. Stephens. 2008. "Decommodification and Activation in Social Democratic Policy: Resolving the Paradox." *Journal of European Social Policy* 18(1): 5–20.

Jamison, D.T., M.E. Sandbu, and J. Wang. 2004. "Why Has Infant Mortality Decreased at Such Different Rates in Different Countries?" Washington: Disease Control Priorities Project, U.S. National Institutes of Health and the World Bank. <http://www.dcp2.org/file/36/wp21.pdf>.

Judge, K.S. Platt, C. Costongs, and K. Jurczak. 2005. *Health Inequalities: a Challenge for Europe*. Expert Report Commissioned by the U.K. N.p.: Presidency of the EU. <http://ec.europa.eu/health/ph_determinants/socio_economics/documents/ev_060302_rd05_en.pdf>.

Kannisto, V., M. Nieminen, and O. Turpeinen. 1999. "Finnish Life Tables Since 1751." *Demographic Research* 1(1). <http://www.demographic-research.org/volumes/vol1/1>.

Kawachi, I., B. Kennedy, and R.G. Wilkinson (eds.). 1999. *The Society and Population Health Reader: Income Inequality and Health*. New York: The New Press.

Kenworthy, L. 1999. "Do Social-welfare Policies Reduce Poverty? A Cross-national Assessment." *Social Forces* 77(3): 1119–39.

Korpi, W., and J. Palme. 1998. "The Paradox of Redistribution and Strategies of Equality: Welfare State Institutions, Inequality and Poverty in the Western Countries." *American Sociological Review* 63(5): 661–87.

Labonte, R., T. Schrecker, and A. Sen Gupta. 2005. *Health for Some: Death, Disease and Disparity in a Globalizing World*. Toronto: Centre for Social Justice.

Labonte, R., and R. Torgerson. 2005. "Interrogating Globalization, Health and Development: Towards a Comprehensive Framework for Research, Policy and Political Action." *Critical Public Health* 15(2): 157–79.

Lee, C.-S., F. Nielsen, and A.S. Alderson. 2007. "Income Inequality, Global Economy and the State." *Social Forces* 86(1): 77–112.

Lindert, P.H. 2004. *Social Spending and Economic Growth Since the Eighteenth Century*. Cambridge: Cambridge University Press.

Luxembourg Income Studies. Working Paper Series. <http://www.lisproject. org>.

Lynch, J.W., G. Davey Smith, G.A. Kaplan, and J.S. House. 2000. "Income Inequality and Mortality: Importance to Health of Individual Income, Psychosocial Environment or Material Conditions." *British Medical Journal* 320: 1200–1204.

Mackenbach, J. 2005. *Health Inequalities: Europe in Profile*. Expert Report to the U.K. N.p.: Presidency of the EU. <http://ec.europa.eu/health/ ph_determinants/socio_economics/documents/ev_060302_rd06_en.pdf>.

McKeown, T. 1976a. *The Role of Medicine: Dream, Mirage or Nemesis*. London: Nuffield Provincial Hospitals Trust.

McKeown, T. 1976b. *The Modern Rise of Population*. New York: Academic Press.

Moore, S. 2006. "Peripherality, Income Inequality, and Life Expectancy: Revisiting the Income Inequality Hypothesis." *International Journal of Epidemiology* 35: 623–32.

Moore, S., A.C. Teixeira, and A. Shiell. 2006. "The Health of Nations in a Global Context: Trade, Global Stratification, and Infant Mortality Rates." *Social Science and Medicine* 63(1): 165–78.

Muntaner, C., and J. Lynch. 1999. "Income Inequality, Social Cohesion and Class Relations: A Critique of Wilkinson's Neo-Durkheimian Research Program." *International Journal of Health Services* 29(1): 59–81.

Navarro, V. 1998. "Neoliberalism, 'Globalization', Unemployment, Inequalities, and the Welfare State." *International Journal of Health Services* 28(4): 607–82.

——. 1989. "Why Some Countries Have National Health Insurance, Others Have National Health Services, and the U.S. Has Neither." *Social Science and Medicine* 28(9): 887–98.

—— (ed.). 2002. *The Political Economy of Social Inequalities*. Amityville, NY: Baywood Publishing.

Navarro, V., C. Borrell, J. Benach, C. Muntaner, A. Quioga, M. Rodriquez-Sanz, N. Verges, M. Jordia Guma, and I. Posarin. 2003. "The Importance of the Political and the Social in Explaining Mortality Differentials among the Countries of the OECD, 1950–1998." *International Journal of Health Services* 33(3): 419–94.

Navarro, V., and J. Schmitt. 2005. "Economic Efficiency versus Social Equality? The U.S. Liberal Model versus the European Social Model." *International Journal of Health Services* 35(4): 613–30.

Navarro, V., and L. Shi. 2001. "The Political Context of Social Inequalities and Health." *Social Science and Medicine* 52: 481–91.

O'Connor, J.S., and G.M. Olsen (eds.). 1998. *Power Resources Theory and the Welfare State: A Critical Approach.* Toronto: University of Toronto Press.

OECD Health Data. 2007. CD-ROM. The most recent statistics are available at <http://www.oecd.org/health/healthdata>.

Oeppen, J., and J.W. Vaupel. 2002. "Broken Limits to Life Expectancy." *Science* 296(10): 1029–31.

Poland, B., D. Coburn, A. Robertson, and J. Eakin. 1998. "Wealth, Equity and Health Care: A Critique of a 'Population Health' Perspective on the Determinants of Health." *Social Science and Medicine* 46(7): 785–98.

Polanyi, K. 2001 [1944]. *The Great Transformation.* Boston: Beacon Press.

Preston, S.H. 1976. *Mortality Patterns in National Populations.* New York: Academic Press.

Pryor, F.L. 2004. "Market economic systems." Luxembourg Income Studies, Working Paper No. 404. <http://www.lisproject.org/publications/liswps/404.pdf>.

Raphael, D., T. Bryan and M. Rioux. 2006. *Staying Alive: Critical Perspectives on Health, Illness and Health Care.* Toronto: Canadian Scholars' Press.

Ratner, R.S. 1997. "Afterword." In W. Carroll (ed.), *Organizing Dissent,* 2nd ed. Toronto: Garamond Press.

Riley, J.C. 2001. *Rising Life Expectancy: A Global History.* Cambridge: Cambridge University Press.

Ross, N.A., D. Dorling, J.R. Dunn, G. Henriksson, J. Glover, J. Lynch, and G.R. Weitoft. 2005. "Metropolitan Income Inequality and Working Age Mortality: A Cross-national Analysis using Comparable Data from Five Countries." *Journal of Urban Health* 82(1): 101–10.

Ross, R.J.S., and K.C. Trachte. 1990. *Global Capitalism—The New Leviathan.* Albany: State University of New York Press.

Sachs, J. 2008. *Common Wealth.* New York: Penguin Press.

———. 2005. *The End of Poverty.* New York: Penguin Books.

Saint-Arnaud, S., and P. Bernard. 2003. "Convergence or Resilience? A Hierarchical Cluster Analysis of the Welfare Regimes in Advanced Countries." *Current Sociology* 51(5): 499–529.

Sayer, A. 2002. "Markets, Embeddedness and Trust: Problems of Polysemy and Idealism." In J.S. Metcalfe and A. Warde (eds.), *Market Relations and the Competitive Process.* Manchester: Manchester University Press. 41–57.

Scruggs, L., and J. Allan. 2006. "Welfare-state Decommodification in 18 OECD Countries: A Replication and Revision." *Journal of European Social Policy* 16(1): 55–72.

Shaw, M., D. Dorling, D. Gordon, and G. Davey Smith. 1999. *The Widening Gap: Health Inequalities and Policy in Britain.* Bristol: The Policy Press.

Siddiqi, A., and C. Hertzman. 2007. "Towards an Epidemiological Understanding of the Effects of Long-term Institutional Changes on Population Health: A Case Study of Canada versus the USA." *Social Science and Medicine* 64(3): 589–603.

Singh, G.K., and M. Siahpush. 2006. "Widening Inequalities in US Life Expectancy, 1980–2000." *International Journal of Epidemiology* 35(4): 969–79.

——. 2002. "Increasing Inequalities in All-cause and Cardiovascular Mortality Among US Adults Aged 25–64 Years by Area Socioeconomic Status, 1969–1998." *International Journal of Epidemiology* 31(3): 600–13.

Sridhar, D. 2007. "Economic Ideology and Politics in the World Bank: Defining Hunger." *New Political Economy* 12(4): 499–516.

Starfield, B., and A.-E. Birn. 2007. "Income Distribution is not Enough: Income Inequality, Social Welfare Programs, and Achieving Equity in Health." *Journal of Epidemiology and Community Health* 61(12): 1038–41.

Statistics Canada. 2000. "Health Reports: How Healthy are Canadians?" *The Daily*. Statistics Canada 31 March. Statistics Canada Cat. No. 11–001E.

Stiglitz, J.E. 2007. *Making Globalization Work*. New York: Norton.

——. 2003. *Globalization and Its Discontents*. New York: Norton.

Stubbs, R., and G.R.D. Underhill (eds.). 2000. *Political Economy and the Changing Global Order*. 2nd ed. Toronto: Oxford University Press.

Szreter, S. 2002. "Rethinking McKeown: The Relationship Between Public Health and Social Change." *American Journal of Public Health* 92(5): 722–25.

——. 1988. "The Importance of Social Intervention in Britain's Mortality Decline c. 1850–1914: A Reinterpretation of the Role of Public Health." *Social History of Medicine* 1: 1–38.

Tapia Granados, J.A., and E.L. Ionides. 2008. "The Reversal of the Relationship between Economic Growth and Health Progress: Sweden in the 19th and 20th Centuries." *Journal of Health Economics* 27(3): 544–63.

Teeple, G. 2000. *Globalization and the Decline of Social Reform*. 2nd ed. Toronto: Garamond Press.

Thirkell-White, B. 2007. "The International Financial Architecture and the Limits to Neoliberal Hegemony." *New Political Economy* 12(1): 19–41.

——. 2004. "The International Monetary Fund and Civil Society." *New Political Economy* 9(2): 251–70.

Travis, A. 2007. "1,500 to be Released Early as Prison Crisis Bites." *The Guardian* online. 20 June. <http://www.guardian.co.uk/uk/2007/jun/20/politics.ukcrime>.

United Nations World Mortality Report. Various years. New York: Department of Economic and Social Affairs, United Nations. <http://www.un.org/esa/population>.

United Nations Human Development Report. Various years. <http://hdr.undp.org/en/reports>.

Wacquant, L. 2001. "The Penalisation of Poverty and the Rise of Neo-liberalism." *European Journal on Criminal Policy and Research* 9(4): 401–12.

Wagstaff. A. 2000. "Socioeconomic Inequalities in Child Mortality: Comparisons Across Nine Developing Countries." *Bulletin of the World Health Organization* 78(1): 19–29.

WHO. 2005. "Action on the Social Determinants of Health: Learning from Previous Experience." Background Paper. Commission on the Social Determinants of Health. Geneva. <http://www.who.int/social_determinants/resources/action_sd.pdf>.

———. 2001. *Macroeconomics and Health: Investing in Health for Economic Development*. Commission on Macroeconomics and Health. Chair: Jeffrey D. Sachs. Geneva: WHO.

WHO. Commission on the Social Determinants of Health. 2007. *Achieving Health Equity: From Root Causes to Fair Outcomes*. Interim Statement of the Commission on the Social Determinants of Health. Geneva. <http://www.who.int/social_determinants/resources/csdh_media/csdh_interim_statement_final_07.pdf>.

WHO. Commission on the Social Determinants Of Health. 2008. *Closing the Gap in a Generation: Health Equity through Action on the Social Determinants of Health*. Final Report of the Commission on the Social Determinants of Health. Geneva: WHO.

WHO. Life Tables for WHO Member States. Annual. <http://www.who.int/healthinfo/statistics/mortality_life_tables/en>.

WHO. World Health Report. Various years. <http://www.who.int/whr/en>.

Wilkinson, R.G. 2005. *The Impact of Inequality: How to Make Sick Societies Healthier*. New York: The New Press.

———. 1996. *Unhealthy Societies: The Afflictions of Inequality*. London: Routledge.

Wilkinson, R.G., and M. Marmot (eds.). 2003. *Social Determinants of Health: The Solid Facts*. 2nd ed. Geneva: WHO.

Wilkinson, R.G., and K.E. Pickett. 2007. "The Problems of Relative Deprivation: Why Some Societies Do Better than Others." *Social Science and Medicine* 65(9): 1965–78.

Wood, G., and I. Gough. 2006. "A Comparative Welfare Regime Approach to Global Social Policy." *World Development* 34(10): 1696–1712.

World Bank. World Development Report. Various years. <http://econ.worldbank.org/wdr>.

Yamey, G. 1999. "Study Shows Growing Inequalities in Health in Britain." *British Medical Journal* 319: 1453.

8

Castles in the Air
"Universal" Human Rights in the Global Political Economy

TONY EVANS

The image of universal human rights is widely acknowledged as a seminal characteristic of the current global order. At the centre of this claim are the Universal Declaration of Human Rights and the two major covenants, one on economic, social and cultural rights and the other on civil and political rights. National and international leaders of all political persuasions, with few exceptions, are prone to exalt the great achievements of the global human-rights regime. Such exuberance is also common in academic circles, where claims of "amazing" and "revolutionary" progress in the field of human rights often accompany analysis of the global and regional human-rights regimes. The emergence of globalization in recent decades, which has seen the expansion of capitalist social relations and the near universal endorsement of liberal democratic institutions, has further encouraged enthusiasm for progress on human rights. Within this context, human rights is claimed to provide the moral foundations for social action, "valorising individualism, autonomy and liberty, and comfortably occupying the global moral high ground" (Robinson 1998: 58).

Two traditions support the view that the current world order provides the necessary conditions for promoting human rights. First, the philosophy-of-rights tradition has investigated the foundations upon which an appeal to human rights might be justified. This investigation has explored many avenues, including the existence of a deity, self-evidence, and human need. Although these competing arguments have stimulated debate on the nature of human rights, natural-rights foundationalism remains the dominant tradition that informs mainstream human-rights talk today (Freeman 2002). Neither the postmodernist turn in philosophy, which has sought to expose all claims to universal and transcendental "truth" claims as illusory, nor Karl Marx's critique of rights and citizenship, seems to have invaded the consciousness of those engaged in mainstream human-rights talk (Alves 2000; Arslan 1999; Marx 2002; Rorty 1993).

Second, the tradition of international law provides the focus for claims of progress on human rights during the last seven decades. Much of the discussion within this tradition applies legal reason to the Universal Declaration of Human Rights (UDHR) and the two major covenants. In particular, comment and criticism within the legal discourse of human rights are concerned with disagreements over the nature and status of international human-rights law in a world that is no longer easily characterized by state sovereignty, non-intervention, or domestic jurisdiction (Chinkin 1998). Within this discourse, it is common to see the assertion that international human-rights law takes priority over all other legal rules, including national law. The dominance of the legal discourse has also been recognized in several surveys of the literature. Furthermore, degree-level programs on human rights are taught mostly in departments of law (Freeman 2002).

What is missing from this bipartite rationale for the claim that human rights are the idea of our time is politics (Evans 2005). Included within this third discourse are epistemological and ontological questions about how and why dominant forms of philosophical and legal reason are created, sustained, and presented as the final "truth" of universal human rights. To include the politics of rights is therefore to question the power and interests associated with the dominant conception of rights and the expression of those interests within international law. While the historic contribution of both the philosophy of natural law and the tradition of international law thrives on claims of neutrality, the politics of rights is often seen as a value-laden, ideological project that brings only confusion and conflict, rather than further clarity and agreement. Furthermore, to include the politics of rights threatens to raise the spectre of past conflicts over foundationalism, foster doubts about the "settled norms" of human rights (Frost 1996), offer comfort to cultural relativists, raise questions over the efficacy of international law, and thus bring down the whole post–World War II project for universal human rights. The politics of rights is therefore relegated to the margins of human-rights talk.

The abstract, moral, utopian approach of philosophy, which offers a glimpse of some future world order, together with the empirical, neutral, norm-driven approach of international law, reassures us that international society is moving inexorably toward realizing universal human rights. Together, the discourses of philosophy and law conspire to marginalize the politics of rights and thus exclude consideration of prevailing economic, social, and political structures and practices that support particular interests, which in turn sustain the conditions for many human-rights violations. In short, the dominant philosophical and legal discourses inspire a level of optimism that masks the causes of many human-rights violations characteristic of the current global order.

In this chapter I am concerned with the politics of rights, and more specifically the political economy of human rights. I argue that the dominant form of rights that has emerged in the age of globalization reflects interests associated with global free-market principles that promote the private property interests of dominant groups. The reification of human rights within international law, and the consequent marginalization of the political discourse on rights, has closed the possibility of a wider political discourse that could have better served the interests of the poor, workers, women, and socially excluded groups. I conclude by asserting that the failure to include the politics of rights deflects attention from investigating the structural causes of violations, causes that are characteristic of the neoliberal global political economy.

THE NEO-LIBERAL CONSENSUS

Claims of progress found in the literature on human rights often seem at odds with daily reports of civil, political, economic, social, and cultural violations in all parts of the world. What this situation reveals is the failure to take full account of the social and political context of rights, the particular configuration of world order in which the current human-rights regime operates, and the interests that the current regime serves. Given the political context of both the French and American Revolutions, which are widely understood as seminal moments in the history of human rights, this is a puzzling omission. These revolutions represent the climax of the struggle to overthrow an old social order and legitimate the new. They are revolutions in the sense that they brought a radical transformation of the accepted principles of social organization, rather than a seizure of power within the existing order. The principles of the new order—the people as sovereign, the authority of civil administration, and the rights of the citizen—replaced the principle of the old order—the divine right of kings, the authority of the Church, and duty to the Crown.

Following the success of these revolutions, the old order was condemned as oppressive and tyrannical, in contrast to the new order which was said to secure the conditions for human dignity, personal freedoms, and the rights of the citizen. As Neil Stammers has observed, the conclusion to be drawn from the French and American revolutions is that "ideas and practices concerning human rights are *created* by people in particular historical, social and economic circumstances" (Stammers 1995: 488; emphasis in original).

Patterns of rights therefore "mirror the struggles and concerns of dominant groups in society at a particular time as those groups organize and reorganize to maintain their position" (Shivji 1999: 253). In this reading, shifts in prevailing socioeconomic relations are accompanied by shifts in rights claims intended to legitimate and sustain the new order. Given this relationship between rights and interests, the contemporary version of natural rights, and the current international legal regime that claims to offer protection against violations of human rights, can both be seen as an attribute of the move toward a global, free-market, capitalist order.

The relationship between rights and interests within capitalist society was noted by Karl Marx. Marx argued that civil society holds the key to questions of rights: "the so-called human rights, the rights of *droits de l'homme* in contrast to the *droits de citoyen*, are nothing but the rights of members of civil society" (O'Malley 1994: 44). Since civil society represents the private sphere, a sphere intended to guarantee the liberty necessary to pursue private satisfaction, human rights describe the egotistic, atomized, isolated individual, separated from community. The exercise of human rights in civil society is therefore concerned with rights to enjoy and dispose of private property arbitrarily, free of all social or political responsibilities, except those commensurate with the equal rights of others (Marx 2002: 45).

In such a society, where the individual is free to exploit others and is presented with the social framework to do so, the possibility of developing the necessary emotional ties associated with community is severely constrained. As Kees van der Pijl (1997) has observed, community and exploitation are incompatible. Nonetheless, to maintain social order there remains a need to create an imaginary space, the state, in which to fabricate the institutions of unity, including those associated with equality, democracy, and rights (Furet 1995). Human rights therefore offer an ethical and moral rationale in support of the egotistic individual, withdrawn into private interests and separated from community. For Marx, all that is left to hold people together is "natural necessity, need and private interests, the conservation of their property and their egoistic person" (O'Malley 1994: 46). With the emergence of economic globalization, which moves to eclipse all national economies, the prospect for community seems even less possible.

From this perspective, power is located within the private sphere of civil society through the legitimation of individual rights. Although it is far from monolithic, Wood describes civil society as "a particular network of social relations that does not simply stand in opposition to the coercive 'policing' and 'administrative' functions of the state but represents the *relocation* of these function, or at least some significant part of them" (Wood 1996: 254; emphasis in original). The role of the state is to oversee the existing order, to act as "nightwatchman" for guaranteeing "fair play" and the "rules of the game," rather than to initiate change, which is the role of civil society (Gramsci 1996: 262–63). All thought of transforming civil society through the formal political processes represented by the state is illusory (Furet 1995). Although the image of the state as the guardian of individual rights is widely accepted—including the image of the state as acting as the agent of civil society in fulfilling the citizen's duty to deal with unacceptable inequalities—in this reading of civil society the state is more concerned with private property, appropriation, exploitation, and securing the economic interests of dominant groups. In short, the separation of public from private life, politics from economics, and the state from civil society provides a context where "political emancipation emancipates civil society from politics and opens the way for the unfettered materialism of interests" (Furet 1995: 19).

Within the current neoliberal world order, human rights associated with civil society are limited to civil and political rights, claims that secure a sphere of freedom in which the egotistic individual pursues economic interests. In the event that these rights and freedoms are deployed by disadvantaged groups to challenge the characteristic inequalities found within capitalist society, three possible counter-strategies are available. The first of these is tolerance, which is exercised only to the point where those who challenge the general principles of the dominant economic, social, and political order "do not seek to make the transition from word to deed, from speech to action" (Marcuse 1969, 85–86). Second is the use of legal and judicial machinery created to protect the property interest of civil society, as both private property and property as natural rights (Collins 1990). Third, in the event that neither tolerance nor the law succeeds in overcoming perceived threats to the dominant order, police and military violence is mobilized (Cox 1997). In these ways, civil society appeals to the state to defend the neoliberal order by summoning means that violate the rights and freedoms said to describe that order. To paraphrase Marx, the rights that describe civil society are aimed at those who want to receive the freedom of property or the egotism of trade, not to those who desire to free themselves from property and trade.

The conclusion drawn from these arguments suggests a hegemony of civil and political rights, which support free-market policies reflected in the recent push to liberalize global trade. Although the unity of all rights is often stressed in UN resolutions and in the policy statements of governments, economic and social rights remain little more than aspirations, to be achieved once the rights associated with private property have served the greater goal of wealth creation. In this sense, while civil and political rights are treated as the property of the individual—as essential characteristics that describe what it means to be human—claims for economic and social rights are not recognized as possessions: as rights to forms of property that sustain life itself. Alternative claims that seek to enlist economic and social rights in the cause of human development seem to have evaporated in the post–Cold War order that stresses the right of the individual to pursue free-market economic interests, unfettered by concerns over social inequalities. In short, it is the economic interests of civil society that constitute the limits, form, and extent of rights, not the state, international society, or international law. Although the unity of all rights is often claimed, the politics of right ensures that economic, social, and cultural rights are downgraded to the level of "aspirations," thus removing an important threat to neoliberal principles.

THE POLITICAL ECONOMY OF HUMAN RIGHTS

Stephen Gill (1995) has referred to practices of "normalization," "common sense," and the institutionalization of particular "truth" claims associated with the current period of globalization as "market discipline." Market discipline stresses economic growth and development, deregulation, the free market, the privatization of public services, and minimum government. It describes a set of normative relationships with a global reach, which are manifest at both the domestic and global level, for instance, in national and international economic planning, market-based solutions for environmental degradation, the move to privatize social-welfare provision, and the drive to privatize life itself, seen in the scramble to patent genes from both human and non-human life forms. The governance of world order is conducted by what Robert Cox (1995) has referred to as the *nébuleuse*, a group of formally and informally constituted institutions without democratic pretensions. The "authentic" voice of market discipline is found within the World Trade

Organization (WTO), the European Union (EU), the North American Free Trade Agreement (NAFTA), the World Bank, the International Monetary Fund (IMF), and less formal institutions such as Davos and Bilderberg. Although the state continues to claim the role of government, the *nébuleuse* conducts the governance of world order.

Within the sphere of market discipline, as opposed to that of international law, human rights are conceptualized as the freedoms necessary to maintain and legitimate particular forms of production and exchange. These are a set of negative rights associated with liberty, security, and private property, which offer a moral and normative foundation for justifying actions within the current global political economy. Although the global legal human-rights regime accepts the unity of rights, including economic, social, and cultural rights, market discipline pursues only those rights necessary to sustain legitimate claims for liberal freedoms. The catalogue of rights associated with market discipline therefore describes human beings as individuals and agents of a particular type and kind. For critics, the human-rights regime is partial. It represents the "Eden of the innate rights of man," where free will, equality within exchange relations, and property converge to create social relations characteristic of selfishness, gain, and private interests, rather than the pursuit of rights, human dignity, and community (Marx 2002). Despite market discipline's propensity to foster self-discipline, there remains a need for authoritative pronouncements to guard against transgressions (Prado 1995). This is the central role of international law, which itself reflects self-discipline through the international legal principle of reciprocity.

Although the contemporary discourse of human rights, which is predominantly a legal discourse, is presented as a unified, natural, and neutral set of rules, the predominance of rules associated with market discipline suggests that human life is valued as a means to an end, rather than as an end in itself (Watkins 1996). This is seen in the greater attention given to trade, private property, and finance, compared to that concerned with humanitarian issues. For critics, market discipline denotes that the supreme value found in the current global order is profit for investors. All else must be subordinated to this cause, including the value we place on human life, which is endorsed only in as far as it contributes to this end (Chomsky 1994). The creation of authoritative international organizations provides the professionalized voice for sustaining the legitimacy of the global neoliberal order. These organizations fulfil the task of surveillance, ensuring adherence to market disciplinary norms, and acting to maintain a particular set of rights and freedoms that are integral to reproducing the values that sustain the neoliberal political economy. If human rights have any significance within the contemporary global order, they offer a set of values delimited by an assumed normative consensus that legitimates activities associated with market discipline, specifically negative rights and those associated with private property.

Three issues illustrate the primacy of market discipline over human rights. First, the tensions between the norms of market discipline and international law are manifest in the changing role of the state under conditions of globalization. Critics of economic globalization argue that the current world order should be seen as a complex of social relations where the social core and periphery cut across national boundaries, creating new patterns of economic growth and consumption. While in the previous stage of world history it was assumed that the state could adopt national strategies for ordering the national economy, today the global organization of production and finance means that states assume the role of administrators, with the mission to ensure the smooth, efficient, uncontested operation of the global economy (Cox 1999). The state no longer assumes its traditional role as guardian of rights but, instead, acts to create and manage a global order that expresses the values found in an emerging global civil society, which is informed by market discipline (Evans 2000; Panitch 1995). In this way market discipline provides the guide for action within self-defining parameters, which include human rights that describe the good neoliberal citizen. International human-rights law, particularly the law concerning economic and social rights, takes second place to the project for expanding and maintaining the values of market discipline.

Second, the centrality of market discipline within the current world order can be seen in the work of the WTO, which is concerned with arguments over the exercise of liberal freedoms. Indeed, the WTO was intended not merely to secure the old rights and freedoms associated with liberal trade, but to extend the agenda into new areas of private property rights not previously explored, for example, intellectual property rights and investment rights (WHO 1997). Some commentators have suggested that the powers given to the WTO, including the authority to strike down the decisions of sovereign states (George 1999), signal the dawning of a new legal system, based not upon the normative order of states or concern for human dignity and freedom, but upon the normative order of market discipline (Camilleri 1990). The authority given to the international human-rights regime will therefore depend upon its relevance to achieving the aims of market discipline, while all claims outside this aim are rejected.

Third, a further indication of the consequences of market discipline is seen in what I will refer to later as the "Dutch auction" of human rights. Under the terms of this auction, the force of market discipline sees countries performing their administrative role by bidding against each other to provide a low-cost, low-risk economic environment that is attractive to investors. Policy decisions taken for this purpose include low or non-existent levels of environmental protection, employment law, trade-union law, human-rights regulation, and protection for health and safety (Millen, Lyon & Irwin 2000). Similarly, aid conditionality brings consequences for human rights when, for example, less developed countries are asked to reduce substantially, or withdraw completely, from social programs on health, education, and housing. Such programs are seen by international banks as a drain on resources better directed at future economic growth, which is a central tenet of market discipline (Waters 1995). In both the case of the "Dutch auction" and that of conditionality, priority is given to the exigencies of market discipline, ignoring the duty to protect and promote human rights, dignity, and welfare. When critics accuse companies of engaging in activities that make them complicit in human-rights violations, environmental degradation, and increasing incidents of ill health, corporate managers remain confident that "normal" business practices remain largely immune from punishment. In the rare cases where legal action is brought, corporations are fully aware that their investment and financial muscle provide powerful arguments in their defence.

It must be stressed that the consequences of such examples are not restricted to economic and social rights. The low social standards offered as a magnet for investment lead the disadvantaged, dispossessed, marginalized, and excluded to organize politically, perhaps by creating independent trade unions and citizen groups to resist the harsher consequences of market discipline. In such cases, violence and the threat of violence are often used against those daring to challenge market-disciplinary principles and the neoliberal rationale for economic development. Since all governments take economic growth and development as a central policy objective, the deprivations suffered by those whose environment is degraded, culture devastated, freedom to protest peacefully suppressed, and traditional ties with the land forcibly severed are seen less as the victims of human rights violations and more as the generation who must bear the cost of economic progress for the good of the wider, future community (Kotheri 1994). Those who continue to protest are referred to pejoratively as insular, conservative, or traditionalists, bent on denying the benefits of modernization to the mass of the people.

Consequently, developing countries often defend their human rights record with a market-discipline response, rather than by reference to international law. For example, a Singapore Ministerial Declaration in

1998 stated that the developed economies' invocation of human rights was merely an attempt to "overcome the comparative advantage of low-wage developing counties," rather than a genuine concern for humanity (WTO Ministerial Declaration 1998).

Caught between the demand for market discipline from above, and the demand for human rights from below, the rhetoric of the international human-rights discourse offers a pacifying response that need not necessarily damage the prospect of achieving economic growth and development. As Mittelman observes, although in theory governments are assumed to protect their citizens' human rights, "in practice leaders are accountable to market forces, most notably debt structures and structural adjustment programs" (1996: 7). Thus, the necessity to respond to market discipline has seen many governments of less developed states plead for special tolerance of their human-rights record. Many of these governments argue that their attitude to human rights is conditioned by two important factors that set them apart from developed countries. The first is the need to build a nation on the remains of colonial institutions, which were themselves created with no concern for human rights and dignity. Given this legacy, many less developed states stress the need for a transitional period, which will allow the necessary conditions for economic and social stability to be implemented. From this perspective, questions of human rights should be framed within the context of whether a particular human right helps or hinders the process of nation-building and the move from a post-colonial to a mature state?

Second, in common with all states, less developed countries embrace the idea that economic growth and development, in accordance with the discipline of market principles, is of paramount importance to achieving the goal of long-term stability and security. Hence, governments are obliged to challenge traditional values, alternative versions of development, and dissident voices, which attempt to deflect the nation from achieving the goal of prosperity through full integration within the neoliberal global market order. Therefore, all measures to bring about the social, economic, and cultural transformations necessary to achieve this goal are legitimate. Violations of human rights, suppression, and the coercion of those who attempt to stand in the way of these radical changes may offend against international human-rights law, but they must be tolerated (Tamilmoran 1992).

Typical of this approach is that of Kishore Mahbubani, who argues that conditions in most developing states necessitate a "period of strong and firm government," committed to radical social reform in order to "break out of the vicious circle of poverty sustained by social structures contained in vested interests opposed to real change" (Mahbubani

1992: 8). Those who support this approach point to the success of authoritarian governments that achieved the so-called East Asian "miracle," wherein governments promoted a very circumscribed definition of democracy and human rights. Economic collapse in these countries during late 1997 and early 1998, which coincided with a growing demand for democracy and human rights, only served to remind political leaders and economic interests that such demands may damage the prospect of further economic growth. Thus, whenever over-exuberant demands for human rights occur, they should be countered by measures to strengthen "market-preserving authoritarianism" (Davies 1998).

Market discipline therefore provides a deep structure for the conduct of the global political economy, where political promotion of human rights plays the role of legitimating neoliberal values. Vivid evidence of the dominance of market discipline was seen at the press conference given at the opening of the United Nations 2000 annual human rights assembly. Although the representatives of the world's press questioned the High Commissioner on Human Rights, Mary Robinson, on a wide range of high-profile abuses of civil and political rights, not one question was asked about economic and social rights (Singh 2000). While the international law formally recognizes the unity of human rights, global civil society promotes only those rights that support market discipline, through rhetoric, policy, and action. These are the embedded principles upon which global action is secured.

STRUCTURAL VIOLATIONS OF HUMAN RIGHTS

Although many commentators recognize that the conditions of globalization provided a new political context for the protection of human rights, including recognition that the structures of the global political economy present new challenges, the tradition of individual agency remains a central assumption. According to Galtung (1994), the focus on individualism offers one of the greatest barriers to conducting research into the causes of human-rights violations. The priority afforded to civil and political rights, as individual possessions, supports the interests of free-market principles that seek to promote a socioeconomic environment for innovation, endeavour, enterprise, and the generation of personal wealth. Given this understanding and purpose of personal freedom, it follows that we must also hold the individual responsible for all of his or her actions, including violations of human rights. Scholars and practitioners routinely take the individual as both the claimant and violator of human rights. This convention, which has its roots in the Judeo-Christian notion of sin, deflects attention from those economic, social, and political structures that support the interests of particular groups. Consequently, investigations into the causes of human rights violations seldom go beyond the assumption that all violations can be explained by reference to the wilful acts of evil, brutal, despotic, and cruel individuals. The possibility that the structures of global political economy (including trade, production, and financial structures) offer a greater threat to human rights is seldom seen as a potential cause of violations.

However, Roy Bhaskar argues that achieving the goal of human rights "depends upon the transformation of structures rather than just the amelioration of states of affairs" (1991: 76). Following the earlier discussion, the structures of market discipline provide an organizing framework for legitimating those rights that support global capital while marginalizing those that offer a potential threat. Many examples of this are offered in the literature on globalization (e.g., Hoogvelt 2001; Thomas 1998). Furthermore, as an examination of western media and the speeches of political leaders attests, struggles for food, shelter, and the necessities for sustaining life are reported mostly in the language of crop failure, overpopulation, natural disaster, and environmental degradation, rather than as violations of human rights. The observation that these "causes" of the failure to protect basic rights are themselves a consequence of global socioeconomic structures is recognized only rarely.

Accordingly, the right to security infers a commitment to something more than liberal forbearance. It must also include a commitment to both *protect* those whose rights are threatened and to *avoid* taking any action that might lead to violations. If global neoliberal institutions provide a legitimate context for transnational corporations to deprive people of the means of subsistence, or if the WTO, NAFTA, and the EU implement free-trade rules, practices, and procedures that deprive people of the means to achieve subsistence for themselves, this is also a denial of human rights. Consequently, "those who deny rights can have no complaint when the denial ... is resisted" (Shue 1996: 14). In this view of structural violations, international institutions, the state and its agents, and transnational corporations have a duty not to engage in practices that indirectly violate human rights (Addo 1987).

Taking account of structural causes of human-rights violations exposes the current neoliberal global order to the charge that its much-vaunted concern for human rights is partial. The neoliberal order is presented as "common sense" habits that are a "natural," "normal," and "rational" approach toward social conduct. It is these "common-sense" practices that provide the rationale for denying responsibility for socioeconomic rights and for absolving international organizations, states, and transnational corporations of all responsibility for activity described by the neo-realist order. However, critics argue that the neolib-eral order cannot facilitate the duty to protect against, or avoid, violat-ing the rights of others (Muzaffar 1995). It is no defence to point to the corpus of international law on human rights, because, as both Katerina Tomasevski and Christine Chinkin have observed, while international law may have the capacity for redressing consequences, it cannot address causes (Chinkin 1998; Tomasevski 1993). Structures cannot be judi-cial persons with intentions and capabilities, nor can they be arrested, put before a court, punished for their crimes, or subjected to sanctions (Galtung 1994). Consequently, it can be argued that the dominance of the legal discourse of rights itself offers a barrier to investigating the causes of human-rights violations. The creation of an International Criminal Court, following the experience of tribunals for Rwanda and the former Yugoslavia, may therefore have little impact on patterns of human rights violations.

CASTLES IN THE AIR

The title of this chapter, "castles in the air," is intended to reflect the difference between the formal human-rights regime and the practice of rights in the global political economy. While the former is built upon foundations developed through the application of philosophical and legal reason, the later is built upon relations of power characteristic of the capitalist global order. If there are any universal values within the current order, they are the values of market discipline, not the full range of human rights found in international law and the rhetoric of political leaders. Should there be any attempt to use the freedoms offered by the promise of human rights to challenge market discipline, it is resisted, sometimes brutally. The imperative of economic growth and develop-ment, which is at the heart of market discipline, takes priority over all other considerations, including human rights.

Consequently, those who attempt to oppose the "irresistible and irre-versible" (Blair 1998) consequences of economic globalization, in an effort to "freely pursue their economic, social and cultural develop-ment" (International Covenant on Economic Social and Cultural Rights [ICESCR] Art. 1: 1), often find their right to self-determination abused. In some cases, resistance to agricultural, industrial, and infrastructural projects associated with market discipline ends in the violation of the human right to "life, liberty and the security of the person" (UDHR Art. 3). The right to form and join trade unions "for the promotion and pro-tection of ... economic and social interests" (ICESCR Art. 8) is often a target for oppressive measures by state and corporate interests. The right to subsistence is violated when people are excluded from their traditional means of feeding, clothing, and housing themselves (ICESCR Art. 11). The special protection afforded to women under the Convention on the Elimination of Discrimination Against Women (CEDAW) seems to attract little respect when there is a need for low-paid, obedient, and non–trade-union labour to engage in the production of export goods (HRW 1996). The rights of children, articulated in the Convention on the Rights of the Child, often suffer a similar fate (Christian Aid 1997).

Finally, the discussion here has sought to raise questions about the claim that we are living in the age of universal human rights. However, although the dominant legal and philosophical discourses present human rights as a concept that empowers those threatened by state violence, the concept is also an instrument for domination. The political construction of universal human rights, which is presented in the language of personal freedoms, reflects relations of power and domination characteristic of the current global political economy. Seen in this light, the politics of human rights stifles the possibility of engaging in critique.

REFERENCES

Addo, M.K. 1987. *The Implications for Some Aspects of Contemporary International Economic Law on International Human Rights Law*. Ph.D. thesis, University of Essex, Colchester.

Alves, J.A.L. 2000. "The Declaration of Human Rights in Postmodernity." *Human Rights Quarterly* 22(2): 478–500.

Arslan, Z. 1999. "Taking Rights Less Seriously: Postmodernism and Human Rights." *Res Publica* 5(2): 195–215.

Bhaskar, R. 1991. *Philosophy and the Idea of Freedom*. Oxford: Blackwell.

Blair, T. 1998. Speech at the WTO. 19 May.

Camilleri, J. 1990. "Rethinking Sovereignty in a Shrinking, Fragmented World." In R.B.J. Walker and S. Mendlovitz (eds.), *Contending Sovereignties*. Boston: Lynne Rienner. 13–44.

Chinkin, C. 1998. "International Law and Human Rights." In T. Evans (ed.), *Human Rights Fifty Years On: A Reappraisal*. Manchester: Manchester University Press. 105–29.

Chomsky, N. 1994. *World Orders Old and New*. London: Pluto Press.

Christian Aid. 1997. *A Sporting Chance*. London: Christian Aid.

Collins, H. 1982. *Marxism and Law*. Oxford: Oxford University Press.

Cox, R. 1999. "Civil Society at the Turn of the Millennium: Prospects for an Alternative World Order." *Review of International Studies* 25(1): 3–28.

———. 1997. "Democracy in Hard Times: Economic Globalization and the Limits to Liberal Democracy." In A. McGrew (ed.), *The Transformation of Democracy*. Cambridge: Polity Press. 49–72.

——. 1996. "A Perspective on Globalization." In J.H. Mittelman (ed.), *Globalization: Critical Reflections*. Boulder, CO: Lynne Rienner.

Davies, M.C. 1998. "The Price of Rights: Constitution and East Asian Economic Development." *Human Rights Quarterly* 20(2): 303–37.

Evans, T. 2005. "International Human Rights Law as Power and Knowledge." *Human Rights Quarterly* 27(3): 1046–68.

——. 2000. "Citizenship and Human Rights in the Age of Globalization." *Alternatives* 25(4): 415–38.

Freeman, M. 2002. *Human Rights*. Cambridge: Polity Press.

Frost, M. 1996. *Ethics in International Relations: A Constitutive Theory*. Cambridge: Cambridge University Press.

Furet, F. 1995. *Marx and the French Revolution*. London: University of Chicago Press.

Galtung, J. 1994. *Human Rights in Another Key*. Cambridge: Polity Press.

George, S. 1999. *The Lugano Report*. London: Pluto Press.

Gill, S. 1995. "Globalization, Market Civilisation, and Disciplinary Neoliberalism." *Millennium: Journal of International Studies* 24(3): 399–423.

Gramsci, A. 1996. *Selections from the Prison Notebooks*. In Q. Hoare and G. Smith (eds.). London: Lawrence and Wisehart.

Hoogvelt, A. 2001. *Globalization and the Postcolonial World: The New Political Economy of Development*. 2nd ed. Basingstoke: Palgrave.

Human Rights Watch. 1996. *No Guarantee: Sex Discrimination in Mexico's Maquiladora Sector*. No. 8: 6(B). Human Rights Watch, Women's Rights Project.

International Covenant on Economic, Social and Cultural Rights (ICESCR). G.A. res. 2200A (XXI), 21 U.N. GAOR Supp.

Kotheri, S. 1994. "Global Economic Institutions and Democracy: A View from India." In J. Cavanagh, D. Wysham, and M. Arrunda (eds.), *Beyond Bretton Woods*. London: Pluto Press. 39–54.

Mahbubani, K. 1992. "The West and the Rest." *The National Interest* 28(Summer): 3–12.

Marcuse, H. 1969. "Repressive Tolerance." In R.P. Wolff, B. Moore, and H. Marcuse (eds.), *A Critique of Pure Tolerance*. Boston: Beacon Press. 81–123.

Marx, K. 2002. *Karl Marx: Selected Writings*. Oxford: Oxford University Press.

Millen, J.V., E. Lyon, E. and A. Irwin. 2000. "Dying for Growth: The Political Influence of National and Transnational Corporations." In J.Y. Kim, J.V. Millen, A. Irwin, and J. Gershaw (eds.), *Dying For Growth: Global Inequality and the Health of the Poor*. Monroe, ME: Common Courage Press. 225–33.

Mittelman, J. 1996. "The Dynamics of Globalization." In J. Mittelman (ed.), *Globalization: Critical Reflections*. Boulder, CO: Lynne Rienner. 1–19.

Muzaffar, C. 1995. "From Human Rights to Human Dignity." *Bulletin of Concerned Asian Scholars* 27(4): 6–8.

O'Malley, J. 1994. *Marx: Early Political Writings*. Cambridge: Cambridge University Press.

Panitch, L. 1996. "Rethinking the Role of the State." In J. Mittelman (ed.), *Globalization: Critical Reflections*. Boulder, CO: Lynne Rienner. 83–116.

Prado, C.G. 1995. *Starting with Foucault: An Introduction to Genealogy*. Boulder, CO: Westview.

Robinson, F. 1998. "The Limits of a Rights Based Approach to International Ethics." In T. Evans (ed.), *Human Rights Fifty Years On: A Reappraisal*. Manchester: Manchester University Press. 58–76.

Rorty, R. 1993. "Human Rights, Rationality, and Sentimentality." In S. Shute and S. Hurley (eds.), *On Human Rights: The Oxford Amnesty Lectures 1993*. New York: Basic Books. 111–34.

Shivji, I. 1999. "Constructing a New Rights Regime: Promises, Problems and Prospects." *Social and Legal Studies* 8(2): 253–76.

Shue, H. 1996. *Basic Rights: Subsistence, Affluence, and U.S. Foreign Policy*. 2nd ed. Princeton, NJ: Princeton University Press.

Singh, S. 2000. "Human Rights—A Charade of the Virtuous." *Third World Resurgence* 116: 40–41.

Stammers, N. 1995. "A Critique of Social Approaches to Human Rights." *Human Rights Quarterly* 17(3): 488–508.

Tamilmaran, V.T. 1992. *Human Rights in Third World Perspective*. New Delhi: Har-Anand Publications.

Thomas, C. 1998. "International Financial Institutions and Social and Economic Rights: An Exploration." In T. Evans (ed.), *Human Rights Fifty Years On: A Reappraisal*. Manchester: Manchester University Press. 161–87.

Tomasevski, K. 1993. *Development Aid and Human Rights Revisited*. London: Pinter.

Universal Declaration of Human Rights (UDHR). G.A. res. 217A (III).

van der Pijl, K. 1997. "Transnational Class Formation and State Forms." In S. Gill and J. Mittelman (eds.), *Innovation and Transformation in International Studies*. Cambridge: Cambridge University Press. 115–35.

Waters, M. 1995. *Globalization*. London: Routledge.

Watkins, K. 1996. *The Oxfam Poverty Report*. Oxford: Oxfam.

WHO. 1997. *Health and Environment in Sustainable Development: Five Years After the Earth Summit*. Geneva: World Health Organization.

Wood, E.M. 1996. *Democracy Against Capitalism*. Cambridge: Cambridge University Press.

WTO Ministerial Declaration. 1998. <http://www.wto.org/english/thewto_e/minist_e/min98_e/mindec_e.htm>.

Military Power, Hegemonic Power
A Neglected Issue of International Political Economy

JAMES M. CYPHER

CONTEXTUALIZING ARMAMENTS PRODUCTION AND MILITARY POWER

This chapter is focused on an analysis of a prime function of the US state—the use and management of the civilian and non-civilian institutions that comprise the country's constellation of military weapons-system production and power projection. A subject I explore in this chapter is the manner and degree to which US strategic policy has strayed from an underlying premise regarding the established postwar state–military relationship: the national state is not an instrument of particular interests; its relative autonomy is deployed within the structural confines of a national and global system that imposes strategies and limits on the implementations of military-related activities. When these conditions are not met, when the dominant national state serves as a unilateral instrument of particular interests (material and/or ideological), a period of hegemonic instability is to be anticipated.

My analysis takes as a point of departure the premise that there are three forms of state power in international affairs: economic power, diplomatic/ideological power, and military power. An initial assumption adopted here is that these three forms of power are deployed constantly by powerful states, and that they are normally interdependent and interrelated. Particular states in given moments mix these three components of national power as they can, to maximize their effectiveness in an environment where other rival states do the same to the degree they are able. Therefore, an additional initial premise is that military outlays are not generally conceived to be an expression of the "burden" of defence—a sort of passive receptacle into which nations must relegate a troubling portion of their society's treasure, human and material. Rather, at least for the hegemon, military spending is an "active" category, a necessary means to accumulate further international power, or under some conditions simply to maintain such power. Rather than being a "burden," military power is a most vital "asset." This is not to say that hegemonic powers in the past have never "overreached," nor is it to argue that everywhere and always the actual use of military power can be accurately directed toward further national aggrandizement. If anything, military power is generally a more precise instrument to the degree that it is used very sparingly, through "shows of force," or implicitly. Warfare opens the door to the so-called "fog of war"—a situation wherein great powers are known to blunder, as the US did in the cases of the Korean War, the Vietnam War, the Afghanistan War, and the second Iraq War. The use of force also opens wide the likelihood of "blowback," as subjected nations or factions seek asymmetrical means for retaliation.

There are two principal areas of focus in this chapter: the national context and the international sphere. First, I maintain that in the new internationalized political economy that took shape in the 1980s, the role of the state has not been diminished, but structurally altered. For the US state, a new set of global limits and constraints has necessitated new forms of action and reaction. In this regard, the issue of competitiveness has come to the foreground. Military power, in its domestic dimension, plays a fundamental role in the reproduction of the capacity for competitiveness. This happens primarily through the linkage of new weapons systems to spin-offs into the civilian economy that permit US corporations (through patents and acquired knowledge) to maintain an edge in terms of new products and production processes. In some respects the connection between military spending and national competitiveness is quite direct, such as the sale of new or aging surplus weaponry, which bolsters the balance of payment and substantially reduces the trade deficit from levels that would otherwise arise. Another relationship, rarely noted, is that military spending tends to bolster US economic growth and (when applied countercyclically, i.e., to counteract the contraction phase of the business cycle) can slow or even reverse recession. This serves to keep the vast US market open to foreign nations, which in turn facilitates state leverage over many nations. Access to the US market varies from significant to vital, depending on the foreign nation. Facilitating such access permits the US state to pursue (at minimum) reciprocity or (more likely) asymmetrical advantage in many areas of international relations such as internal state policy. Such policy varies in time and place and can include commercial considerations, currency issues, and cooperation in international forums such as the World Bank or the United Nations. Here the line of causality runs from the national implications and impacts of military spending to the international leverage given to the state by military spending. Thus, while military spending plays a vital role in propping up the macroeconomic trajectory of the US, and in advancing its technological edge, its importance extends far beyond "military Keynesian" effects, fundamentally conditioning the international political economy of structural power relationships between nations.

My second area of focus, the international sphere, pertains to the utilization of state power through the expression of military policy. Military power is a prime means for the maintenance and reproduction of hegemonic power, and numerous forms of policy expression are exercised for a variety of purposes. For example, maintaining the world's largest navy to dominate the sea lanes and key "choke points" for international commerce confers upon the US a degree of tutelary power. Less powerful nations are under a certain obligation to act in an obsequious manner in some or many areas; however, these are difficult to reveal since no sovereign nation will willingly acknowledge the forms of homage or supplicant positions it is forced to adopt. The same line of analysis can be applied to other areas, such as seeking the ability to guarantee the control of the world's most vital commodity: oil. Maintaining the sea lanes and expending vast treasure to control the global flow of oil can be a means to leverage the US's position regarding another element of hegemonic power: seigniorage—or the maintenance of the US dollar as the world's key currency. Positioning bases is another aspect of the grand strategy utilized by the US to maintain, reproduce or expand the suzerainty of power. Host nations often can lower their military expenditures and/or ensure stability in the face of hostile forces, internal or external. Payments for basing "rights" can support oligarchs, who, in turn, are willing to provide access to important resources, markets, intelligence, etc.

My objective in the chapter will not be to catalogue the various forms in which military power is translatable into elements that support the maintenance of hegemonic power. Rather, it is to reveal the structural logic behind the massive outlays on military systems and the command centers the US has positioned around much of the globe. To assert the vital role that military power entails does not in any way call into question the strategic role of diplomacy or "soft power." Neither is it designed to displace the vital significance of international economic policy-making. Instead, the purpose is to recast the role of military power, placing it at least on a level of equivalence with the other two commonly understood and recognized forms of international power.

The contemporary "logic" of the US military system is to be understood within the structural characteristics and elements of US capitalism as contextualized by the current conjuncture of the *internationalization of capital* arising from the 1970s onward. These structural characteristics include, but are not limited to the following: (1) a broad array of oligopolistic industrial corporations that increasingly emphasize external markets and offshore production sites as crucial components of their strategy to maximize profits; (2) a grouping of financial corporations whose significance to US capital has grown relative to that of industrial capital and whose reliance on international capital flows and access to international financial markets are crucial to its existence and expansion; (3) a state that combines two central roles conducive to US capital accumulation: the underwriting of scientific research via direct and indirect means (particularly through military contracting) that in turn boosts the competitiveness of US industrial capital, and the deployment of its vast economic leverage within a variety of national and multilateral institutions such as the US Departments of Defense and State, the World Bank, and the IMF to pursue an aggressive policy of neoliberal restructuring, particularly of peripheral nations; (4) the decimation of the capital–labour accord of the 1940s, empowered through the linked processes of deunionization, offshoring, and outsourcing, which enabled neoliberal economic restructuring strategies both in the US and abroad.[1]

THEORY IN THE APPLICATION OF STATE POWER

Currently, a profound dispute rages over the application of US military power. This dispute arose within the context of the end of the Cold War, when the then-conventional wisdom regarding a massive reduction in military capabilities was challenged by a rightist neoconservative insurgency that has (until recently) steadily gained force and legitimacy since the mid-1970s. In order to analyze this policy realignment, discussed in the next section of this chapter, some contextual observations regarding the structural nature of the US "National Security State" (often referred to as the Iron Triangle) are necessary.

The "Iron Triangle" forms the US military establishment's decision-making structure and includes its major interest groups. One side of the triangle includes the "civilian" agencies that shape US military policy:

the Office of the President, the National Security Council, the Senate and House Armed Services Committees, and civilian intelligence agencies such as the Central Intelligence Agency (CIA) and the National Security Administration (NSA). A second side includes the military institutions: the Joint Chiefs of Staff; the top brass of the Air Force, Army, Marines, and Navy; the "proconsul" regional commands (the powerful commanders-in-chief or CINCs); and, in a supporting role, veterans' organizations such as the American Legion and the Veterans of Foreign Wars. At the base of the triangle are the 85,000 private firms that profit from the military contracting system and that use their sway over millions of defence workers to push for ever-higher military budgets.

Few of the Fortune 500–level corporations involved in military contracting are bankrolling the main think-tanks of the neoconservatives, such as the American Enterprise Institute, the Heritage Foundation, and the Cato Institute. The many within the 500 who contract with the Pentagon have seen their longest uninterrupted year-on-year profit increases on record from 1999 through fiscal year 2011. Yet no documents have surfaced in which a clear and simple line can be connected between the neoconservative policy-makers and US-based oil transnationals or military contracting corporations. In other words, the recently emerged neoconservative policy is not an instrument of military-industrial corporations, oil corporations, or of finance and manufacturing capital in general.

In viewing the relationship between military contracting firms, the Pentagon, and the civilian centres of national political power, it is useful to retain the context of the theory of the relative autonomy of the state (Cypher 1992). This relative autonomy (from the lobbying interests and vested interests of the largest entities of capital—as well as from other interests such as small and medium-sized businesses, ideological groupings, citizens' advocacy groups, and organized labour) has allowed for the limited ascendancy of the "state within the state": the national security state composed of the defence intellectuals, the strategic policy think-tanks (such as the RAND corporation), the vast network of military academies, colleges, and postgraduate programs, the National Security Council, the Joint Chiefs of Staff, the global military commands (the CINCs), the intelligence network (16 entities), the US State Department, key congressional security specialists, and some national universities where scientific labs and/or policy-making analysts play crucial consulting roles to the vast complex of military institutions that have evolved since World War II. Yet this "state within the state" must contend with its relative (rather than absolute) condition. It is embedded within a complex institutional network—primarily national, but also international—and must confront certain resource constraints. In this context, pushed along by the tailwind created by 9/11, the neo-conservatives were able to carry the day and inaugurate their war of choice in Iraq. Since then, however, they have steadily lost ground. This tendency is best expressed by the fact that the wars in Afghanistan and Iraq have become quagmires that have resulted in an incessant process of distancing (by various elements of the power elite, the technostruc-ture, and the "informed public") from the neoconservative doctrine of the use of force as a first-order option of grand strategy and geopolit-ical policy.

By late 2007 the situation in the state resembled Bonapartism: no fac-tion (among them realists, liberals, and neoconservatives—all of which are discussed in the next section) was clearly dominant. Indicative of this situation, in December 2006 the Bush administration selected Robert Gates, a seasoned realist, as Secretary of Defense. By then those neocon-servatives who had played the formative role of the key defence intel-lectuals, such as Paul Wolfowitz and Richard Perle, along with a host of neoconservative policy-makers (and their close allies such as Donald Rumsfeld), had left the administration. Adventurism had taken a toll ideologically, politically, militarily, and perhaps (in a long-term context) economically. US "soft power" had collapsed worldwide in the wake of the use of extreme, unsanctioned methods to coerce prisoners taken in Afghanistan, Iraq, and elsewhere.

While neoconservatives' dominance has ebbed, in the closing stages of the Bush Administration they remained as creative and persistent as ever, now promoting the idea of an inevitable war with Iran, and touting the presumed "success" of their surge strategy in Iraq.[2] While Gates does not believe that US intervention constitutes a viable strategy regarding Iran, and nor does the head of the Joint Chiefs of Staff of the US mili-tary (Admiral Mullen) or the former head of the US Central Command (Admiral Fallon), Vice-President Cheney and numerous neoconserva-tive leaders managed to receive congressional funding for a massive covert offensive involving the CIA, the Joint Special Forces Operation Command, and at least two dissident groups within Iran (Hersh 2008: 1). The strategic topic of the moment, in mid-2008, was the looming pos-sibility of widening the wars in the Middle East and south-central Asia.

It is too soon to understand in its entirety the nature of President Obama's emerging military policy. What is known suggests that conti-nuity, rather than fundamental change, will define his administration. In one important respect, however, Obama will swing the national secu-rity state back to its long-term posture, entailing the calculated use of military power projection. Preemptive wars of choice will cease to be a

pivotal policy position. Nonetheless, Obama's designs on the national
security state point to a multi-year commitment to pursue military victory in Afghanistan and a willingness to carry armed conflict into the
border regions of Pakistan.

Obama's appointments to key positions within the national security state reflect the return of the realist segment of policy makers, with
a strong orientation toward an ongoing prioritization for deliberate
power projection. For example, General Jones, a former commandant
of the Marine Corps, was appointed National Security Advisor (often
viewed as the second most powerful position in the US state). Robert
Gates, Bush's realist Secretary of Defense, received reappointment
amid the change of presidential power for the first time in US history.
The second ranking position in the Pentagon was given to Raytheon
Corporation's chief lobbyist. (Raytheon was the fifth-ranking Pentagon
contractor in 2007.) Occupying the all-important number three position, Undersecretary of Defense for Policy, Michèle Flournoy is a former high-level Defense Department official from the realist Clinton
Administration, who argued in 2008 that "The US must prepare for a
broad range of future contingencies, from sustained small-unit irregu-
lar warfare missions to military-to-military training and advising missions to high-end warfare against regional powers armed with weapons
of mass destruction and other asymmetric means" (Flournoy 2008: 1).
Meanwhile, Secretary of State Hilary Clinton has put forward the idea
of "smart power," combining military and economic power with "soft
power." As the economic crisis deepened in 2009 and Obama quickly
exhausted much of his $787-billion Keynesian "stimulus" program, and
as the US war in Afghanistan widens, structural economic and geopolitical forces will likely drive US military spending upward once again.

The "stimulus" program made a down payment on this tendency
with $20.16 billion allocated to the military sector. At the same time in
early 2009, Obama pushed up troop levels in Afghanistan to 33,000,
along with at least 5,000 mercenaries. By May 2010 he had requested
"supplemental" funding for Afghanistan of $33 billion, after having
obtained the highest military budget ever during the normal funding
cycle. Abandoning "regime change," "nation building," and preemptive wars of choice, Obama has accepted the structural imperatives of
the imperial project, continuing global militarism and countercyclical
military spending. Nonetheless, as in the early 1990s, should fear of
financing a surging national debt escalate, military expenditures could
be moderated in the closing months of the first Obama Administration.

In regard to the shifting sands of doctrine and policy formation, a final
issue deserves comment, if not resolution: the neoconservative moment of

dominance, running roughly from 2002 through 2006, has yielded few or no results of a concrete positive nature in terms of meeting stated strategic, geopolitical, and economic goals. Afghanistan remains in dispute; the war in Iraq is without foreseeable end and there is no viable resolution of their indigenous contestations; Iran has become a lightning rod for the neoconservatives, promising much future tension; the US strategy of saturating Iraq with military bases large and small has provided forward deployment strength while failing to stabilize the global oil market; while Pakistan's fractured social structure shows no particular tendency toward cohesion. This list is far from exhausting the various critical security matters in but one region in the world. On the economic front it is relatively easy to anticipate the neoconservative (and conservative nationalist) response: our ideas were not correctly applied; our ideas have not had sufficient time to work. These have been the constant stock responses of the neoliberal Chicago School economists from whom the neoconservatives have drawn their "free market" economic ideas.

It is both common and reasonable to anticipate some correspondence between the realm of the economy and the realms of public policy and ideology. The neoconservatives, however, are ideologist—unconstrained by considerations regarding the structural needs and necessities of the US and the global economy. Without exploring this point in detail, it may suffice to single out the impact of neoconservative policies on the global petroleum industry. Military tensions in the Middle East, and the probability of even greater interventions, pushed oil and gas prices in 2008 to levels unimagined in 2001, engendering an uneven global economic slowdown that particularly impacted US producers and their employees. Neoconservative strategic policy has engineered one of the largest and most rapid transfers of wealth in history, to resource-rich nations. At the same time, the economic slowdown has reduced state capacity due to falling tax revenues, necessitating ever more international borrowing to meet both the growing demands thrust upon the Pentagon and to maintain routine public-sector activities. The fact that these matters were never foreseen (even as contingencies) of US interventions in the Middle East, and the fact that they are neither addressed nor even seriously acknowledged and analyzed by neoconservatives and conservative nationalists, points to the structural limitations of a national security policy based on an ideology-in-command perspective.

Clearly, ideology can become, and in this instance became, an independent force and a critical determinant of strategic policy. One can easily find, in other previous social formations, instances where an ideology-in-command perspective was never adequately curbed and the social system spiralled downward.

It was no simple task to construct the social and strategic structure of US Cold War policy—what has become known as military Keynesianism. The end of the Cold War created the opportunity and necessity for a vast institutional realignment. At the same time it opened the door to the inner sanctuaries of power to the "first strike," "rollback" advocates of the far right.[3] Were ideologies merely a reflection of objective social conditions and realities, one could anticipate that the neoconservatives have had their fling with power policy formations. Such, however, is not the case. A recrudescence of neoconservatism is a matter that cannot be dismissed in spite of the objective failures of this faction to obtain its stated goals.

THE PRESENT STATUS OF US MILITARY POWER: REALIST, LIBERAL, AND NEOCONSERVATIVE APPLICATIONS

While, since the closing days of World War II, US military power has been unparalleled, the economic turbulence and restructuring beginning in the 1970s coincided with a reconfiguration of US military power—a process that has continued into the first decade of the twenty-first century. The political right that empowered Ronald Reagan's campaign for the presidency in the late 1970s used graphic imagery and deception to create the widespread perception within the electorate of the US that the Soviet Union was out in front in the arms race (Cypher 1981). And, at the same time, the "centrist" regime of Jimmy Carter successfully rode and manipulated events in central Asia in order to embroil the USSR in its very own Vietnam in Afghanistan. A crucial outcome of this era of tension was the "Carter Doctrine," which essentially extended the Monroe Doctrine from the Western Hemisphere to the Middle East. The US declared it would be the military arbiter and guarantor of oil flows in that region. Rapid Deployment Forces, rather than a massive string of US bases, were thought to be the technological innovation ensuring a new era of control. The rise in tensions and arms expenditures directed at the Soviet Union and the determination to exercise military power in Afghanistan set off the "Second Cold War" (Halliday 1983).

As the second Cold War wound down in the late 1980s, it was assumed that a giant "peace dividend" would accrue to the US economy. The US seemed to be doubly blessed in the early 1990s—the threat of "Japan as number one" had evaporated, and the USSR had melted away. US hegemony in the global economy, a structured outcome of World War II, appeared to be undergoing a new stage of consolidation and invigoration.

With the election of Bill Clinton in 1992, the impression that the US was crossing a threshold into a new era crowned with "superpower" capacities, not strictly limited to the realm of strategic/military concerns, but extending into unquestioned economic and ideological dominance, was palpable. Yet, a sour note was to be heard amidst the triumphalist celebration of the 1990s: the rise of the conservative forces that can be dated either to Barry Goldwater's failed bid for the presidency in 1964, or Ronald Reagan's unexpected victory in California's governor's race in 1966, set the course for a new politics of national security and power projection. This new vector had displaced the bipartisan consensus on national security issues in the run-up to Reagan's electoral victory in 1980. Throughout the 1990s, remnants of the hard-right forces that had marched with Goldwater and then Reagan metamorphosed into the neo-conservative forces that would derail Clinton's political momentum in the congressional election of 1994, when both the Senate and the House of Representatives turned to the extreme right. This new constellation of the right, particularly in the House, gave a public face to an innovative group, soon generally to be known as the "neoconservatives."

In fact, however, the new rightist faction actually contained two elements: the "conservative nationalists" and the "neoconservatives" (Hurst 2005; Rothburn 2008). The former supported a doctrine of unilateral military interventionism, particularly to maintain the control of oil. They constituted a rather clear break from the dominance since World War II of the "realist" posture wherein the unsentimental pursuit of national interest took place within the context of the status quo balance of power. Under this prior context the use of violence (at least in principle) was to be limited to self-defence, while all-out strategies of unilateralist global hegemony were to be eschewed out of respect for and cooperation with the multilateral institutions created during and after World War II.

Visible in the election of 1994, but much more so after 9/11, the neoconservatives vociferously champion what they self-consciously define as the US empire (Kagan 2008; Sterling-Folker 2008). They are perhaps most distinguished for their ability to encode an old, marginalized idea of the extreme right during the Cold War: the doctrine of "first strike" or "rollback" became official US military policy by way of the 2002 "Bush Doctrine," which declares the US commander-in-chief entitled to wage *preventive* war. Further, the neoconservatives were able to move the George W. Bush administration (2001–09) to adopt the "Freedom Agenda" whereby the US could elect to manipulate, coerce, or invade a nation in order to reset its political institutions to coincide with US ideas of justified political rule (normally simply called "democracy").

In addition to a focus on nation-building, the neoconservatives champion a volunteeristic "will to power" doctrine: they espouse an unconstrained will to use violence and, via the influence of Leo Straus,[4] an advocacy for deception as a justified weapon to be used *against* the US public in order to advance their agenda. Both the conservative nationalists and the neoconservatives imagine that the US, through the doctrine of exceptionalism, would inevitably use its military force for the "good." Therefore, the application of US military power *should* be welcomed by those who are on the receiving end. Important in the neoconservatives' rise to prominence was the general acceptance of their specious assertion that high levels of US military spending had destroyed the social fabric of the Soviet Union, thereby disintegrating the Soviet Bloc and thus creating the "unipolar moment" of unbounded opportunity for the expansion of US power. In contrast, the realists assumed that the use of US military power was always solely in pursuit of tangible US national interests (not essentially metaphysical ideas such as delivering "freedom") and would be understood as such by rival powers.[5]

This rightist faction of conservative nationalists and neoconservatives was not a mere rump faction of extreme sectarian political and ideological leaders: it included many powerful political figures that rose to prominence within the confines of the old bipartisan (or realist) Cold War elite from the late 1970s onward. For this group, the idea of the "Peace Dividend"—that the US should systematically cut back on its military might, increase social spending on many public priorities, and adjust to a multi-polar world of power sharing as the Cold War ended—was anathema. Meanwhile, Clinton's economic and strategic advisors (realists who put much emphasis on economic rather than strategic factors) were enamoured with a neoclassical/neoliberal vision of global harmony and order based on an undefined concept commonly termed "globalization." What exactly globalization was (or is) has defied crystallization. Many analysts have insisted that the main thrust of the concept is the withering of state power and the creation of transnational webs of organization and power, a perspective certain to alienate the state-centred/power-centred rightists (Barkawi 2006). The Clinton administration sought consolidation of rising international levels of trade, investment, and financial flows, which (assuming that the Bretton Woods institutions [the IMF and World Bank] and the newly created World Trade Organization performed their functions) would constitute a new "regime of accumulation" or "social structure of accumulation," thus ending the economic turbulence of the 1973–92 period.

By the end of the Cold War it was possible to discern a fourfold division regarding international policy, with some factions of the political class placing more emphasis on strategic issues while others focused largely on international economic forces. First were the "liberal internationalists," who centred their analysis on "globalization," advocating an all-out offensive to open international markets to industrial and financial capital under the banner of "free trade." The second grouping was the realists, who maintained their posture but lost clout to the "liberal internationalists," particularly during the Clinton administration. Third, the neoconservatives recoiled from the posture of the "liberal internationalists" and their willingness to systematically reduce US military spending. For them, the end of the Cold War was the "unilateral moment" not to be squandered through a flighty approach to global military strategy. Pushing on themes such as "preparedness," the neoconservatives falsely claimed that the US military was suffering a funding crisis that left the US with weakened defences, even as external threats mounted. Finally, the ever more aggressive discourse of the neoconservatives pulled many within the venerable realist camp to the right, creating a fourth alignment regarding strategic policy—the conservative nationalists.[6] The rise of the Bush administration in 2001 brought this latter new constellation to power, but it also opened the door to the temporary capture of US strategic policy by the neoconservative defence intellectuals and their allies after 9/11.

This complex transition can be best understood in the context of dramatically changing economic circumstances, particularly in the 1990s. For a brief moment between 1993 and 1999, many felt that the new "NASDAQ/bubble economy" would underwrite a new long wave of expansion. At its base, the new economy had been bolstered by adroit Wall Street financial manoeuvres combined with commercial products spun off from electronics and information technology innovations that had originated in the bowels of the military-industrial complex—such as the computer and the internet. Not all of the longest economic expansion in US history was fluff, but productivity growth levels were modest by historical standards, as was overall economic growth. (Almost all of this growth was captured by those in the top ten per cent of the income distribution—a trend that accelerated in the early years of the twenty-first century.) By 1999, if not before, any careful observer could see that the economic expansion was coming to an ungraceful end, but there were few who met this qualification.

The rightist faction was content that the ideas they had long championed regarding neoliberal economic doctrine were now being zealously promoted by the political "centrists" within the Clinton administration. But they were deeply alarmed by the lax focus on the Pentagon. The "unipolar" moment, they maintained, was being squandered. By

1998, the Clinton administration—yielding to a barrage of criticism for its allegedly limp military posture—shifted on military policy. An historically unprecedented post–World War II military buildup began in 1999, funded at least through fiscal year 2011. This buildup, now longer than any period since 1947, has engendered current policy pressure from the neoconservatives to push baseline military expenditures from the 2007 levels of roughly 3.8 per cent of GDP to a *permanent* level of 4, 5, or 6 per cent.[7] This initiative, backed by the Heritage Foundation, the American Enterprise Institute, and many "defence intellectuals," is notable for three reasons. First and foremost, the idea of a permanent military expenditures/GDP level is new and audacious. This is the case because, like the neoliberal Washington Consensus "reforms" imposed on developing nations since the early 1980s, it is structured to be irreversible. Second, the concept, again like the so-called reforms of the Washington Consensus, removes from the political-economic realm the public decision to fund the level of military outlays, replacing it with a blank mandate. (Imagine the outcry if centrist policy-makers attempted to increase social expenditures by as much as one-third—while leaving room for "supplemental" outlays that could push such expenditures upward by as much as 40 per cent.) Third, it asserts that the military sector is underfunded even as military outlays have surged every year for over a decade.

In late 2000, George W. Bush was elected to preside over the executive office for the 2001–05 period. The campaign had not turned on distinctions between the centrist/realist vs. conservative nationalist/neoconservative perspectives on military expenditures. However, Bush's top national security advisors—Dick Cheney, Donald Rumsfeld (a conservative nationalist), and Paul Wolfowitz (a neoconservative)—formed the core of what would be known as the "Vulcans." This group not only wanted large increases in military outlays (Johnson 2004, 2006; Kolko 2006; Mann 2004; Suskind 2006), but more importantly, these advisors wanted to employ military capabilities as their first-order option— shifting drastically away from the neoclassical policy structures that had guided the Clinton administration with their riveted focus on homogenizing the global circuits of trade, financial, and production capital. To be sure, experienced political "realists" such as James Baker and Brent Scowcroft sought to gain ascendancy within the small circle of key advisors, and they did manage to place Scowcroft's protégé, Condoleezza Rice, in the key position of national security advisor while General Colin Powell—a long-time Clinton functionary—took the helm at the State Department. Rice, however, was weak and inexperienced and exercised no formative power at the key National Security Council. Powell was constrained by the Vulcans—a group that Rice soon joined.

As the centrist Secretary of the Treasury Paul O'Neill pointed out in his revealing biography, President Bush's first cabinet meeting in 2001 was dominated by the Vulcans, who were focused on the extension of US military power in Iraq—what would become known as "regime change" (Suskind 2004). Neoconservative defence intellectuals, foremost among them the adroit Richard Perle, had sought to capture the high ground of grand strategy and geopolitical policy-making. Grand strategy is to be understood as the combination of national policies that entail the application of military power as a prime means to achieve the international political and economic objectives of the state. Barry Posen maintains that "a grand strategy enumerates and prioritizes threats and adduces political and military remedies for them. A grand strategy also explains why some threats attain a certain priority, and why and how the remedies proposed could work" (Posen 2007: 6). Although complementary and regionalized, "geopolitical policies seek to establish national or imperial control over space and other resources, routeways, industrial capacity and population the territory contains" (Streusand 2002: 41). Posen argues that the rightist faction achieved its goal of defining the current thrust of grand strategy, which he describes in two short paragraphs:

Democratic and Republican strategists alike hold that the most imminent threats today are threats to US safety. Terrorism, basically Islamist in origin, is the key problem. It is caused by something that is wrong with Arab society in particular, but also the societies of other Islamic countries such as Pakistan, Iran and Afghanistan. "Rogue" states ... are a closely related threat because they may assist terrorists. "Failed" states ... produce or nurture terrorists, and they produce human rights violations, refugees and crime....

Based on this threat analysis, the consensus therefore supports a US grand strategy of international activism. The United States must remain the strongest military power in the world by a wide margin. It should be willing to use force—even preventively, if need be—on a range of issues. The United States should directly manage regional security relationships in any corner of the world that matters strategically, which seems increasingly to be every corner of the world. The risk that nuclear weapons could fall into the hands of violent non-state actors is so great that the United States should be willing to take extraordinary measures to keep suspicious countries possibly or even potentially in league with such actors from acquiring these weapons. Beyond uses of force, the United States should endeavour to change other societies so that they look more like its own. A world of democracies would be the safest outcome, and the United States should be willing to pay considerable costs to produce such a world.[8] (Posen 2007: 6)

This bipartisan policy consensus was, to a great degree, the result of the work of Perle, Robert Kagan, and William Kristol—three of the most influential neoconservatives on military policy. They have produced many tracts urging the dramatic use of military power, such as *Present Danger: Crisis and Opportunity in American Foreign and Defense Policy*, which features an article by Perle advocating US intervention in Iraq (Kagan and Kristol 2000). Works such as these were well known to Wolfowitz, Rumsfeld, and Cheney, all of whom were partisans in the struggle to bring new ideas of grand strategy and geopolitical policy into the highest circles of power in the US. Older centrist/realist ideas, commonly associated with writings linked to the Council on Foreign Relations, the Brookings Institution, and other conventional centres of Cold War analysis were marginalized—while key policy-makers in these conventional centres steadily moved toward the new position of an unilateral, expansionist strategy. Even before the commonly presumed key doctrine of the neoconservative defence intellectuals, produced by the Project for a New American Century in 1998, had surfaced, Council on Foreign Relations scholar and former national security advisor Zbigniew Brzezinski became an advocate of US "global supremacy" (Brzezinski 1997: 3).

But even as the centrists were pulled toward a new, unilateralist conception of grand strategy and geopolitical control, particularly in the Middle East and Africa, the neoconservatives heightened a focus on "values over interests" that rests on distant and near precedents: Italy's successful war of colonization in Ethiopia under Mussolini, for example, was putatively carried out to achieve humanitarian goals—particularly the eradication of slavery; the US war of colonization in the Philippines was putatively carried out to Christianize the indigenous population—an act largely undertaken by the Spanish some centuries before. By 1998, if not before, it was the Clinton administration that was seeking to define a new norm of post–Cold War intervention: "humanitarian intervention." Noam Chomsky, for one, sought to cut through the Wilsonian rhetoric and posturing of the Clinton administration as it orchestrated NATO's intervention in Kosovo. For Chomsky there were five reasons for the intervention, where humanitarian concerns were no more than cosmetic. First, it was necessary for NATO to maintain its "credibility" in the post–Cold War era and to extend its suzerainty to the Mediterranean. In so doing NATO reclaimed its "purpose," which it had lost at the end of the Cold War, while the US reasserted its claim to lead this organization. Second, victory in the former Yugoslavia was instrumental in the achievement of western control over a key geopolitical region that strategically formed a bridge between the Middle East and Europe. Third, in Chomsky's view, the war in Kosovo ramped up military expenditures to the benefit of the industrial base of the "iron triangle." Fourth, western corporations (overwhelmingly American) have been in a position to feast from a cornucopia of large infrastructure projects to rebuild the damage from NATO's "surgical" bombing. Finally, it appeared that NATO would remain subordinated to the US lead, squelching plans for Europe to construct an independent unified command as a complement to the EU (Chomsky 1999: 74–75, 135–43). Subsequent to Chomsky's effort, one could add to his list another major outcome of the intervention: the US seized one thousand acres of land in Kosovo to build Camp Bondsteel, which became, prior to the massive bases constructed in Iraq, the "largest and most expensive base constructed since the Vietnam War" (Johnson 2004: 143). While Chomsky discounted issues of resource control in the case of the war in Kosovo, subsequently it was learned that Camp Bondsteel

> ... is actually located astride the route of the proposed AMBO [Albania, Macedonia, Bulgaria Oil] Trans-Balkan pipeline. This $1.3 billion project, if built, will pump Caspian Basin oil brought by tanker from a pipeline terminus in Georgia across the Black Sea to the Bulgarian oil port at Burgas, where it will be piped through Macedonia to the Albanian Adriatic port of Vlore. From there, super-tankers would take it to Europe and the United States, thus bypassing the congested Bosphorous Strait—as of now the only route out of the Black Sea by ship.... In 2003 the US began to construct two additional military bases in Burgas, Bulgaria, while the US Air Force built a garrison nearby to support air incursions in Iraq. Another similar facility was constructed close-by, in Romania, both located amidst large oil-refining regions which supplied vital petroleum products to the military efforts in Iraq and Afghanistan. (Johnson 2004: 145–46)

Revisiting some of the salient elements of the war in Kosovo is instructive because it casts the neoconservative-led intervention in Iraq in a different light than is normally conceived: clearly, as the work of Chomsky, Johnson, and others has shown, the vaunted "humanitarian" incursion into Kosovo carried with it a broad variety of "realist" elements. The same can be seen in the neoconservative-led incursions into Afghanistan and Iraq. Here we primarily find other examples of the "shock doctrine" as articulated by Naomi Klein (2007). That is, the neoconservative military campaigns are tightly wrapped in the trappings of good and evil, but the inside contents are simply the neoliberal agenda that opens up the Middle East and central Asia to the "free"-market ideology of the Chicago School, the trade regime to US (and other) transnationals—the Open Door, and grants access to all areas of the Afghanistan and Iraqi economies to Foreign Direct Investment, doing away with all elements of the social safety net and privatizing all public goods as far as possible. At the same time, as seen in the region of the former Yugoslavia, very large US military bases have been quickly constructed to serve as a platform for regional geopolitical control and power projection to nearby regions.

And, although delayed, the allegations that the wars in Afghanistan and Iraq had much to do with US corporate access to and control over oil has become better understood: in July 2008, the Iraqi government opened six of its major existing oil fields to foreign investors, granting access to roughly one-half of its existing oil reserves to foreign oil corporations. This is a context in which it is considered that US-based oil giants such as ExxonMobil, Chevron, and Shell (which is also partially British and Dutch) will have the inside track, with foreign firms being allowed to retain an unprecedented 75 per cent of the value of the contracts (Klein 2008: 10). Meanwhile, a trans-Afghan gas pipeline, originally to be built by a US oil major prior to the intervention in 2001, is now moving toward fruition: the TAPI (Turkmenistan, Afghanistan, Pakistan, India) pipeline project to route natural gas over 1,700 kilometres through Afghanistan, entailing $7.6 billion in construction costs, was conceptually approved in 2008 and continues to be viewed as likely to be "Afghanistan's largest development project" (Foster 2010).

If there are fundamental, rather than formal, distinctions to be found regarding grand strategy and geopolitical initiatives, it would appear that they have to do with risk. Many realists, as has been noted, shifted over to the conservative nationalist or even the neoconservative position with the end of the Cold War. Yet an important part of US policy-making remains in the Pentagon. Neoconservative defence intellectuals such as Wolfowitz held sway and shaped important Pentagon policies only so long as their patrons (in this case Rumsfeld) were able to cling to power. At a more fundamental level, it is important to note that realists of the centrist persuasion within the power elite—particularly important within the Pentagon—are leery of adventurism. For these realists, only well-calculated adventures are to be considered, and these are generally enveloped in multilateral formalities. Failure, if it occurs, is shared—or preferably shifted—and international opprobrium becomes muted. When unilateral movement is deemed necessary, great effort is made to employ clandestine tactics. With the events of 9/11 as their armour, the neoconservatives assumed they had a mandate for high-risk actions— unilateral, if necessary. While the neoconservatives may seek the use of force as a first-order option, the vehicle for such use, the US military, has long tended to ostracize and contain advocates of "rollback" or "first-strike" or "preventive war fighting." While the neoconservatives obtained the high ground of policy-making with respect to the globalization liberals of the Clinton era, they could not dislodge the realist bias at the Pentagon. With the gradual distancing of the George W. Bush administration from this faction in Bush's final months of power, and with the election of Obama, the realist/centrist position has now regained its position of dominance.

GRAND STRATEGY AND GEOPOLITICAL POLICY

While the neoconservatives are losing ground, the question of their fate tends to displace the analysis from the central focus on the current dominant perspective regarding US military power. This perspective is, according to grand strategy, a policy of "enlargement," as mentioned by both Brzezinski in 1997 and Anthony Lake, Clinton's national security advisor, in 2003 (Foster 2006: 10–11). Foster expresses what I have termed the policy of "global militarism" (Cypher 1991), a policy that has undergone evolutionary refinement. It has been applied by realists, liberals, and neoconservatives with increasing determination and scope, beginning in the late 1980s. As Foster maintains, global militarism is a result of the restructuring of the national economy in light of declining profit margins and increasing international economic rivalry from the late 1970s through the early 1990s:

> US imperial grand strategy is less a product of policies generated in Washington by this or that wing of the ruling class, than an inevitable result of the power position that US capitalism finds itself in at the commencement of the twenty-first century. US economic strength ... has been ebbing fairly steadily.... At the same time US world military power has increased relatively with the demise of the Soviet Union. The United States now accounts for about half of all of the world's military spending—a proportion two or more times its share of world output. The goal of the new ... strategy is to use this unprecedented military strength to preempt emerging historical forces by creating a sphere of full-spectrum dominance so vast, now encompassing every continent, that no potential rivals will be able to challenge the United States.... (2006: 11)

If we step back from these sweeping statements for a moment, and view the role of US military power projection from the perspective of a key component of the US military—the US Navy—there is a strong correspondence to the ideas emphasized above. In 2002 the National Defense University published *Globalization and Maritime Power*. In this realist treatment it is assumed that all "great" nations seek a "disproportionate share" (the words of Captain Alfred Thayer Mahan in 1902) of ocean-going trade, because this forms a vital basis for the wealth and economic strength of a nation. For some observers, recalling Mahan's linking of economic power with dominance in sea commerce might seem quaint in an era of "knowledge-based economies." It is important to note, however, that 90 per cent of all international trade, including trade in vital natural resources—particularly oil—travels by sea. The US Navy is the very embodiment of sea power, here defined as

> ... the control of international trade and commerce; the usage and control of ocean resources; the operation of navies in war; and the use of navies and maritime economic power as instruments of diplomacy, deterrence, and political influence in time of peace.... Sea power can never be quite separated from its geo-economic purposes....
> Maritime shipping, seaport operations, undersea resources (such as oil), fisheries and other forms of commerce and communications ... can all be seen as integral to a nation's sea power. (Tangredi 2002: 2)

The US Navy regards itself as the "sole global navy in existence today" and "the benchmark and dominant standard for all things naval" thereby providing a vital linchpin between sea power and the ability to successfully participate in the process labelled "globalization." Sea power is not passive or merely structural, rather it conditions a nation's ability to control oceanic resources and to engage in the circuits of international trade and production. Equally important, sea power entails an ability to project power *into and from* the sea in order to control or influence the course of events both on water and land. The US Navy is truly global—major fleets are simultaneously present in the Mediterranean, Arabian Sea, and the Western Pacific "and it has individual ships and squadrons in almost *every major locale*" (Tangredi 2002: 6; emphasis mine).[9]
Tangredi goes on,

> Of course, freedom of the seas can be said to benefit the dominant sea power ... in ways similar to how critics (and even proponents) see globalization as benefiting the dominant economic power. As a globalized service, the US Navy can—within certain limits—determine the

location, timing, and procedures of the world's maritime exchanges, as well as control access to land regions. This represents an *omnipresent influence of US sea power* on the global economy and the overall globalization process. (Tangredi 2002: 6; emphasis mine)

MAINTAINING HEGEMONIC POWER?

The analysis spread through *Globalization and Maritime Power* affirms a major point that is all but excluded from international political economy—that there are direct linkages between US military expenditures and national hegemonic power. This view stands in direct opposition to most attempts to analyze US military expenditures that commence with the premise that arms production constitutes a drain on the economy that reduces national competitiveness and international capacities.[10] The arguments made above regarding the functional role of military expenditures needs to be expanded to capture the scope of their interrelationship with the maintenance and expansion of hegemonic power. The use of power in a geopolitical area redounds upon the US in indirect ways. To the degree that the US uses military power to control a region, such as the Middle East, direct benefits flow to Europe and Japan, which are the major buyers of oil from that region. The benefit to the US is indirect—greater access to the markets of Europe and Japan, greater ability to make Foreign Direct Investments on favourable terms, greater access to financial markets or greater flexibility in those markets. These benefits can take many other forms, such as a greater willingness to follow US-based initiatives regarding policies at international financial institutions, at the WTO, or within the OECD. National political policies can be more easily moulded or swayed to conform to US diplomatic objectives or geostrategic tactics regarding NATO, the expansion of the EU, policies toward China or Russia, space weaponry, technological applications across borders, support for neoliberal free trade agreements, and so on. Much of the external benefit of massive levels of military spending would presumably flow in a North-South direction, granting the US leverage and favourable access (particularly to vital minerals and other resources) otherwise unavailable. Activities such as sharing technology in the military sphere can easily translate into better access or better tax treatment for US-based transnational corporations.

Power also has very much to do with precluding policies and actions on the part of other nations that are particularly oppositional. Military power is, therefore, fungible. Providing the "public good" of military "stability"—naval or other—is both directly and indirectly beneficial (through the asymmetrical reciprocal or responsive actions of other nations) to the US economic system. Hegemonic power is, then, self-generating. A "virtuous" circle, from the hegemon's perspective, is set in motion through its "selfless" provision of "defense" functions in the international arena. The national state is not an instrument of particular interests—its relative autonomy is deployed within the structural confines of a global system that imposes strategies designed to obtain a "disproportionate share" of global production for the hegemonic power—as a study of the global oil industry demonstrates (Stokes 2007).

These "externalities" befalling the US as a collateral residual of military outlays are extremely important, because without them there is a high likelihood of losing the multiple advantages enjoyed by the holder of hegemonic power. This is particularly the case because most, if not all, of the other registries of hegemonic power (particularly as analyzed in a classic study by Robert Keohane that enumerated the several conditions necessary to attain the status of the hegemon) are slipping from the grasp of the US. These include the control of the dominant commodity in world trade, holding the dominant foreign-investment position, attaining dominance in the financial markets, and maintaining the dominant or "key" currency (Keohane 1991).

The US lost its self-sufficiency in oil production and consumption roughly fifty years ago. Every year its oil import requirement rises, and it has not developed an alternative-fuels policy. As to investment, Table 9.1 illustrates the declining role of US corporations. This is reinforced by a complementary trend: in 1980 the US accounted for 217 of the world's largest corporations, while in 2005 the number had withered to 170, only slightly above the 165 associated with the European Union (Fry 2007: 3). In the financial realm it is now widely accepted that London is beginning to rival New York as the financial capital of the world economy. One popular metric used to capture this trend is London's share of global hedge-fund assets, which rose from 12 per cent in 2002 to 26 per cent in 2006. Meanwhile, the US share has plummeted from 82 to 63 per cent (New York Times 2007: C6). Financial markets have been affected by repeated waves of turbulence since the rupture of the subprime market strategy engineered by Wall Street investment banks in August 2007. At every turn since that date the incentives to shift finance capital to the City of London have grown, as British policy-makers are well aware. London is doing everything within its power to undermine, discreetly yet successfully, US financial hegemony. The US has become the world's largest debtor nation—a $2.7-trillion net (negative) foreign asset position was registered in 2005. In 1980, US assets owned abroad exceeded foreign-owned assets in the US by a ratio of nearly 2:1 (Fry

2007: 3). By late 2007, the G7 finance ministers and central bankers had reached a consensus that the competitive depreciation of the US dollar in the 2005–07 period would have to be addressed (Bennhold and Castle 2007: C10). Data from eighteen months earlier illuminated a financial trend that could have only accelerated: in 2000, 55 per cent of the foreign-exchange holdings were in US dollars, but by early 2006 this had fallen to 44 per cent, while the total value of corporate bonds denominated in Euros exceeded those in US dollars (Fry 2007: 19). By the widely accepted standards of Keohane, the US should *not* now be the hegemonic power. The fallout from the Great Recession of 2007–09 remains to be understood, yet the degree of external dependence in the areas of oil and the financing of the national debt continues to rise. The trade deficit continues as well, and the "parallel banking system" was swept away in the Wall Street crash of late 2008.

TABLE 9.1 Share of Stock of World Foreign Direct Investment (FDI) (percentage of world total)

COUNTRY	1914	1960	1978	1992	2000	2005
France	12.2	6.1	3.8	8.3	8.3	8.0
Germany	10.5	1.2	7.3	9.2	7.4	9.1
Japan	0.1	0.7	6.8	13.0	4.7	3.6
United Kingdom	45.5	16.2	12.9	11.4	15.0	11.6
United States	18.5	49.2	41.4	25.3	20.8	19.2

Source: UNCTAD 1994: 131; 2001: 307; 2006: 303.

This calculation, however, omits the crucial role of military power in the sustainability of a hegemonic position. As the economic power variables all move against the US, the relative level of military power rises. The US has developed through more than fifty years a carefully nurtured competitive advantage in armaments production and power projection. This counterweight to relative economic loss in the international arena has been insufficiently incorporated into the field of IPE. In the late 1980s and early 1990s, before the "new economy" boom, "declinist" projections were rampant in the international relations literature. Once again, economistic dirges are to be heard. Recasting the discussion to take full account of the structural role of arms production and power projection constitutes a necessary amendment to the models and metrics used to measure hegemonic power—as Mahan maintained more than a century ago.

NOTES

1 The complex structural characteristics of the era defined by the internationalization of capital since the 1970s have proved difficult to encapsulate in
a classic formulation such as that offered by Paul Baran and Paul Sweezy
in their paradigmatic statement of the US economy in the "Keynesian"
1945–65 period (Baran & Sweezy 1966). The crises of the 1970s marked
the close of the first postwar era, while economic, institutional, and technological factors opened the way for the new era of internationalization—
commonly termed "globalization." For an attempt to capture the dynamics
of the current era, see McDonough et al. (2006).

2 Writing in *The American Conservative,* Andrew Bacevich argues that the
US surge in Iraq cannot be termed a success. Rather it is the result of vast
concessions, including arms and money to various factions in Iraq whose
fundamental long-term interests are at odds with US policy. The surge has
bought time to encourage a political settlement among the Iraqis, but results
are difficult to demonstrate (Bacevich 2008).

3 The complex world of warfighting strategies, particularly nuclear, is discussed in Kaplan (1983) and McMahan (1985).

4 Philosophy professor Straus held court at the University of Chicago from
1949 to 1968, impressing student zealots such as Paul Wolfowitz with his
advocacy of unrestrained power as a "right" to be exercised by powerful
nations over subordinated ones.

5 Regarding the Middle East, the neoconservatives are tightly entwined with
the most adventuristic factions of the Israeli political class and their allies
in AIPAC. This is the prism through which the dynamics of the Middle East
are to be understood—a perspective generally closely followed by the conservative nationalists.

6 The rightward nationalist shift of many former realists in the course of
the 1990s is well-illustrated through an examination of key policy making
documents such as that of the US government's Commission on National
Security/21st Century, convened in October 1998, which brought together
leaders from industry, government, and military—that is, of the country's
power elite. Former Senators Gary Hart and Warren Rudman chaired the
Commission. Its commissioners included Martin Marietta CEO Norm
Augustine, realists such as Lee Hamilton (co-author of the 2006 Baker-
Hamilton [Iraq Study Group] report to realign US strategy in Iraq in con-
sonance with realist ideas, a step rejected by President Bush in favour of
Robert Kagan's urging of a surge strategy), and a leading neoconservative—
former House Speaker Newt Gingrich. Its 29 "study group members" came
from top universities like MIT and Princeton, and think tanks including the
RAND Corporation, the Cato Institute, and the Brookings Institution. The
Commission also enjoyed the cooperation of the Departments of Defense
and State, as well as the top intelligence agencies like the CIA and the
National Security Agency (NSA). In 1998, the Commission began a major
review of US military strategy. Its aim was to redesign the institutional structure of the military for the post–Cold War era.

The Commission's 1999 report "New World Coming: American Security in the 21st Century", outlined a strategy for the United States to "remain the principal military power in the world." (U.S. Commission on National Security 1999: 3). In the coming century, the report argued, the United States will become increasingly vulnerable to direct "nontraditional" attacks— against its information-technology infrastructure, for example. It will have to intervene abroad more frequently to deal with state fragmentation, as it did in the Balkans and Africa, or to ensure an "uninterrupted" supply of oil from the Persian Gulf region, or elsewhere. And, it will face rivals in its drive to dominate space. The report concluded that to ensure continued US dominance, US military spending will have to rise dramatically.

7 "Baseline" refers to annual military appropriations. This excludes such related expenditures as those devoted to Homeland Security and particularly to Supplemental appropriations that have been used since 2001 to fund the ongoing wars in Afghanistan and Iraq.

8 It is important to note that this synopsis of the conservative nationalist and neoconservative view of the strategic situation facing the US does not reflect Posen's assessment of current military realities: Posen's article, in fact, is devoted to the following perspective: "The United States needs to be more reticent about the use of military force; more modest about the scope for political transformation within and among countries; and more distant politically and militarily from traditional allies. We thus face a choice between habit and sentiment on the one side, realism and rationality on the other" (2007: 6). His position regarding Israel is that the US needs to cut its military assistance to that nation to zero within ten years. Posen was a study-group member for the US Commission on National Security's 1999 report.

9 A new regional US military command, AFRICOM, was announced in 2007. This command will bring expanded US seapower to the seas surrounding Africa. In 2008 the US Navy announced the rejuvenation of the Fourth Fleet to be assigned to the Southern Command, to eventually expand the reach of seapower projection into the Atlantic and Pacific Oceans on the East and West coasts of Latin America.

10 As cogently argued by Baran and Sweezy (1966), in theory a nation that does not spend funds on the military but rather on pursuits that directly increase the productive base, or directly increase the economic well-being of its populace (through programs that cannot be adequately provided via the market due to income limits on the working class and those too old, too young, disabled, unemployed, etc.), will increase its economic or social well-being, or both, depending on how funds are redirected from the military. Yet, within the specific historical context of US capitalism, when military spending has been cut, very little is directed to such objectives. Instead, the economy shrinks. Socioeconomic, ideological, and political resistance to public expenditures has been a structural component of the US economy— only momentarily side-stepped during the Depression of the 1930s.

REFERENCES

Bacevich, A. 2008. "Surging to Defeat." *The American Conservative*. April 21.

Barkawi, T. 2006. *Globalization and War*. Lanham, MD: Rowman and Littlefield.

Baran, P., and P. Sweezy. 1966. *Monopoly Capital*. New York: Monthly Review Press.

Bennhold, K., and S. Castle. 2007. "Europeans Toughen Line on the Dollar's Weakness." *New York Times* 5 December: C10.

Brzezinski, Z. 1997. *The Grand Chessboard*. New York: Basic Books.

Chomsky, N. 1999. *The New Military Humanism*. Monroe, ME: Common Courage Press.

Cypher, J. 1992. "Institutions, Arms Spending and the State." In William Dugger and William Waller (eds.), *The Stratified State*. Armonk, NY: M.E. Sharpe. 217–43.

———. 1991. "Military Spending after the Cold War." *Journal of Economic Issues* 25(2): 607–15.

———. 1981. "The Basic Economics of 'Rearming America.'" *Monthly Review* 33(6): 11–27.

Flournoy, M. 2008. "Strengthening the Readiness of the U.S. Military." Prepared Statement before the U.S. House Arms Services Committee (February 14): 1–9. <http://armedservices.house.gov/pdfs/FC021408/Flournoy_Testimony021408.pdf >.

Foster, J. 2010. "Afghanistan, the TAPI Pipeline, and Energy Geopolitics" *Journal of Energy Security* (March). <http://www.ensec.org/index.php?option=com_content&view=article&id=233:afghanistan-the-tapi-pipeline-and-energy-geopolitics&catid=103:energysecurityissuecontent&Itemid=358>.

Foster, J.B. 2006. "A Warning to Africa: The New U.S. Imperial Grand Strategy." *Monthly Review* 58(2): 1–12.

Fry, E. 2007. "The Decline of the American Superpower." *The Forum: Berkeley Electronic Press* 5(2): 1–24.

Halliday, F. 1983. *The Making of the Second Cold War*. London: Verso.

Hersh, S. 2008. "Preparing the Battlefield." *The New Yorker* 7 July. <http://www.newyorker.com/reporting/2008/07/07/080707fa_fact_hersh>.

Hurst, S. 2005. "Myths of Neoconservatism." *International Politics* 42(1): 76–96.

Johnson, C. 2006. *Nemesis*. New York: Metropolitan Books.

———. 2004. *The Sorrows of Empire*. New York: Metropolitan Books.

Kagan, R. 2008. "Dangerous Nation." *International Politics* 45: 403–12.

Kagan, R., and W. Kristol (eds.). 2000. *Present Dangers: Crisis and Opportunity in American Foreign and Defense Policy*. San Francisco: Encounter Books.

Kaplan, F. 1983. *The Wizards of Armageddon*. New York: Simon & Schuster.

Keohane, R. 1991. "The Theory of Hegemonic Stability." In G. Crane and A. Amawi (eds.), *The Theoretical Evolution of International Political Economy*. Oxford: Oxford University Press. 245–62.

Klein, N. 2008. "Disaster Capitalism: State of Extortion." *The Nation* 21 July: 10–11.

———. 2007. *The Shock Doctrine: The Rise of Disaster Capitalism*. New York: Henry Holt & Company.

Kolko, G. 2006. *The Age of War*. Boulder, CO: Lynne Reinner.

Mann, J. 2004. *Rise of the Vulcans*. New York: Viking.

McDonough, T., M. Reich, D. Kotz, and M.A. Gonzalez-Pérez. 2006. *Growth and Crisis, Social Structure of Accumulation: Theory and Analysis*. E-book, National University of Ireland, Galway.

McMahan, J. 1985. *Reagan and the World*. New York: Monthly Review.

New York Times. 2007. "Back of the Envelope." April 4: C6.

Posen, B. 2007. "The Case for Restraint." *The American Interest* 3(2): 6–12. <http://www.the-american-interest.com/article.cfm?piece=331>.

Rothburn, B. 2008. "Does One Right Make a Realist?" *Political Science Quarterly* 123(2): 271–99.

Sterling-Folker, J. 2008. "The Emperor Wore Cowboy Boots." *International Studies Perspectives* 9(3): 319–30.

Stokes, D. 2007. "Blood for Oil? Global Capital, Counter-Insurgency and the Dual Logic of American Energy Security." *Review of International Studies* 33(2): 245–64.

Streusand, D. 2002. "Geopolitics vs. Globalization." In S. Tangredi (ed.), *Globalization and Maritime Power*. Washington, DC: National Defense University Press. 41–56.

Suskind, R. 2006. *The One Percent Doctrine*. New York: Simon & Schuster.

———. 2004. *The Price of Loyalty*. New York: Simon & Schuster.

Tangredi, S. 2002. "Globalization and Sea Power." In S. Tangredi (ed.), *Globalization and Maritime Power*. Washington, DC: National Defense University Press. 1–26.

UNCTAD (United Nations Conference on Trade and Development). Various years. World Investment Report. Geneva: United Nations.

United States Commission on National Security. 1999. "New World Coming: American Security in the 21st Century".

10

Resisting Neoliberal Capitalism
Insights from Marxist Political Economy[1]

ELAINE COBURN

Two insights of Marxist political economy inform this chapter. The first is that political life is partly determined or conditioned by the economic system within which it takes place—not just any kind of politics or social life is possible within a given historical moment. Instead, how people get together in order to make what is necessary to live, what Marx called the mode of production, limits the range of political possibilities. Of course, this does not mean that variety is not possible within given economic systems. At least since Esping-Andersen (1990), for example, it has been clear that there are varieties of capitalist welfare states, and now, varieties of neoliberal, market-dominated states within a world capitalist system. Nonetheless, the boundaries of political life and even what is considered politically possible are profoundly shaped by the economy. Indeed, the mode of production shapes all aspects of social life, including human beings' most intimate thoughts and hopes, with important implications for political struggle.

The second insight is that economies are not natural and inevitable. Social reality is ultimately contingent: human beings make (and re-make) the economic world and therefore can change the rules of the game to which they are, at any given time, collectively and individually subject. No political economy is forever. Feudal economies preceded capitalist economies, and capitalist economies, in all their variations, will one day be superseded by different ways of organizing social life. If econo-mies *seem* natural and inevitable, they are, in fact, ultimately political and social, contingent and changeable.

In what follows, these two insights of Marxist political economy are the starting point for a discussion of contemporary battles over neolib-eral capitalism, particularly the role played by the movements oppos-ing neoliberal capitalism. In what ways do these movements reflect the dynamics and constraints of the neoliberal societies from which they emerge? What are their contradictions and limits? How, and to what extent, do they alter the balance of political (class) forces, both chal-lenging the common sense of neoliberal precepts and reclaiming social spaces from the market—and so potentially foreshadowing a non-cap-italist future? Considered against the historically specific phase of con-temporary neoliberal capitalism, at once the context and object of the transnational movement analyzed here, in this chapter I draw atten-tion to the movement's many faces, its contradictions, its limits, and its emancipatory possibilities.

NEOLIBERAL CAPITALISM: A MATERIAL AND IDEOLOGICAL PROJECT

Capitalism has undergone several major transformations following recurrent, structural crises, with the most recent, neoliberal phase of capitalism emerging in the wake of various events of the 1970s. In particular, the oil crises of 1973 and 1979, along with "stagflation," a hitherto unseen combination of slow economic growth, unemploy-ment, and inflation, marked the beginning of the undoing of the variet-ies of welfare states that had developed in the world economy's core in the postwar period. At the same time, the crises helped precipitate the death of the national liberation movements in many of the developing countries, as the world periphery sank under debts and came, in large measure, under the tutelage of the International Monetary Fund (IMF) and World Bank. Later, 1989 marked the beginning of the collapse of the officially communist or "state capitalist" regimes, leaving Western market economies unchallenged by any existing alternatives. By 1992, Francis Fukuyama had announced the "end of History," arguing that the triumph of liberal democracies and liberal economics worldwide marked the final stage in an evolutionary process. Human beings, he argued, could not hope to find more perfect principles along which to organize society: if actually existing liberal democratic economies might be improved in practice, the struggle to improve everyday life would be carried out within the possibilities offered by liberal politi-cal and economic theory.

Although linked with capitalism's structural crisis in the 1970s, the advent of contemporary neoliberal capitalism is not the *spontaneous* expression of underlying economic relations. Instead, its emergence has depended upon a number of factors in conjuncture with the crisis, in particular, the mobilization of organized fractions of capital and the "technical" support of networks of semi-autonomous neoliberal economists, often holding vital positions in national and international financial bodies (Dezalay & Garth 2002). Moreover, if neoliberal capitalism is partly the result of informal regimes operating across transnational corporations (Cutler 2003), it is frequently conjured through favourable rules negotiated, elaborated, and enforced by states and the reconfigured postwar International Financial Institutions, notably the IMF, World Bank, and more recently the World Trade Organization (Coburn 2003: 160–61). Indeed, neoliberal capitalism arguably requires a muscular state, not limited to the policing of populations marginalized by neoliberal policies (Wacquant 2006). Finally, in some cases, neoliberalism has been imposed by military force (Petras & Veltmeyer 2001). In short, fractions of neoliberal capital, or "technocrats" acting on their behalf, if not at their behest, succeeded in institutionalizing rules reproducing and extending further the relative power of capital over labour and the state, often with muscular or even military action.

The role of the declining economic and military hegemon, the United States, is probably difficult to overstate in the emergence of a neoliberal phase of capitalism. The US plays a central if not determining role in the International Financial Institutions (IFIs), supplies many of the world's intellectual and economic elite through its better-known universities (Dezalay & Garth 2002), can use its market power to coerce nations or entice and bribe their elites, and is able to credibly threaten military action when negotiated outcomes fail. In this respect, the well-known circumstances of Chile's precocious conversion to neoliberalism is instructive: following a CIA backed coup against Salvador Allende's democratically elected socialist government in 1973, dictator Augusto Pinochet pursued an austerity policy designed by alumni of the Chicago School of Economics, with the guidance of monetarist and Nobel-prize–winning economist Milton Friedman. In short, the contemporary phase of neoliberal capitalism is the reconfiguration of the capitalist world system to better accommodate the interests of organized, international fractions of capital. Yet this outcome is not the automatic expression of structural factors. Rather, it is the result of opportunistic political struggle by organized capital and other actors, including collaboration between the dominant class in the core and periphery (Navarro 2007: 54–56), in a moment of generalized economic crisis.

Why characterize as neoliberal the contemporary phase of capitalism that Fukuyama celebrated? If classical economic liberalism is about the operation of unfettered markets, neoliberalism is about (re)establishing markets as *the* organizing principle of social life. Typically, this includes commitments to the privatization of formerly public goods and services, the liberalization of trade and financial capital flows, and the dismantling of labour, environmental, and other regulations that are costly for capital. Domestic fiscal reform favourable to national capitalist fractions includes reduced revenue, inheritance, and capital gains and other taxes for the (very) wealthy (Piketty 2001: 547–52; Sutcliffe 2005). Such costly measures are then used to justify the imposition of new constraints on access to "unaffordable" welfare programs, such as unemployment insurance and health care, for instance by imposing user fees or making the criteria for access much stricter. Whether it is pursued "autonomously" by states in the developed core or at the behest of the IFIs, as in much of the world periphery, the general consequence of this reorganization is to shrink alternatives to participation in market relationships. Although greater exposure to the market is supposed to foster individual responsibility and entrepreneurialism while eliminating government waste, its major consequence is to leave the world's vast majority more vulnerable to market vicissitudes, with precarious access to basic "goods" such as adequate food, clean water, health, housing, safe working conditions, and education (Coburn & Coburn 2007).

Of course, there are important variations across and within different parts of the world system regarding the extent to which neoliberal policies are translated into practice. These variations are not idiosyncratic. Instead, they reflect factors like the differential ability of class coalitions to pressure states to resist specific neoliberal policies, as well as the differential ability of state actors to circumvent neoliberal principles unfavourable to its domestic capital fractions. For example, the United States has successfully resisted free trade with respect to the vulnerable domestic textile and agricultural sectors. In Kerala, since the Communist Party of India came to power in 1957 through an alliance of poor tenants and landless labourers on a strong platform of social justice—a platform informed by the struggle for independence—the state has consistently supported an expanded welfare state and protection for the lowest social classes, resisting neoliberal measures sought by the IMF and World Bank (Sandbrook et al. 2007: 65–92). Other important variations in the breadth and types of neoliberal policies implemented exist across the former communist countries, which have embraced "varieties of Eastern European capitalism" (Buchen 2005). In some cases, as in Hungary, they have embarked upon technocratic versions of neoliberalism marked by "ritual calls for sacrifice" (Eyal, Szelényi & Townsley 1998: 103), although heavy-handed moralistic overtones accompanying neoliberal reforms may not be as unique to Eastern Europe as these authors assume. The class coalitions that historically enabled the Scandinavian countries to establish social democratic welfare states, providing citizens with strong alternatives to participation in the market, now allow these states to resist many neoliberal policies (Lindbom & Rothstein 2004). In short, there are important, ongoing, nontrivial differences among state regimes across the world system. Still, in general—if unevenly—varieties of neoliberal states are replacing the varieties of postwar states.

The neoliberal phase of capitalism is a material project embedding goods and services within market relationships, thus shrinking "the commons" and reducing protections from, and alternatives to, market participation. Yet neoliberal capitalism is also an ideological project, a utopia "en voie de réalisation," in the process of becoming (Bourdieu 1998: 108). The same market formulas of privatization, liberalization, deregulation, and tax reforms are applied worldwide, regardless of the specificities of regional, national, and local circumstances. It is taken for granted that the introduction of market mechanisms frees capital, so stimulating entrepreneurialism, economic growth, employment, and, in a virtuous cascade, adequate food, clean water, health, and so on. The underlying assumption is that markets are intrinsically efficient, given a minimum of "good governance" by states. Typically, negative outcomes are explained, not as a result of market failures but rather as a consequence of residual state interference. Although the IMF conceded that the 1997 Asian crisis was *mainly* the result of financial systems' weaknesses, for example, the same "factsheet" adds that it was "made worse by governance issues, notably government involvement in the private sector" (IMF External Relations Department 1999), a remark that likewise denies one main insight of political economy in assuming that markets function outside of state rules. Thus, neoliberal institutions combine with neoliberal ideology in what Smith (2004) has characterized as the "relations of ruling" (73–95).

Less visibly and less formally, neoliberal capitalism's reorganization of social life along market principles means a "colonization of the lifeworld" by market logics (Habermas 1987; Hackett & Carroll 2006: 52–53). As Polanyi (1957) reminds us, markets exist in market *societies*. All aspects of societies are transformed by the fundamental fact of markets as the central organizing principle for social life. It should not be surprising, then, that in a world of commodity exchange there are "black markets" in which almost anything can be bought and sold, including subjects and objects typically formally excluded from the market nexus, such as children and human organs. Market logics seep into every pore of society, transforming the way we appreciate human beings, abstracting them so that they become a commodity like any other, weighted literally as well as metaphorically in terms of costs and benefits. All market societies tend in this direction, but this may be especially true in an era of neoliberalism when the market expands unchallenged by the spectre of the alternative communist system or by national liberation movements. The contemporary phase of neoliberal capitalism, in all its variations, is the worldwide material and ideological terrain within and against which resistance has arisen.

BEYOND THE MARKET: INTERNATIONAL MOVEMENTS AGAINST NEOLIBERAL CAPITALISM

Marxist political economy has a long-standing concern with the potential for movements to fundamentally transform social life. Indeed, one of Marx's major insights was to explain the transition from one mode of production to another as the result of political struggle between opposing classes, struggles themselves related to structural contradictions within the mode of production. Thus, the feudal mode of production was unable to contain the new class dynamics of the emerging bourgeoisie, leading to the breakdown of feudalism and the emergence of early industrial capitalism. Ultimately, Marx predicted the demise of the capitalist mode of production, in its turn, as the result of working-class struggle, arguing that workers concentrated together on assembly lines would recognize their shared interest in overthrowing private ownership of the means of production. This struggle does not triumph in a vacuum, but within the broader context of a capitalist system that is not stable, but subject to recurrent crises. At the same time, it should be emphasized that working-class mobilization is not automatic. Ideologically, the working class must overcome the apparently natural, rational, and inevitable character of the capitalist mode of production, as well as claims that the capitalist system is "in the general interest" (Marx 1978: 172–74). Indeed, Marx's own writings, both scholarly and journalistic, sought to contribute to developing workers' consciousness as distinct from hegemonic bourgeois consciousness. Materially, revolutionary class struggle ultimately seeks to overthrow the institution of private property as *the* major source of inequality, although in practice this must be confronted alongside other forms of inequality organically intertwined with capitalism, including racism and sexism. As Marx cautions, it is the economic structure that is the ultimate guarantor of the bourgeoisie's ideological hegemony, since ownership of the means of mental production enables the exclusion of what Gramsci (1971) called counter-hegemonic voices. If class struggle is the engine of social change, this struggle is inevitably both ideological and material, with the success of the movement partly dependent upon the propitious fragilities of a crisis-ridden capitalist system.

What's in a Name? Describing Contemporary Movements against Capitalism

Yet if Marxist political economy emphasizes the essential role of class struggle in overthrowing capitalism, it must consider actually-existing contemporary movements against capitalism, whether or not they take the anticipated revolutionary form of a self-conscious international working-class movement. The concern here is not "resistance" in its myriad, day-to-day, and sometimes ambiguous forms, although such acts of resistance, both individual and collective, clearly matter. Rather, the concern—at once empirical and analytic—is with organized, self-consciously political, public mobilizations that directly seek to challenge contemporary capitalism. In the last decade, the movement that has arguably most captured the attention of Marxist political economists, among others, as at least potentially filling this role is the "alternative globalization movement," also known in the popular press, less accurately, as the "antiglobalization movement." Announced by the Zapatista uprising in Mexico in 1994, the movement came to the attention of the developed nations with the 1999 protests in Seattle, Washington, against the World Trade Organization and then took on a new form with the first-ever World Social Forum, held in Porto Alegre, Brazil, in January 2001. I will discuss these events in more detail below.

Within the Marxist tradition, both old and new linguistic terms have been mobilized to describe the alternative globalization coalition.[2] Of course, this vocabulary is not innocent but rather expresses theoretical commitments and empirical judgements, making varying assessments about the movement's revolutionary or reactionary potential, its inherited or novel character, its material and ideological contributions and limits. In particular, it questions whether the movement is a contemporary working-class movement, and what this suggests about the movement's likely impact. Indeed, the alternative globalization movement is interesting partly because the tensions within it reveal important controversies in Marxist political economy; such controversies are never "merely" theoretical, since interpretation has crucial implications for political practice. Below, I briefly review central contributions by several Marxist political economists specifically concerned with the alternative globalization movement, considering the insights and arguments of individual authors separately at first, and then together.

Making a case for the ongoing relevance of the working class as *the* engine of social change, the editors of *The Monthly Review* wonder if the "Battle in Seattle" against the World Trade Organization marked "a new internationalism" (Sweezy & Magdoff 2000). Here, the suggestion is that the alternative globalization movement *may* be the latest development in a long history of international working-class movements, dating back at least to Marx's nineteenth-century rallying cry, "Workers of the world, unite!", a call that both participated in and sought to encourage working-class struggle. By raising the possibility of a "new internationalism," *The Monthly Review* editors consider the likelihood of a revived worldwide labour movement that finally includes overt class struggle in the hegemonic world power, the United States, where class conflict is typically submerged within classless nationalist rhetoric (resurgent following the September 11 attacks on the World Trade Center). Despite nationalistic and xenophobic temptations, not least within the American labour movement, the alternative globalization movement is seen as at least potentially representing a new international working-class coalition that challenges capitalism from the hegemonic centre.

David McNally (2002) focuses on the prefigurative potential of the alternative globalization movement, highlighting dynamics that appear most favourable to a socialist project. He writes about "socialism from below: radical democracy for the age of globalization" (238), a characterization that simultaneously contrasts the movement with a world capitalist system inevitability organized "from above" and with the authoritarian, bureaucratic postwar communist states. In particular, McNally highlights the autonomously organized Landless Workers Movement in Brazil, one of the few self-proclaimed socialist currents within the movement; the contingent unfurled a banner containing the words "Another World Is Possible—Only As Socialism" at an early World Social Forum (cited in Callinicos 2003: 85). Yet McNally is cautious about the leading role of labour, narrowly defined, within the movement and within a socialist democratic project more generally. He argues that radical democracy is possible only when the working class mobilizes its most marginalized elements, including women and people of colour; socialist struggle must be grounded in the actual experiences of gendered, racialized, working-class people (221–23). At the same time, "radical activists" within the movement that have too often dismissed unions as merely bureaucratic must support organized labour, taking the struggles of working people seriously and, through their involvement, helping to transform union practices, particularly in the world's core, to become more radical and democratic (264). Despite the movement's ideological success in putting neoliberal institutions

like the World Trade Organization on the defensive (258), McNally
suggests that its future material success will depend upon democratizing organized labour and struggling against the various forms of injus-
tice—including racial and gender discrimination—to which workers
are actually subject.

For Immanuel Wallerstein, the alternative globalization movement is
best understood as the latest development in a long history of "antisys-
temic" struggles that seek to deepen freedom and equality by revolution-
izing a world capitalist system that is antagonistic to both (Wallerstein
2002). Like McNally, and in keeping with his earlier work, Wallerstein
rejects the idea that the movement will be led by an ideal-typical pro-
letariat: the adult, male, salaried factory worker (Wallerstein & Zukin
1989: 438). Reacting against the failure of historical anti-systemic movements in power, including Communist, national liberation, left-popu-
list, and social democratic governments in the former Soviet Union,
Africa, Latin America, and Europe, the 1968 anti-systemic movements
emerged in diverse guises, notably including the once-powerful Maoist
movements, and the "new social movements"—that is, environmentalist, feminist and various "minority" movements such as those of Beurs
in France or Indigenous people in North America and elsewhere. The
Maoists fizzled out, for various reasons, but the other anti-systemic
movements persisted in various forms, ensuring that the main challenge
to world capitalism will emerge from diverse "minorities"—labour, in
its different occupational guises, but also ecological, sexual, feminist,
and other "minority" movements. In this account, the much-remarked
diversity of the alternative globalization movement is not unprecedented,
but the legacy of the prior anti-systemic mobilizations.

Yet, compared to previous anti-systemic movements, alternative
globalization does have particular responsibilities. Given the relatively imminent collapse of the 500-year-old world capitalist system
due to internal contradictions, including the unsustainable use of natural resources, the alternative globalization movement is critical to
deciding the shape of a post-capitalist future (Wallerstein 2005: 38).
Of course, the movement, at least as embodied in the World Social
Forums, has important shortcomings, including a lack of transparency
in decision-making and a stated unwillingness to embrace formal politics. Yet Wallerstein argues that it is the only body that may plausibly
contribute to building a new, democratic, and egalitarian world-system
to replace a world capitalist system that was, in any case, never eternal
and is now entering its terminal phase. This involves not only the collective, democratic imagining of different visions of an egalitarian and
democratic future, but also political action directed toward achieving

egalitarian, democratic social relations at multiple levels, from the local to the transnational (39–40).

William K. Carroll (2006) suggests that, at its best, the "global justice movement" is a counter-hegemonic bloc (see also Evans 2005). This characterization does not imply a purely "idealistic" or discursive vocation, since an effective counter-hegemonic challenge must lay bare the material bases for capital's ideological dominance, as well as tackling the substance of capitalist ideology. Given the hydra-headed nature of capitalist discourse, achieving the latter (like dealing with the former) is not a simple task: there is no single, unitary, transhistorical, and transcultural hegemonic capitalist "story" to defeat. Rather, a variety of myths, motivations, and social roles for various groups are admitted, as long as they are compatible with capital accumulation, encourage consumption, and discourage scrutiny of basic, unequal social relationships (Carroll 2006: 12). Yet neoliberalism, as a particular set of ideological claims, is vulnerable, with its celebration of individual rights and freedoms narrowly interpreted (e.g., to mean consumer choice), its characterization of society as no more than a sum of interacting individuals, its understanding of the state as little more than a guarantor of private property protection (15), and an assemblage of coercive, disciplining practices exercised in the name of "security" (18–19). Against this, the movement is well positioned to reclaim community, solidarity, and justice as positive values, an ideological challenge that must be linked with political action that reclaims the state, as well as local and transnational spaces. At the same time, Carroll suggests, the movement should *embody* solidarity, refusing to celebrate (individual) difference for its own sake and instead articulating common action across working people in both their "old labour" and "new social movement" guises (26). Without such an articulation, both old labour and new social movements, as diverse expressions of the human needs of workers, remain trapped: "ecology," for example, simply becomes green consumerism, and labour "rights" remain premised on ever-increasing, unsustainable consumption. Articulating struggles across working people's movements means recognizing that unalienated human existence requires *fundamental* transformation of social relationships, beyond capitalism.

Finally, although Alex Callinicos (2003) refers to the alternative globalization movement as an "anti-capitalist" movement, he is skeptical of its transformative potential. At present, he argues, the movement is dominated by currents that espouse, at best, ambiguous and contradictory positions as they react against different aspects of the capitalist political economy. First, there are "bourgeois anti-capitalists," who encourage consumers to pressure corporations to carry out less exploitative practices, a stance that, in Callinicos's view, dangerously positions corporations, rather than states, as privileged sites for progressive "development" policies (70–73). Second, there are "localists" who celebrate "good markets," seeking to challenge corporate monopolies by favouring small-scale local producers selling to "the socially aware consumer," as in the Fair Trade movement, for example (74–76). To Callinicos, this stance naively posits normally functioning capitalism, including corporate monopolies, as anomalous. Third, "reformists" focus on humanizing capitalism by redesigning institutions such as the IMF and World Bank, an approach that specifically eschews the transformation of basic capitalist commitments to private property. Finally, "autonomists," although explicitly condemning capitalism, celebrate highly individualized, decentralized acts of resistance. Callinicos regards this approach, theorized in Hardt and Negri's (2004) celebration of the revolutionary potential of "the multitude," as hopelessly utopian in its rejection of coordinated political action. Thus, the alternative globalization movement is seen as multifaceted and contradictory, although with a latent socialist potential—indeed, Callinicos sees his contribution as part of the struggle for a decisive socialist turn within the movement. This turn may be achieved partly through a "transitional programme" (2003: 132–39) of reforms (e.g., cancellation of Third World debt, reduction of the working week) whose combined logic challenges the principles of capitalist social organization.

"A new internationalism," "socialism from below," "anti-systemic movements," "counter-hegemonic bloc," and "anti-capitalist movement": these terms, and the accompanying accounts, combine descriptive statements of the movement as it is with analytical judgements about what might be, if the movement's most promising dynamics—from the point of view of achieving a democratic, socialist future—are encouraged. The descriptive project requires a frank analysis of the movement's limits, including, for example, a tendency to disperse political energies around disarticulated specific "causes." Yet such critical assessments sit alongside a fundamental optimism about the alternative globalization movement's existence—the emergence, however flawed, of an international movement challenging neoliberal forms of capitalism, if less often capitalism itself.

Together, contemporary Marxist political economists suggest that the alternative globalization movement is an ideological project, attacking the taken-for-granted nature of neoliberal common sense, as the contemporary version of a flexible capitalist ideology. The many different movement participants agree at least on this, that "Another World Is Possible" (the official slogan of the World Social Forum), firmly rejecting the notion that there is no alternative to neoliberalism as *the* approach to organizing the world political economy. Still, the movement has many currents, and not all of them question the principle of markets as a basis for organizing human relationships. Instead, some, perhaps a majority, seek relatively limited reforms of corporate behaviour, e.g., via pressure applied directly to for-profit enterprises or through reform of international financial institutions. Such approaches do not entail a critique of capitalism and at the same time typically underestimate the importance of the state as a site for struggle. As a whole, the movement is committed to participative, democratic decision-making, against the inevitably top-down nature of decision-making within capitalism. Although such commitments are not always met with truly democratic practice, they act as prefigurative experiments in collective, democratic decision-making, as well as marking the movement's distance from the bureaucratic totalitarian states of official Communism.

With the possible exception of Magdoff and Sweezy, none of the authors expect that a successful transformative movement against capitalism will be spearheaded by organized, white, male, salaried workers in the world's developed core. They point out that the vast majority of participants in the alternative globalization movement are workers, at least in the sense of selling their labour power in order to make a living (see, for example, Carroll 2006: 25). But they argue that workers' varied occupational status, the historically specific reality of workers' gendered, racialized existences, and the fact that as human beings, workers have multiple capacities for creative, unalienated expression that capitalism cannot satisfy, mean that labour's struggle is inevitably multifaceted. Thus, the alternative globalization movement is acknowledged to be "diverse," and this diversity is not seen as inherently problematic—although the authors warn against depoliticized, postmodern celebrations of "difference" and autonomist celebrations of highly individualized "microresistance" that prevent effective unified political action. Finally, the movement's transnational dimension, both in fact and as a desirable component of the movement as it develops, seems acquired, if not irreversible, continuing a long anti-capitalist tradition of internationalism, going back at least until Marx. Yet the future successes of the movement will depend upon the recognition that internationalism should be pursued alongside, not at the expense of, state and local activism.

Defining Moments in the Movement against Neoliberal Capitalism
At its best, then, the alternative globalization movement is a diverse, transnational movement committed to democratic participatory methods

that challenge contemporary capitalism both ideologically and materially. Of course, in practice, the movement is not this straightforward, with tensions, for example, between a commitment to internationalism and the danger that this might result in abandoning serious efforts to reclaim the state from capital. But before returning to a consideration of the movement's potential and limits, it is worth asking: How did this movement, with its ambitions, its socialist democratic potential, but also its weaknesses, emerge?

An exhaustive approach to this question would chronicle the many struggles against a centuries-old world capitalist system by participants in the alternative globalization movement. These struggles have, of course, been punctuated by many different events, in many different parts of the world system, including, for example, illegal occupations of agricultural territory by landless workers in Brazil, strikes by South Korean labour unions, social and cultural mobilizations by dalits in India, the organization of women's non-profit cooperatives in rural China, the establishment of transnational associations such as the Third World Network based in Malaysia, South African and international movements against the privatization of water, the protests of the Ogoni against foreign oil companies in Nigeria, and so on (for an overview, see Amin & Houtart 2002; Forum mondial des alternatives 2004). Many of these events have long histories; for example, the occupation of agricultural land by landless workers in Brazil has occurred sporadically for decades, across both democratic and authoritarian state regimes. Rather than attempt such an exhaustive history of the different participants within the movement, I sketch a brief history of three of the movement's emblematic moments. The aim is *not* to reduce the alternative globalization movement to a series of recent "events," but simply to juxtapose these moments with their commonalities and contradictions as one entry point into the description and analysis of the movement.

THE ZAPATISTA UPRISING: LINKING LOCAL AND GLOBAL STRUGGLES

Arguably, the initial event that announced the emergence of an international movement against neoliberalism was the military uprising by the Zapatista National Liberation Army (Ejército Zapatista de Liberación Nacional or EZLN) in Chiapas, Mexico, on January 1, 1994, the date that the North American Free Trade Agreement (NAFTA) entered into force (Le Bot 2003). The movement's implicit articulation between a local, mainly indigenous movement and broader struggles against neoliberalism, as exemplified in NAFTA, was made explicit two years later with the "First Intercontinental Gathering for Humanity and against Neo-liberalism," held in 1996. The gathering attracted several thousand people, mostly youth from the United States, Canada, and South America. In the declaration announcing the conference, the Zapatistas denounced neoliberalism as an "historic crime in the concentration of privileges, wealth and impunities, [which] democratizes misery and hopelessness" and called for an opposition movement, "an international of hope" (EZLN 1996). The Zapatistas, somewhat surprised by the international resonance of their uprising, nonetheless rejected the idea of setting an example for others:

> ... don't follow [our example]. We think that everyone has to build his and her own experience and not repeat models.... We think that the people have enough courage and wisdom to build their own process and their own movements, because they have their own histories. (Subcomandante Marcos, spokesperson for the ELZN, quoted in Muñoz Ramírez 2004)

As an organization of armed resistance, the Zapatistas were subsequently excluded from the World Social Forum and other events premised on non-violence. However, the armed rebellion and subsequent conference were arguably among the first to receive broad international attention for linking local struggles with the potential for an international movement against liberalization. Prefiguring later developments, the Zapatistas insisted upon the importance of decentralized, participatory methods of organizing, despite the visibility and media popularity of Subcomandante Marcos, as well as the value of differentiated identities and strategies.

THE BATTLE IN SEATTLE: BRINGING DISSENT TO THE DEVELOPED CORE
The second main event in the history of the movement was the "Battle in Seattle," the protest against the "Millenium Round" negotiations of the World Trade Organization held in Seattle, Washington, in November and December 1999 (see Coburn 2003 for a brief analysis of the protest). The negotiations within the WTO, established in 1995 as the successor to the postwar General Agreement on Tariffs and Trade (GATT), were ambitious, seeking agreement among the more than one hundred member states on a wide range of measures from trade liberalization to protection for intellectual property and equal treatment for foreign and domestic investors. In opposition to this wide-ranging program, tens of thousands of protestors descended into the streets, marching under banners with slogans such as "No New Round, Instead Turnaround!", also the title of a petition endorsed by more than 1,500 organizations; "WTO/Democracy," with arrows pointing in opposing directions; and

"Teamsters and Turtles Together at Last!", an allusion to the presence of the Teamsters' unions alongside environmental activists. The protestors successfully blocked the opening speech and disrupted access to the conference. A state of emergency was declared, nearly a hundred activists were hospitalized because of police violence, and hundreds of others were arrested. The meetings, already facing important obstacles because of disagreements among member states over textile and agricultural subsidies, investment rules, and other topics, collapsed with an admission by the organizers that the discussions had been a "failure." Not least because the protests took place in the United States, the (declining) hegemon, the "Battle in Seattle" became an explicit reference for subsequent protests organized "in the spirit of Seattle": for example, against the IMF and World Bank in Prague on September 26, 2000; during the Asia-European Union meetings in Seoul on October 20–21, 2000; and in Genoa on July 20–21, 2000, during the meeting of the G8, the eight wealthiest developed nations, when an activist, Carlo Giuliani, was killed by police.

THE WORLD SOCIAL FORUM: SEIZING THE INITIATIVE BACK FROM CAPITAL

The third defining moment in the history of the movement was the establishment of the "World Social Forums," initiated principally by the Landless Workers Movement in Brazil and, in France, by ATTAC,[3] an association advocating a tax on speculative financial capital movements, using the proceeds for a development fund (Evans 2000). Initially held January 25–31, 2001, in Porto Alegre, Brazil, a municipality that had experimented successfully with participatory budgets for a decade, the WSF was convened in parallel with the World Economic Forum of business leaders traditionally held in Davos, Switzerland. The Forum was an attempt to move beyond reacting to initiatives taken by representatives of capital, to fostering autonomous discussion and organizing among movement participants. Held annually, the World Social Forum officially summarizes itself as an "open meeting place where social movements, networks, NGOs and other civil society organizations opposed to neo-liberalism and a world dominated by capital or by any form of imperialism come together to pursue their thinking, to debate ideas democratically, for formulate proposals, share their experiences freely and network for effective action" (WSF 2007).

In principle, the World Social Forum does not allow the participation of political parties, although members of such parties are allowed to participate as "private persons." As a forum, the WSF does not issue any common platforms, including from its 100-strong international organizing council, although various organizations operating from within the WSF have issued charters, sometimes misrepresented as official Forum statements, e.g., the Call of Social Movements at Porto Alegre II, and the Bamako Appeal. Following the first gatherings, the WSF moved to Mumbai, India, in 2004, then took place in a "polycentric form" in Bamako (Mali), Caracas (Venezuela), and Karachi (Pakistan) in 2006, and finally was organized in 2007 in Nairobi, Kenya. Many of these events attracted large numbers. For example, the Mumbai WSF had approximately 75,000 participants and 1,500 organizations representing 115 countries (Morgan 2006: 93). During this period, the WSF inspired other social forums, including the European and Asian Social Forums, as well as smaller events such as the 2005 Russian Social Forum. In 2008, the World Social Forum was replaced by a Global Day of Action on January 26, to coincide with the World Economic Forum in Davos, with mostly small, local, and regional protests autonomously proposed and organized, in some eighty countries, under the slogan "Act together for another world" (WSF 2008). Following the February 2009 forum in Belém, Brazil, the next World Social Forum will be held in Dakar, Senegal, in 2011.

The Alternative Globalization Movement: Tensions and Contradictions

As even this cursory summary suggests, the alternative globalization movement already has a history that is not without its tensions and contradictions. In inaugurating the World Social Forums, the movement sought to increase its autonomy, both *vis-à-vis* governments and political parties, but also from capital. The aim was to seize the initiative back from capital, a shift that the change in vocabulary from "antiglobalization" to "alterglobalization" and "alternative globalization" sought to capture. In this, the WSF has been only partially successful. Indeed, the decision to hold the WSF in parallel with the World Economic Forum, at least initially, arguably implies symmetry between these events, when clearly the two Forums have vastly unequal financial and organizational resources, as well as unequal access to political power. Notably, the WEF can translate its discussions into policies in ways that the WSF cannot. Arguably, this asymmetry is exacerbated, since the WSF specifically rejects the idea of (official) alliances between the movement and political parties, making the kind of class alliance central to the most important achievements of social democratic welfare state—i.e., in health, literacy, the schooling of female children, and so on (Esping-Andersen 1990; Sandbrook et al. 2007)—more difficult. The unofficial presence of politicians and political parties, including President Luis "Lula" Da Silva of Brazil and President Hugo Chávez of

Venezuela, among others—with Chávez unofficially "closing" the WSF
at Porto Alegre in 2005 by giving a speech in Gigantinho stadium—suggests that efforts to hermetically seal off the Forum from political parties are, in any case, difficult if not impossible to maintain in practice.
Since progressive political parties need close connections with grassroots organizations if they are to counterbalance capital and a mostly
hostile media when in government (Carroll & Ratner 2005), the price
of the WSF's principled, official exclusion of political parties may represent a missed opportunity to generate support for progressive governments and policies nationally. Seizing back the political initiative from
capital is complicated when alliances with formal political parties are
a priori excluded.

The ability of the World Social Forum and the alternative globalization movement to maintain the initiative in a world where it is structurally disadvantaged compared to capital is not simple, as the aftermath
of the September 11th attacks on the United States illustrates. Until
September 11th, the movement's main success had been ideological,
changing the international political climate so that neoliberal capitalism became debatable, rather than taken-for-granted "common sense."
Following September 11th, the US government, in particular, sought to
make this debate irrelevant, partly by discrediting the opposition: *the
major world struggle was now to be defined* (once again) in nationalistic terms, as between the United States and its allies against (Islamic)
terrorists, a struggle sometimes cast in essentialist cultural terms as a
"clash of civilizations." In this calculus, criticism of the United States'
neoliberal policies and capitalism are un-American, making the alternative globalization movement a functional partner with terrorists. At the
same time, materially, aggressive attacks on civil liberties in the name of
"security" and the "war against terror," particularly targeting migrants
and people of colour, have circumscribed the space for social protest,
especially in the Anglo-Saxon world where neoliberal measures have
been historically the strongest (Beaudet 2002; Zarifian 2002).[4] For the
rest of the world, September 11th became justification for further armed
intervention by the United States, with the wars in Afghanistan and Iraq,
but also accentuated militarization, especially marked in South and
Latin America (as in the Colombia Plan, for example). In this respect,
the events of September 11th were less an excuse for a radical new politics than justification for ongoing American military interventionism
(Achar 2002: 263). In short, the events of September 11th were used
by the American government, in particular, to make counter-hegemonic
initiatives more difficult, particularly within the US and elsewhere in
the Anglo-Saxon world.

The alternative globalization movement's initial response was to wage a defensive ideological battle. Two 2002 reports of the World Social Forum International Council mentioned the events. These were far from being the focus of the reports, however, which instead rejected the notion of a functional alliance between the alternative globalization movement and the authors of the attack and simultaneously insisted upon the movement's ongoing relevance. Specifically, the first report emphasized that "all the members of the World Social Forum have unanimously condemned ... the criminal attacks" (WSF International Council 2002a), while the second insisted that "September 11th did not ... interrupt the struggle of movements" (WSF International Council 2002b)—i.e., since the 2002 World Social Forum went ahead as planned, with more participants from a wider range of countries than at the inaugural Forum. The movement, which had hitherto been relatively silent on security and military questions (Achar 2002: 263), now noted that "[t]he struggle for peace ... does not cancel out the struggle against neoliberal globalization. Both are core elements of our agenda" (WSF International Council 2002b). At the same time, both activists and organic intellectuals for the movement began to theorize contemporary American imperialism and "political Islam," often building upon a Marxist political economy long critical of imperialism as an integral part of the world capitalist system. Therefore, among others, Amin (2002) argued that the true "functional alliance" is not between alternative globalization activists and terrorism, but between capital and political Islam: historically, insofar as the United States armed political Islamists during the Cold War and supported them against national-liberation movements, and ideologically, since both the US and political Islamists displace social (class) struggles by focussing on conflict between supposedly transhistorical cultural communities (Amin 2002: 99; see also Achar 2002; Zarifian 2002: 197). Yet such critical analytical efforts and huge anti-war protests, overlapping with the alternative globalization movement, did not succeed in stopping the wars in Afghanistan or Iraq, nor have they had major success in limiting legislation attacking basic civil liberties in the name of the "war on terror."

Another source of tension within the movement is the imbalance between activists and organizations from the global core and those from the periphery. In particular, decisions about where to hold the WSFs reflect a desire to recognize struggles in the periphery, where the vast majority of the world's people live, where the inequalities linked with neoliberal capitalism are among the most striking, and where many of the most dynamic, committed struggles against capitalism take place. Symbolically, then, this shift recognized the central role of movements from these areas while pragmatically enabling the participation of local movements and activists from the "global South" who—like the disadvantaged in the world's core—may otherwise have difficulties meeting basic travel and other costs associated with attending the Forum. Certainly, the evidence suggests that the protests prior to the WSFs were heavily dominated by organizations and activists from the developed nations: a petition that circulated at the Seattle protests against the WTO was dominated by organizational signatories from just three countries— the United States, Canada, and the United Kingdom (40 per cent)—and the vast majority (about 70 per cent) of organizations that signed were from developed nations. Least developed and Eastern European countries combined comprised fewer than 5 per cent of the organizational signatories (Coburn 2003: 172). Furthermore, albeit on a much smaller scale, the 2005 Hong Kong protest against the WTO was dominated by 1,500 Korean workers who had travelled to continue the "offshore struggle" against the WTO (Sohi 2006: 356), suggesting that participation is heavily biased toward local and regional activists. Therefore, the decision to move the WSF amongst various locations in the global periphery, besides helping it resist institutionalization, has allowed for more participation from organizations and activists from these areas. Indeed, one of the (few?) positive outcomes of the WSF in Nairobi— which was plagued by important problems, including a remote location, heavily armed private security guards, prohibitive entry fees, corporate-sponsored telecommunications, and high charges for food and even water (Oloo 2007)—was that the Forum enabled African participation and exchanges, although with relatively few Kenyan participants.

Finally, there is some question about the extent to which the movement successfully differentiates itself from capital and the "ruling relations." Earlier, I noted that the establishment of the WSF was partly an attempt to ensure the autonomy of the movement, both from capital and from formal political parties. Yet Dezalay and Garth (2005) have suggested that it is increasingly possible to have a "career" as an activist, drawing "symbolic capital," as well as actual wages and other benefits, such as subsidized travel, from working for non-governmental organizations (NGOs). Certainly, there is a danger that frequenting the United Nations, for example, becomes a full-time engagement for actors who then become decreasingly engaged with everyday protest and actions. Symptomatic of this danger, a few well-known "activists" at one of the Porto Alegre Forums issued a declaration from the lobby of a luxury hotel (Pleyers 2006). At the same time, the movement against neoliberal capitalism is not parallel with the universe of NGOs, which is much larger than the movement, having grown exponentially from the 1970s to the 1990s (Tarrow 2005: 188–89); NGOs are only one element in the movement, which also includes much more decentralized associations, "affinity groups," and so on. These have widely varying degrees of engagement with states, IFIs, and other official bodies—a source of considerable tension within the movement, as more professionalized NGOs seek to influence, for example, World Trade Organization proceedings as officially invited guests while more horizontal groups reject such engagement as potentially legitimizing the decisions taken within such institutions. Ultimately, the movement's rich organizational ecology may be protective: the movement is vast and varied enough that it cannot be reduced to those actors closest to institutionalized sources of power, the circuits of capital.

LOCAL, NATIONAL, GLOBAL

The WSF, the Battle in Seattle, and the Zapatista uprising and conference against neoliberalism are among the more visible events marking the movement's history. Behind these there are less visible moments, in particular the processes by which mainly local, national, and regional movements became articulated, to varying degrees and with varying consistency, with an international movement against neoliberal capitalism.

Clearly, there are objective reasons why different movements might be expected to protest neoliberal capitalism. To artificially disaggregate components of the movement for the sake of analysis, the cases of labour, women, and the environmental movement are instructive. Among other factors, labour faces increasing exploitation in a neoliberal era where the relative power of capital is enhanced, partly through the increasingly credible threat of transnational capital mobility (Ross & Trachte 1990). With the important exception of the European Union,[5] free trade and investment agreements that specifically facilitate the mobility of goods, capital, and business persons rarely contain parallel provisions for working-class labour mobility. At the same time, women are confronted with a shrinking welfare state, simultaneously depriving them of formal employment in the public sector where women's paid labour is concentrated, while increasingly burdening women with caregiving tasks that were formerly partly socialized in the welfare state (Coburn 2005). For their part, environmental groups are confronted with the "deregulation" of environmental laws costly to capital. For example, enhanced trade liberalization rules specifically forbid the enforcement of "protectionist" national environmental regulations (Coburn 2003), while at the national level state environmental agencies are deprived of funds, making enforcement of environmental laws difficult. In short, processes of privatization, liberalization, and deregulation central to neoliberal capitalism create enlarged market spaces that threaten the interests of workers, women, and those acting out of concern for the environment, among others.

To such "objective" reasons for the emergence of opposition to neoliberalism may be added the relative *visibility* of many neoliberal policy measures, internationally as well as nationally. Thus, for example, free trade and investment agreements must be negotiated and ratified by states. Cuts to welfare programs, from health to education, are frequently formally announced by governments. The privatization of nationalized industries and the lifting of subsidies on basic foodstuffs are not easily disguised. Of course, other neoliberal policies may be less visible or implemented in less visible ways. For example, tax credits for the very wealthy may pass relatively unperceived, at least in the short and medium term. Governments may choose *not* to announce cuts to public services, instead reducing funding with the consequence that the standards of care deteriorate. Subsequently, the formerly supportive middle class may withdraw political support for degraded public services. In this case, the decision to privatize services may then appear less brutal. Still, many neoliberal policies are relatively formalized, direct, and visible. Because they typically have important negative effects on the vast majority, including labour and women as well as the environment, there are good reasons to expect popular opposition to neoliberalism to emerge.

Yet it is clear that significant obstacles to coordinated international activism persist, even given what might appear to be an objective shared interest in forming oppositional coalitions. As Marx reminds us, there are ideological obstacles. This includes the seeming inevitability of neoliberal reforms, at least until the early 1990s: Fukuyama's "end of History" remarks were made at a time when neoliberal market solutions appeared to be the only reasonable, or at least the only possible, route for reform. Yet, there are also conflicts among the dominated classes in the world capitalist system that make international mobilization, in particular, unlikely. Thus, for example, Evans (2000) argues that workers may see workers in other countries primarily as competitors rather than as partners with common labour concerns. Women's organizations face the significant challenges of operating across different regions of the world system with their vastly different histories and unequal material and normative resources. Environmental movements are not welcomed universally as "progressive." In particular, "conservation" efforts initiated in the world core may be perceived as insensitive to basic human needs in the global periphery. Of course, many of these tensions are not new. With the introduction of laws threatening to privatize formerly public commons, Marx sided emphatically with poor people and against new bourgeois property laws hiding behind what he castigated as the artificial "rights of trees" (Marx 2007: 93–94). In sum, an objective interest in opposing neoliberal capitalism may not be sufficient to overcome hegemonic ideologies legitimizing and naturalizing neoliberalism, especially when combined with tensions among the dominated classes. These dominated classes are not homogeneous, but act from differentiated social locations across an uneven world capitalist system.

The Council of Canadians: Local, National, and Transnational Activism

In this context, it is useful to consider an empirical case of how a local, in this case, ostensibly national, social actor became implicated in the transnational movement against neoliberal capitalism. The Council of Canadians (COC) was established in 1985 by a "handful" of prominent Canadians, including novelist Margaret Atwood, Bob White, president of the Canadian Auto Workers' Union and later of the Canadian Labour Congress, and environmentalist David Suzuki, with a focus on "the future of Canada as a nation-state on the North American continent" (COC 2007). In particular, the COC was part of the "Pro-Canada," later Action Canada, network of "labour unions, churches, women, social justice activists, farmers, cultural workers, First Nations peoples and others" (COC 2007), which mobilized unsuccessfully against the Canada-United States Free Trade Agreement, which became law following the re-election of Brian Mulroney's Progressive Conservative government in 1988. Arguing that closer economic integration with the United States threatened Canadian sovereignty, the COC maintained that "the trade agreement would be the first step to the elimination of our social security, our distinct culture, and our stewardship over our natural resources and would make us infinitely weaker as a nation" (COC 2007). Subsequently, the COC continued its struggle against the North American Free Trade Agreement (NAFTA) for Canada, the United States, and Mexico, which was passed on January 1, 1994 under the Liberal government.

Following this second major defeat, the COC suffered an internal crisis and only refrained from disbanding after a poll of its members suggested that the COC could play an important role defending Canada's social programs. Partly as a result of the continent-wide ties that had been formed during the struggle against NAFTA, the COC became increasingly internationalized. Indeed, the unsuccessful mobilization against continental free trade led naturally to campaigns against the Multilateral Agreement on Investment (MAI), which among other measures would have required equal treatment of foreign and domestic investors among signatory nations, and then to the World Trade Organization, where a new investment agreement was proposed following the defeat of the MAI at the level of the Organization for Economic Cooperation and Development (OECD). During this time, new networks led to an increasingly self-conscious embrace of internationalism. The Council writes that

> In building continental and international alliances, we realized that we had more in common with one another than with our own [political] leaders and that to fight for health care or cultural diversity in Canada necessitated fighting for those rights everywhere. Our campaigns were increasingly based on international solidarity and a critique of global corporate rule. And we no longer saw U.S. imperialism as the only place where this corporate tyranny existed. (COC 2007)

The COC has since been embedded in international networks and actions, for example, participating in the International Forum on Globalization, signing petitions and participating in protests against the WTO in Seattle, and, subsequently, building campaigns in coordination with a worldwide movement against the sale of the "global commons" and, in particular, water. The COC now maintains that it would be a "mistake" to return to the nationalism of the 1970s and 1980s, especially insofar as such a perspective excludes a consideration of "class, youth and colour" (COC 2007).

Nonetheless, it would be misleading to suggest that the Council of Canadians has shifted *from* the national *to* the international level. Rather, it remains active locally, through local chapter initiatives, and many of its criticisms and actions target the federal state of Canada, including both Canada-wide legislation but also Canada's positions with respect to international treaties (e.g., Kyoto) and organizations (such as the World Trade Organization). Indeed, the structure of the Council of Canadians mirrors the federal structure of the Canadian state, with a federal office and four regional offices, in addition to defined "campaigns" ("health," "water," "trade," "peace," etc., but not "labour"), each steered by a paid staff person. At the same time, international activism and partnerships with, for example, the worldwide movement against the privatization of water, are pursued *alongside* national and local actions. At times, this articulation has meant a reconceptualization of national concerns. For example, COC chair Maude Barlow argues that while formerly the organization spoke of "protecting Canada's social programmes" against pressures toward downward North American integration, they now (also) speak of fighting for the *principle* of sovereignty, of self-governance (quoted in Patterson 2005: 21). This way of framing the struggle makes the links between the COC's struggles and those of others around the world more obvious: no longer simply a nationalistic defense of specifically Canadian social programs, the COC's activities are, in addition, linked with worldwide struggles for democratic decision-making.

The brief and inevitably incomplete description of this case obviously cannot substitute for a more systematic analysis of the movement as a whole, either at an organizational level or at the level of individual activists. Moreover, the COC has particular characteristics that, despite its nationalistic orientation, might have enabled the organization's shift to include a more international outlook as well. For example, the COC was founded by members with quite different areas of expertise, including labour, culture, and the environment, and, as a member of the Action-Canada Network, was embedded in a transnational community of highly differentiated organizations. This experience likely facilitated later cooperation with international movements with diverse priorities. In addition, the COC has a strong formal structure, which likely enhances the COC's ability to interact with other formal organizations for the purposes of networking, and Barlow has been its chairperson since 1988. This is quite different from the radically decentralized, participatory structures of some of the other currents opposing neoliberal capitalism, yet it may have facilitated, albeit in a highly personalized way, the progressive development of expertise and contacts. Finally, the COC is located in one of the "richest underdeveloped countries in the world" (Levitt 2002: 25). This means certain material-resource advantages for international organizing, from paying for plane tickets to the WSF and other protests, to maintaining and using infrastructures for communications, from traditional mailing to establishing and renewing an important, professional presence on the internet. Of course, relative privilege is not only enabling but may imply certain constraints (Antrobus 2007: 15), particularly when coordinating across class and education lines, whether across or within the "core" or "periphery."

If the COC has particular characteristics that may have facilitated its shift from a national to an international orientation, it is by no means totally idiosyncratic. While remaining aware of its specificities, the organization's trajectory is suggestive. Although initially established with a nationalistic outlook, the COC shifted its "vision"—to use its own terminology—to articulate national alongside international concerns. This was partly as a result of networks, discussions, and contacts forged with others engaged in a struggle against a neoliberal agenda that was itself increasingly internationalized. Thus, neoliberal forms of capitalism were initially organized around national fractions and coordinated through states whose autonomy within capitalism is only ever relative. Even so, such apparently national initiatives were already partially transnationalized in that they included strong elements of mimetism: it is probably not incidental that Mulroney repeatedly and publicly deferred to Ronald Reagan, referring to him as "sir." Subsequently, the internationalization went further and became progressively more institutionalized, first via the continent-wide free trade and investment agreements and then via truly international forums like the OECD and the WTO. The COC's shift from national to also include international activities and outlook is thus a pragmatic shift: resistance became transnational in response to the transnationalization of the neoliberal initiatives on behalf of capital. Although this may not be a necessary outcome of transnationalization, it is worth noting that the COC radicalized and broadened its agenda as it became more international. In particular, the COC shifted from a focus on American corporations to corporate hegemony broadly defined, and from a preoccupation with trade to other issues related to the expansion of the market, notably the privatization of the "global commons." Finally, as remarked earlier, the COC has regretted its early failure to consider the salience of the notion of "class," although its analyses tend to focus, for example, on "citizens" rather than on working people as such. Nonetheless, this recognition suggests some growing appreciation, if mainly rhetorical so far, of the salience of critiques, not just of corporate power, but of a capitalist system that organizes social relationships as unequal class relationships, within Canada and worldwide.

THE ALTERNATIVE GLOBALIZATION MOVEMENT: BEYOND CAPITALISM, TOWARD A BETTER WORLD?

As I noted at the outset of this chapter, the problem for the alternative globalization movement is that the world capitalist system is both the object of struggle and the terrain within which the struggle is being fought. This means that the movement is constantly susceptible to being captured by dynamics and inequalities that work against its aims. This is true across the whole range of its activities and even with respect to the means it uses to coordinate its activities: the movement confronts systemic barriers as it seeks to move "beyond capitalism" and struggles for a better—more just, more democratic, more equal—world.

Thus, for example, the alternative globalization movement has made significant use of the new communications technologies, particularly the internet, to coordinate and make public its activities, reports, debates, protests, as well as to launch alternative media, like indymedia, established during the Seattle protests as a form of independent media refusing all corporate, government, or foundation funding. Yet, inevitably, access to the internet and especially the ability to provide high-quality content to the internet is uneven, reflecting both inequalities between capital and others, as well as inequalities among working people across the world capitalist system (Calhoun 2003). Movements in the world periphery, for example, including the former communist countries, simply do not have the same access and presence as well-funded organizations in the developed core, which in turn may have difficulty competing with capital, for example in terms of having professionalized, accessible content that is frequently updated.

In addition, the movement has its own "organic intellectuals," including Callinicos, Wallerstein, and others cited in these pages, who are sympathetic to the movement's aims and who seek to make rigorous analyses of the movement available to activists. Inevitably, however, these intellectuals are not nearly as well connected with the circuits of power and do not have nearly as many resources (from "independent" foundations, the government, and so on) to make and publish their cases as are those sympathetic to capital. Neoliberal economists hold positions in finance and trade ministries that negotiate international financial and trade agreements and are invited, for example, as experts to the Davos economic summits. In contrast, the organic intellectuals of the alternative globalization movement can only expect to affect political decision-making much more indirectly through their involvement in the movement and, often, in academia (although typically not in the best-funded business and economics departments).

Further, the movement's vocabulary was, in large part, developed within the 500-year-old capitalist system. Such inherited discourses, when they are not rejected outright, must be reinfused with new meanings. The established liberal rhetoric around individual human rights, for example, has been mobilized for the new purpose of limiting the encroachment of markets, as with contemporary efforts to declare access to water a right and restrict its commercialization, or with similar campaigns to protect the right of peasants to produce, use, share, and store seeds, rather than being required to pay agricultural businesses for new seed every year. However, such rights, even if enshrined in charters, are likely to be disregarded in ways that are not idiosyncratic, but reflect capitalism's basic, unequal structures (Teeple 2004). Further, as Teeple also points out, there is the danger that the use of rights rhetoric will mean that questions that should be a matter of democratic discussion become "legal" rights decided by a handful of experts in courts instead. Building counter-hegemonic discourse and practice is susceptible to capture by existing structures in this way.

Finally, the criticism that the alternative globalization movement is simply talk and no action—a criticism confirmed rather than refuted by the relatively small, local, low-profile actions undertaken during the Global Day of Action in January 2008—is similarly linked to the difficulties of manoeuvring in a political world structured in favour of capital. Thus, the refusal to articulate such actions with organized political parties because of a fear of being captured by them is itself informed by the recognition of the limits of "bourgeois" liberal democracy. Radical political action, and even peaceful political protest, often carries a heavy price when capital and capitalism are directly targeted. This is a lesson that may be familiar, say, to the Brazilian Landless Workers' Movement but was less familiar in the developed core—until the death of an activist and the serious injury of many hundreds more in the Genoa 2000 protests. Political activism that matters is therefore discouraged, often by the heavy hand of the state and its representatives.

To these are added further obstacles, not least a flexible capitalist ideology that is arguably already post-neoliberal, insofar as it incorporates some aspects of the critique of neoliberalism. The World Bank, for instance, is now preoccupied by the question of poverty, although it resolutely avoids class analysis. At the same time, the International Financial Institutions and many non-profit foundations have become increasingly concerned with "good governance," particularly with respect to states. It is no longer state interference *per se* that is seen as disturbing the proper functioning of markets; rather, the problem is "incorrect" state behaviour that must be remedied. From this point of view, concerns about "corruption," for example, are simply another way of suggesting that (improperly functioning) states are the problem, and markets the solution. This post-neoliberal ideology, like its neoliberal predecessor, will not be without its internal contradictions and weaknesses, but it means that the alternative globalization movement is struggling against an adaptable, moving target.

Other developments are likely more propitious for the movement. The International Monetary Fund's role has dramatically declined over the last decade, in terms of loans to the developing world, and with it the ability of the organization to demand structural adjustment programs that enhance market structures. The rising importance of China and India and the challenge they represent to American hegemony *may* lead to slightly enhanced autonomy for the developing countries, particularly Africa: states may be able to play off Chinese and American bids for influence, in the same way that Cold War competition created some space for autonomy in the global periphery (although alongside the periphery's militarization, another existing threat). The alternative globalization movement may be able to use this enhanced state autonomy as it struggles for progressive social reforms. The emptying out of the rural areas in the world, so that now more than 50 per cent of humanity lives in cities, means the decreasing ability of capital to relocate to regions where recent urban migrants may be superexploited to maintain profit margins (Wallerstein 2000). In turn, this suggests enhanced relative power for labour over time. The environmental crisis means there are absolute limits to capitalist expansion, although there is also the very real possibility that the profound changes in capitalism required to prevent ecological disaster will come "too late," not so much for the planet, which will continue, but for the existing human, animal, and plant life on it.

In short, there are, as always, recurrent structural antagonisms within capitalism that predictably, result in crisis. However, the exact shape and form of these crises is always specific, reflecting the particular play of class forces within any given historical moment of capitalism. Capital will seek to resolve the current crisis on the backs of the dominated, although the exact form that this capital counteroffensive will take, beyond neoliberalism, is not yet clearly defined. At the same time, crises are moments of uncertainty—not least ideological uncertainty—that may allow the alternative globalization movement some increased, relative power, and not only at the margins.

Despite recognition of the strengths of an adaptable capitalist system and of the limits of the alternative globalization movement, there is optimism around the latest anti-capitalist movement. This optimism is *necessary* as a spur for political action, but it is not merely strategic. Rather, it is based upon the recognition of the ultimately ephemeral nature of any existing political economy, the possibility for change through collective struggle. The direction of change is not certain—a reality underlined by Amin in a recent article entitled "Beyond liberal globalization: a better world—or worse?" (2002). But this uncertainty only underscores the importance of the alternative globalization movement, which, however flawed, seems the only credible candidate to lead an international struggle, articulated with local and national activism, for *progressive* change. In this light, it is simply historical truth to proclaim, with the movement, that another world is possible—and it is an urgent, human necessity that this new world be a better one.

NOTES

1   Thank you to David Coburn for his comments on several drafts of this paper, and to two anonymous referees for helpful comments on an earlier version.

2   Obviously, Marxist political economists do not have a monopoly on naming the movement. An early term, probably bestowed by an unsympathetic media, was "antiglobalization," a label supposed to identify the extent to which activists opposed neoliberal globalization, but simultaneously implying that the only possible form of globalization is neoliberal. Subsequent terms tended to emphasize the movement's oppositional character, although more vaguely, as with "les nouveaux mouvements contestataires," the new contestatory movements (Sommier 2001). Bourdieu (1998) spoke about "la résistance contre l'invasion néo-libérale," the resistance against the neoliberal invasion. Della Porta and Mosca (2007), borrowing from Italian activists, refer to "the movement of movements" and "the global justice movement." Within an elaborate theoretical context, Hardt and Negri (2004) talk about the "multitude," a term that arguably joins neoliberalism in celebrating the individual, rather than class or other social movements as the subject of history (Carroll 2006). Finally, others emphasize the movement in more narrowly political terms, writing of "un mouvement citoyen international," an international citizens' movement (Favreau, Larose & Fall 2004).

3   The ATTAC acronym has not changed, but its name has undergone several permutations. Originally proposed as an "Action pour une taxe Tobin d'aide aux citoyens," it then became "Action pour une taxation des transactions financières pour l'aide aux citoyens," followed by "Action pour une taxation des transactions financières et pour l'aide aux citoyens." The June 2009 ATTAC constitution names the organization the "Association pour la taxation des transactions financières et pour l'action citoyenne."

4   It is worth insisting that the "climate of fear" (Zarifian 2002) fostered by the American government after the September 11th attacks is most pronounced in the anglophone, neoliberal nations of the United States, Canada, the United Kingdom, and possibly also Australia. France, for example, is not especially immune to anti-Arab and anti-Muslim sentiment, especially as connected with youth in the impoverished Parisian suburbs. Nor is France a stranger to "security"-oriented rhetoric, which was successfully employed by the far-right presidential candidate Jean-Marie Le Pen, vaulting him into the final round of the presidential elections in 2002, and which is now used by President Nicolas Sarkozy, partly to justify Draconian policies against illegal immigrants (often working, paying taxes, with children in French schools). But these measures are not (explicitly) linked with "the war on terrorism," nor is the notion of a nation at war omnipresent—perhaps in the absence of Fox News and other channels regularly carrying "terror alerts," and also given the fact that France did not participate in the war in Iraq. The climate of fear found in the Anglo-Saxon countries is not universal, and its relevance to Europe and the rest of the world should not be exaggerated.

5   According to the European Union, "Free movement of persons is one of the most **fundamental freedoms** guaranteed by Community law. It includes

the right for EU nationals **to move** to another EU Member State **to take up employment** and establish themselves in the host State with family members. EU Member States are **precluded** from directly or indirectly **discriminating** against **migrant workers** and their families on the basis of their nationality. EU migrant workers and their families are entitled to **equal treatment** not only in employment related matters, but also as regards public housing, tax advantages and social advantages" (Commission of the European Communities 2006: 3; bold in original). Of course, in practice, states may or may not respect this right; for example, Italy has passed legislation that criminalizes the Roma population and does not recognize their right to free movement of persons.

REFERENCES

Achar, G. 2002. "La militarisation du monde et les nouvelles conditions de la paix." In S. Amin and F. Houtart (eds.), *La mondialisation des résistances: l'état des luttes 2002*. Paris: l'Harmattan. 257–66.

Amin, S. 2002. "Le monde arabe et le moyen-orient." In S. Amin and F. Houtart (eds.), *La mondialisation des résistances: l'état des luttes 2002*. Paris: l'Harmattan. 95–124.

Amin, S. 2006. "Au-delà de la mondialisation libérale: un monde meilleur ou pire?" *Actuel Marx* 40: 102–22.

Amin, S., and F. Houtart (eds.). 2002. *La mondialisation des resistances: l'état des luttes 2002*. Paris: l'Harmattan.

Antrobus, P. 2007. *Le mouvement mondial des femmes*. Paris: Enjeux Planète.

Beaudet, P. 2002. "L'Amérique du nord." In S. Amin and F. Houtart (eds.), *La mondialisation des résistances: l'état des luttes 2002*. Paris: l'Harmattan. 163–74.

Bourdieu, P. 1998. *Contre-feux: Propos pour servir à la résistance contre l'invasion néo-libérale*. Paris: Raisons d'Agir.

Buchen, C. 2005. "East European Antipodes: Varieties of Capitalism in Estonia and Slovenia." Paper presented at the Conference on Varieties of Post-Communist Countries. Paisley University. September 23–25.

Calhoun, C. 2004. "Information Technology and the International Public Sphere." In D. Schuler and P. Day (eds.), *Shaping the Network Society: The New Role of Civil Society in Cyberspace*. Cambridge, MA: MIT Press. 229–51.

Callinicos, A. 2003. *An Anti-capitalist Manifesto*. Cambridge: Polity.

Carroll, W.K. 2006. "Hegemony, Counter-hegemony, Anti-hegemony." *Socialist Studies/Etudes Socialistes* 2(2): 9–43.

Carroll, W.K., and R.S. Ratner. 2005. *Challenges and Perils: Social Democracy in Neoliberal Times*. Halifax: Fernwood.

Coburn, D., and E.S. Coburn. 2007. "Health and Health Inequalities in a Neo-Liberal Global World." In G. Mooney and D. McIntyre (eds.), *The Economics of Health Equity*. Cambridge: Cambridge University Press. 13–35.

Coburn, E. 2005. "Globalization and Women." In L. Biggs and P. Downe (eds.), *Gendered Intersections: A Collection of Readings for Women's and Gender Studies.* Toronto: Fernwood. 393–98.

——. 2003. "La Bataille de Seattle: Portrait d'une manifestation en mouvement." In M. Wieviorka (ed.), *Un autre monde ... : Contestations, dérives et surprises dans l'antimondialisation.* Paris: Balland. 155–75.

Commission of the European Communities. 2006. "Report on the Functioning of the Transitional Arrangements Set Out in the 2003 Accession Treaty (Period 1 May 2004 to 30 April 2006)." Brussels: European Union.

Council of Canadians. 2007. "Vision Statement Background." <http://www.canadians.org/about/BOD/vision_background.html>.

Cutler, A.C. 2003. *Private Power and Global Authority: Transnational Merchant Law and the Global Economy.* Cambridge: Cambridge University Press.

Della Porta, D., and Mosca, L. 2007. "In movimento: 'Contamination' in Action and the Italian Global Justice Movement." *Global Networks* 7(1): 1–27.

Dezalay, Y., and B. Garth. 2005. "Les ONG aux services de la mondialisation? Connivences des élites internationalisées." *Le monde diplomatique* (June): 30–31.

——. 2002. *The Internationalization of Palace Wars: Lawyers, Economists and the Contest to Transform Latin American States.* Chicago: University of Chicago Press.

Evans, P. 2005. "Counterhegemonic Globalization: Transnational Social Movements in the Contemporary Global Political Economy." In T. Janoski, R.R. Alford, A.M. Hicks, and M. Schwartz (eds.), *Handbook of Political Sociology.* Cambridge: Cambridge University Press. 655–70.

Esping-Andersen, G. 1990. *The Three Worlds of Welfare Capitalism.* Princeton, NJ: Princeton University Press.

Eyal, G., I. Szelényi, and E. Townsley. 1998. *Making Capitalism Without Capitalists: The New Ruling Elites in Eastern Europe.* London: Verso.

EZLN. 1996. "First Declaration of La Realidad for Humanity and Against Neoliberalism." <http://www.ezln.org/documentos/1996/19960130.en.htm>. From *La Jornada*, January 30. Link no longer operational; archived copy available from the author.

Favreau, L., G. Gérald Larose, and A.S. Fall. 2004. "Introduction: Mouvement Citoyen, Alternatives Socioéconomiques et Coopération Internationale." In L. Favreau, G. Larose, and A.S. Fall (eds.), *Altermondialisation, économie et coopération internationale.* Québec: Université du Québec. 1–21.

Forum Mondial des Alternatives. 2004. *Mondialisation des résistances: l'état des luttes 2004.* Paris: Edition Syllepse.

Fukuyama. F. 1992. *The End of History and the Last Man.* New York: The Free Press.

Gramsci, A. 1971. *Selections from the Prison Notebooks*. Ed. Q. Hoare and G. Nowell-Smith. New York: International Publishers.

Habermas, J. 1987. *The Theory of Communicative Action*. Boston: Beacon Press.

Hackett, R.A., and W.K. Carroll. 2006. *Remaking Media: The Struggle to Democratize Public Communication*. New York: Routledge.

Hardt, M., and Negri. A. 2004. *Multitude: War and Democracy in the Age of Empire*. New York: Penguin.

International Monetary Fund External Relations Department. 1999. "The IMF's Response to the Asian Crisis." <http://www.imf.org/external/np/exr/facts/asia.htm>.

Le Bot, Y. 2003. "Le zapatisme, première insurrection contre la mondialisation libérale." In M. Wieviorka (ed.), *Un autre monde ... : Contestations, dérives et surprises dans l'antimondialisation*. Paris: Balland. 129–40.

Levitt, K. 2002. *Silent Surrender: The Multinational Corporation in Canada*. Montreal and Kingston: McGill-Queen's University Press.

Lindbom, A., and B. Rothstein. 2004. "The Mysterious Survival of the Scandinavian Welfare States." Paper presented at the annual meeting of the American Political Science Association, Chicago. September 2–5.

Marx, K. 2007. "Débats sur la loi relative au vol du bois." In D. Besaïd, *Les dépossédés: Karl Marx, les voleurs de bois et le droit des pauvres*. Paris: La Fabrique.

——. 1978. "The German Ideology." In R.C. Tucker (ed.), *The Marx-Engels Reader*. 2nd ed. London: W.W. Norton. 146–200.

McNally, D. 2002. *Another World Is Possible: Globalization and Anti-Capitalism*. Winnipeg: Arbeiter Ring.

Morgan, J. 2006. Interview with Michael Hardt. *Theory, Culture and Society* 23(5): 93–113.

Muñoz Ramírez, G. 2004. "A Time to Ask, a Time to Demand, and a Time to Act: Interview with Subcomandante Marcos." Americas Programme. Silver City, New Mexico. Interhemispheric Resource Center. January 16. <http://www.cipamericas.org/archives/1120>.

Navarro, V. 2007. "Neoliberalism as a Class Ideology; Or, the Political Causes of the Growth of Inequalities." *International Journal of Health Services* 37(1): 47–62.

Oloo, O. 2007. *Critical Reflections on WSF Nairobi 2007*. Liège: Committee for the Abolition of Third World Debt. <http://www.cadtm.org/IMG/article_PDF/article_a2544.pdf>.

Patterson, Brent. 2005. "Exciting, Tumultuous, Passionate: Maude Barlow Reflects on the Council of Canadians' 20 Years of Action." *Canadian Perspectives* (Autumn). Ottawa: The Council of Canadians.

Petras, J., and H. Veltmeyer. 2001. *Globalization Unmasked: Imperialism in the 21st Century*. Halifax: Fernwood.

Piketty, T. 2001. *Les hauts revenus en France au XXième siècle: Inégalités et redistributions, 1901–1998*. Paris: Bernard Grasset.

Pleyers, G. 2006. Personal communication.

Polanyi, K. 2001 [1957]. *The Great Transformation: The Political and Economic Origins of Our Time.* Boston: Beacon Press.

Ross, R., and K.C. Trachte. 1990. *Global Capitalism: The New Leviathan.* Albany: State University of New York Press.

Sandbrook, R., M. Edelman, R. Heller, and J. Teichman. 2007. *Social Democracy in the Global Periphery: Origins, Challenges, Prospects.* Cambridge: Cambridge University Press.

Smith, D. 2004. *Writing the Social: Critique, Theory and Investigations.* Toronto: University of Toronto Press.

Sohi, J. 2006. "Anti-WTO Movement in Hong Kong: the 'Battle of Hong Kong' and Implications for Asian Social Movements." *Inter-Asia Cultural Studies* 7(2): 353–58.

Sommier, I. 2001. *Les nouveaux mouvements contestataires.* Paris: Flammarion.

Sutcliffe, B. 2005. "A Converging or a Diverging World?" Department of Economic and Social Affairs. Working Paper No. 2. New York: United Nations Department of Economic and Social Affairs.

Sweezy, P., and H. Magdoff. 2000. "Toward a New Internationalism." *Monthly Review* 52(3): 1–10.

Tarrow, S. 2005. *The New Transnational Activism.* Cambridge: Cambridge University Press.

Teeple, G. 2004. *The Riddle of Human Rights.* Aurora, ON: Garamond.

Wacquant, L. 2006. *Punishing the Poor: The New Government of Social Insecurity.* Durham, NC: Duke University Press.

Wallerstein, I. 2005. "Le Forum social mondial à la croisée des chemins." *Revue du MAUSS* 26: 33–40.

——. 2002. "New Revolts Against the System." *New Left Review* 18: 29–39.

——. 2000. "Globalization or Age of Transition? A Long-Term View of the Trajectory of the World System." *International Sociology* 15(2): 249–65.

Wallerstein, I., and S. Zukin. 1989. "1968, Revolution in the World System: Theses and Queries." *Theory and Society* 18(4): 431–49.

World Social Forum. 2008. "Collected Reports from Around the World [on the January 2007 Global Days of Action]." <http://wsf2008.net/eng/node/6893>. Link no longer operational; archived copy available from the author.

——. 2007. "About the WSF." <http://wsf2008.net/eng/about>. Link no longer operational; archived copy available from the author.

World Social Forum International Council. 2002a. "Document on the Dakar Meeting." <http://www.forumsocialmundial.br>. Link no longer operational; archived copy available from the author.

——. 2002b. "WSF International Council Meeting: Barcelona April 28–30." <http://www.forumsocialmundial.br>. Link no longer operational; archived copy available from the author.

Zarifian, P. 2002. "Le Terrorisme globale et le régime de guerre." *Revue du MAUSS* 20: 195–203.

11

Notes on the Continuing Economic Crisis

GARY TEEPLE

Many analyses of the crisis of 2007–09 place the US subprime mortgages, their securitization, and defaults at the heart of the explanation. They imply that, except for these anomalies, the current regime of accumulation (for a definition see Kotz, McDonough & Reich 1994) would have continued uneventfully into the foreseeable future. Other less sanguine analyses have pointed out that, while the defaults were a contributing factor, the crisis had deep roots that spanned several decades.

On the surface, the crisis can be seen as one of a long series of crises beginning in the 1980s. This chain suggests a new pattern of accumulation that produces a chronic succession of economic breakdowns striking various corporations, economic sectors, nations, or groups of nations with no decisive global economic collapse. The crises differ from the past in their frequency and degree of state involvement.

The roots of the present crisis, we suggest, lie in the postwar regime of accumulation, a Fordist mode of production framed by Keynesian state policies. By the 1970s, the rapid economic growth of this era had ended in stagnation; at the same time, this regime had produced new means of production and new forms of capital that were no longer compatible with its Keynesian framework.

There were many reasons underlying the economic stagnation of the 1970s. After 1945, Western states introduced Keynesian policies to give capitalism a "human face." Among other reasons, persisting memories of the 1930s, the expansion of socialism, colonial liberation struggles, the reconstruction of European capitalism, and new economic and political powers of the working classes all made social reform necessary in this period. At the same time, however, the consequent growth of the state sector and rising real wages and salaries became a barrier to accumulation, leading to a greater share of national income going to the working classes and producing a disincentive to reinvest (Glyn 2006: ch. 1).

Just as the exigencies of social stability in the postwar period left governments little choice but to introduce Keynesian policies, so too other exigencies obliged them to adopt military policies that led to what many have called military Keynesianism (Galbraith 1973). A standing military presence, constant state outlays in military production, and active foreign interventions were required to expand overseas markets, to export superfluous capital and secure raw materials, to keep former colonies in the orbit of Western capital, and to contain the spread of socialism. Military expenditures also became a means to increase aggregate demand during recessions (Mandel 1971: 522), shifting certain social resources from labour to capital, and lessening the need to increase demand through state redistribution to the working classes. A military/industrial complex and its continuing demand for state resources came to be a permanent part of capitalist economies (Melman 1974).

Military Keynesianism in the industrial nations has also had an international impact. It has been a decisive component in global unequal exchange; the value from the Third World in the form of food and other resources that are exchanged for military goods and services from the industrial countries represents value that returns no useful benefits to the Third World. In fact, they take the form of commodities that provide the defence of continued unequal exchange and the suppression of opposition or resistance to it (Mandel 1971: 522–29). The development of a permanent and growing arms industry and military training, moreover, contributes to the need for wars or conflicts (Lutz 2009).

If Fordism and its policy counterparts, Keynesianism and its military expression, constituted the heart of the postwar regime of accumulation, they also produced consequences that helped bring this regime to an end. One of these was the increased share of total income going to the working classes in the form of rising wages and salaries and state redistribution, factors leading to economic stagnation. Another was the transformation of the mode of production, and a third was the growing phenomenon of financialization, the rise of a mass of money capital with declining fields for investment. The expanding influence of money capital shifted the process of accumulation from the national to the global, and to the extraction of surplus as money capital, from all sectors and by any means, without concern for the continuity of economic processes.

FINANCIALIZATION

Financialization began in the postwar period with two main developments: a vast increase in international trade and investment reflecting the productive power of Fordism, and the reconstruction policies of the industrial states. Regarding the former, commodity exchange grew by approximately 800 per cent during this period, which was greater than in any previous period and larger than the growth in global GNP (Cypher 1979: 514). Estimates of US corporate profits from foreign investments rose from about 8.8 per cent in 1960 to approximately 15 per cent of total profit in 1970 (Melman 1974: 268) and to about 25 per cent by the late 1970s (Cypher 1979: 515). The productivity of Fordism created a shift in the ground of accumulation, through trade and foreign direct investment, from the national to the global, greatly expanding the potential for accumulation. It was, moreover, creating surplus capital through overproduction for which speculation and credit were becoming the main outlets because of the growing saturation in productive investment.

The other source of capital separate from productive use lay in the considerable state mobilization of public and private capital necessary for the reconstruction of war-devastated economies. State-leveraged capital via deficit financing, increased taxes, and debased money was provided to the corporate sector and public enterprises. Importantly, economic assistance in the form of UNRRA[1] funds amounted to about $4 billion between 1944 and 1949, and the Marshall Plan alone accounted for about $13 billion given to European nations for reconstruction between 1948 and 1952 (Milward 2006; Hogan 1987).

These vast sums became the basis of what was called Eurocurrency: monies freed from national jurisdictions and regulation, more or less beyond the control of central banks or other regulatory bodies. Between the late 1950s and the 1970s, other sources of capital contributed to Eurocurrency: overseas US spending for the Korean and Vietnam wars and military bases, recycled petro-dollars, the assets of Third World elites, and extraneous illicit funds (Naylor 1994). In 1971, moreover, the end of fixed exchange rates, part of the Bretton Woods agreement, produced an enormous growth in foreign-exchange markets.[2] Similarly, international bond markets grew exponentially, as did transnational securities trading and bank lending. By 1973, the total Eurocurrency market was estimated to be larger than all government international reserves; by 1978 it was said to be twice as large as those reserves. Between 1971 and 1983, Eurocurrencies grew from about $150 billion to over $2 trillion (*Debt Bondage* 1985). In short, by the 1970s, there was a massive expansion of world credit that was free from national jurisdiction, largely unregulated, and without a "lender of last resort" (Hawley 1979: 82–83; Gowland 1983).

These enormous pools of capital were quintessentially global in nature; that is, whatever their denomination (albeit mainly US dollars), their use possessed little if any national meaning. Capital markets were now capable of shifting vast sums of money quickly (the ability to destabilize national currencies) and of creating credit (the power to increase global liquidity), which underlay part of the global inflation of the period. The growing influence of independent money capital was now a reality without any obvious barriers to its continued expansion, other than the persistence of national regulations, which it strove to abolish. Although its instability increased the possibility of crises, it also encouraged the centralization of capital (cartels, monopolies, and oligopolies), narrowed the control, increased pressure to invest in new productive forces, promoted competition and overproduction, demanded more global markets, gave rise to increased transnational banking, and advanced the possibilities for speculation of all sorts. A vast new engine for accumulation had opened up in the form of speculative capital flows, traded by a large number of banks with global networks (Pardee 1987).

With the expansion of global trade and the rise of the Eurocurrency markets, a number of other developments followed suit in this postwar period. The form of foreign investment shifted from portfolio capital to direct or equity investment (moving control from borrower to investor); the number and size of transnational banks and corporations grew very rapidly (foreign assets of US banks and corporations increased more rapidly than domestic assets, facilitating unregulated global money movements); and the de facto integration of the major world stock exchanges took place (affirming the power of global investment), among other changes. In other words, by the end of the 1970s the financial sector was global, composed of large and growing pools of denationalized capital, operating within structures (international bank branches and stock markets) largely outside of national control, and demanding an end to national regulation (Hawley 1979: 82).

Financialization refers to a change within capitalism of the pattern of accumulation that started in the postwar era but grew rapidly beginning in the 1980s.[3] It signals a shift from the use of money capital primarily to facilitate the expansion of the "real" or value-producing sectors of the economy to its use as a mechanism to make profits in the sphere of circulation and to enrich its managers. It marks a shift in the main source of profit from the sphere of value creation to operations of value concentration and centralization.[4] Money capital produces no surplus value itself, but rather shares the surplus value created in the production process; as it grew to assume a position of control over production, it served increasingly to centralize and redistribute existing surplus value to the benefit of its owners/managers and shareholders.

Financialization also points to a decisive shift in the nature of capital: no longer predominantly privately owned, but rather social, composed of stocks, bonds, pension funds, sovereign wealth funds (SWF), state, corporation, and individual debt, embezzled national funds, and other forms of illicit money from many sources. It is social capital in the framework of private property, and in the form of money capital for which profit comes from the manipulation of debt, deferred income, pooled investments, and stolen assets.

Once all the industrial nations began accumulating more than was possible to invest, the global economy became swamped with superfluous capital unable to find profitable investments in the sphere of production. Here began the more or less rapid movement of money capital into every aspect of economic life, fuelling every speculative possibility and coming to prevail over the whole of the system. It was no longer capitalists who were in charge, but managers of money, a "financial aristocracy" that manipulated this money capital in their own interests, without regard for the fate of social capital because it was not theirs, and that came to control the whole of capitalist production through a vast system of credit and speculation (Grossmann 1992: 26, 54; Marx 1981: 569, 570, 572).

Financialization in the 1970s was already pointing to chronic overaccumulation (O'Connor 1986)—i.e., too much capital to be invested profitably in productive ventures, and so remaining as money capital, striving to find new means to extract surplus or capitalize other forms of wealth or redistribute existing assets. It also pointed to the end of national capital markets and to many aspects of national policy that constrained its operations (Eatwell & Taylor 2000: 2). The Eurocurrency system and international branch banking, for example, undermined national counter-inflation policies because they created a chronic global oversupply of money. National economic and social planning and policies, moreover, were thwarted by large volumes of "denationalized" capital that could be moved more or less at will, and by unregulated international credit (Grossmann 1992: 78, 84, 86). In order to offset falling profits, furthermore, these available funds were invested in speculative ventures and in large loans to Third World nations, increasing

their debt loads and helping to cripple their development by siphon-
ing off their surpluses and existing wealth. Currency crises increased
because exchange rates became determined by shifts in this speculative
money capital and by the inadequacy or absence of regulatory mechanisms (Eatwell & Taylor 2000: xi). With global finance able to destabilize national economies, governments began to act in ways to guarantee
the confidence of the "investors," and liberal democracy increasingly
began to appear an empty exercise, recognized implicitly in declining
voter turnouts around the world.

By the 1970s, this growth of superfluous money capital added new
demands to those of the stalled industrial sectors that required an end
to the postwar regime and an opening of new avenues for accumulation, especially in the sphere of circulation, through deregulation and
privatization. The elections of Margaret Thatcher in the UK and Ronald
Reagan in the US signalled the change in the control of the state necessary to effect this regime transformation.

THE "NEW ECONOMY"

Despite the lack of consensus on the meaning of the "new economy"
or post-Fordism, some key characteristics of the new mode of production show its incompatibility with the national political structures and
property relations of its predecessor, Fordism. Above all, this new mode
is computer-based, making it qualitatively different from all the modes
that have come before. Like other machines, computers are compos-
ites of objectified social labour, but unlike others, they are program-
mable, self-activating, and more or less universally applicable to the
full range of production of goods and provision of services. They form
the basis of a permanent revolution in the labour process, communications, and science.

The use of micro-electronics beginning in the 1970s spawned a massive increase in productivity in all spheres; in short order, it revolution-
ized capital goods production, administration, banking, government,
mining, research and design, education, auto production, agriculture,
and so on—nothing was exempt from its application and effects (CSE
1982; Sayer & Walker 1992). Before the end of the 1970s, national markets were appearing anachronistic, along with their political systems,
in the face of the immense mass and variety of goods that now increasingly were being produced in global economic chains.

Part of this post-Fordist knowledge-based economy was the rise of
the so-called "information society," which can be defined as the transformation by computers of every aspect of human interaction (Tapscott &

Caston 1993; Tapscott 1996). The information society can be equated with the arrival of the "virtual" institution: networks of computers and digitized information that can embrace banks, corporate and government administration, universities and schools, and factories. All can be reduced to computer systems that store, distribute, accumulate, and apply information. Even much professional activity in law, medicine, engineering, architecture, and teaching can similarly be transformed by computer applications. With "e-commerce," markets have become virtual, by and large continuous, and global. An enormous number of leisure activities, moreover, have also become virtual. Human communication itself has moved to a virtual form—the internet[5]—which crosses all boundaries.

This "new economy" created the basis for a massive increase in productivity and consequently a relative decline in demand for labour. Increased productivity, in turn, lowered the cost or cheapened the world's supply of goods and services and created an ever-greater impetus for global chains of production and distribution. This cheapening of the costs of production and distribution increased market demand and provided a counter-tendency to stagnation and crisis by offsetting the declining purchasing power of stationary or declining wages and salaries and producing a rise in the mass of profits (Grossmann 1992: 33).

At the same time, it brought its own contradictions. With the globalization of production chains, national economic regulations needed to be harmonized with global demands because national laws inhibited global growth. Global accumulation in a global market, moreover, allowed for vastly greater pooling of capital than ever before, which created more pressure for investment possibilities pushing the pace of state privatization, deregulation, dispossession from the land, and more speculation and economic bubbles. Furthermore, the relative decline in the demand for labour (rising organic composition of capital) produced underemployment and unemployment (an increase in the global reserve of labour), and an incremental levelling of wages and salaries across the globe, which in turn dampened consumer demand.

The Structure of the Working Classes

With a changing mode of production, the structure of the working class followed suit. If Fordism forced a massive shift of labour from the primary sectors to the secondary and tertiary sectors in the 1950s and 1960s, in the 1970s incipient post-Fordism or computer-aided manufacturing and design opened the possibility for the first time in history of doing away with most forms of labour other than the creative. Initially, however, the impact was felt through the de-skilling of many

Fordist occupations, the intensification of work, "lean" production, "flexible" workforces, increased "robotization," and computerization of the entire range of economic activities, followed by growing chronic unemployment, underemployment, and a foreseeable end to well-paying, secure, career-length jobs (Aronowitz & DiFazio 1994; Womack, Jones & Roos 1990). These changes, in turn, gave rise to a new segmentation of the working classes in the industrial world, undermining union strength in the manufacturing sector and leading to increased competition between the working classes in the industrial nations and the Third World, resulting for the former in downward pressure on wages and salaries (Henderson 1989; Cohen 1987).

By the end of the 1970s, the working classes everywhere, defined and confined by laws and regulations as national entities, were increasingly confronting capital operating more and more on the global level with ever fewer restrictions. This new relation undermined their strength with respect to capital, and lessened the leverage they had in national politics. Keynesianism had provided safeguards for the working classes from the unmitigated discipline of the labour market and dictates of employers, and so it contributed to growing wages and squeezed profits; however, the declining political influence of the working classes encouraged attacks on Keynesian policies and programs, the development of which usually reflected the degree of national power of the organized working classes. The growth in real wages that had squeezed profits throughout the postwar era was beginning to level off in the latter half of the 1970s under the effects of changing state policies (Jones 1973), new technology, and increasing competition with production in the so-called newly industrializing countries and the Third World.

The End of Keynesianism

By the 1970s, most of the conditions that had given rise to the Keynesian welfare state were in decline,[6] and the contradictions of Keynesianism and Fordism had brought relative stagnation to industrial capitalism. Western economies had stalled, affected by high wages, high unemployment, inflation, large state sectors, and a profit squeeze. Fordism was being transformed by a growing computer-based mode of production that facilitated global exchange and so began to rub against Keynesian policies, chaffing against the remaining barriers to global production, trade, and capital movements. The increased organic composition of capital contributed to the continuing fall in the rate and mass of profit, which could be offset in part with expanded access to global markets and downward pressure on wages. The rise of vast pools of "denationalized" money capital, moreover, operating outside of national regulation, undermined the nationally defined economy. By this time it was becoming a force in its own right and creating demands for deregulation and greater opportunities for investment. Global and regional markets increasingly confronted national labour and capital markets, which were losing their economic rationale.

In the 1970s, the development of capital had arrived at a juncture. In theory, blocs of capital can expand in several ways. One is through reinvestment of surplus in productive sectors—or accumulation through expansion or reproduction; another is by private appropriation of blocs of state capital—or accumulation by privatization and deregulation; a third is by capitalizing other forms of wealth such as "commons" and a range of pre-capitalist property forms—or accumulation through dispossession or concentration; another is by means of mergers and acquisitions of smaller private corporations or pools of capital—centralization; another form of centralization, and a result of surplus money capital, is through speculation; and lastly, there is accumulation through criminal or extra-legal means. At the end of the 1970s, reinvestment was frustrated because of persisting high wages, a falling rate of profit, and active trade unions; for capital to reinvest, measures had to be taken to counter these developments. The process of dispossession was restricted by non-market or pre-capitalist property relations, which had to be re-cast in the form of private property in order to tie them into the accumulation process. Mergers and acquisitions, which have proceeded rapidly during every recession, now increasingly became a constant feature of capital growth, limited only by the amount of leverage and whatever forms of anti-trust legislation existed. Speculation grew at unprecedented rates, leading to "new financial products" and a series of burst bubbles with damaging consequences for certain corporations, economic sectors, and even whole countries.

A new regime of accumulation was in the making, predicated on denationalized money capital and a computer-based mode of production. Combined, they increased productive power and facilitated distribution, but they also demanded numerous changes in the national structure of economies, the power and size of trade unions, property relations, and state ownership, redistribution, and regulation. They were incompatible with the national Keynesian policies of the state and required that their demands, particularly deregulation and privatization, be formalized in a set of policies. A shift was in the offing, from a degree of class compromise in the postwar regime to the more open class war of the regime that followed. The contradictions of the former that resulted in economic stagnation were to be "solved" by the latter, whose own contradictions would come to the fore in the twenty-first century.

THE POST-FORDIST REGIME OF ACCUMULATION: THE CONTRADICTIONS OF POST-FORDISM, FINANCIALIZATION, AND NEOLIBERALISM

The impasse that arrived in the 1970s was forestalled by extensive accumulation of wealth from the Third World—state indebtedness, destruction of petty commodity producers, privatization of state sectors, elimination or minimization of state expenditures, and expropriation of common property. Now, new policies in the industrial nations that favoured capital over labour had to be introduced to reverse the culminating effects of the contradictions of Keynesianism and Fordism. These new policies in the industrial world would be added to the policies employed to extract surplus from the Third World. Together these policies would over time also stall the system, albeit through the systematic lowering of consumer demand and increasing the overabundance of money capital.

With the elections of Thatcher in 1979 and Reagan in 1980, the ideas of Friedrich von Hayek and Milton Friedman (Hayek 1944; Friedman 1962; Lilley 1977) were brought to the fore in the industrial nations. Designed to counter Keynesianism and its acceptance in the public mind, Thatcherism or Reaganism or neo-liberalism, as these ideas came to be called, had as their objective the destruction of the class compromise that had idled capitalism in the 1970s. Often treated as merely politically inspired policy changes, or simply alternative economic theories, they resembled a form of class war waged in the realm of ideas and by means of government policy.

Keynesianism emphasized the use of fiscal policies (tax levies and state expenditures) to determine in part "aggregate demand," and the "pattern of resource allocation" or income distribution. Using these policies and presupposing national capital controls, the state could influence the direction and pace of economic growth. When employed by a liberal democratic government, which allowed for a degree of working-class political pressure, they produced a certain class compromise. Monetarism, the label given to Hayek's and Friedman's theories, on the other hand, emphasized the use of money supply and interest rates to manage economic policy. These instruments were to be restricted to the powers of the central banks, which were then to be de-coupled from political oversight. Economic policies in the hands of central banks, independent of government, were then relatively free from the influence of working-class political leverage. The intent of monetarism was largely to reduce regulation of the market, to free the corporate sector from the class compromises of the postwar era. Monetarism sought to leave the working class as much as possible to the ruthless discipline of the markets while employing the state for the benefit of capital (Keleher 1998).

The postwar period of class compromise had come to an end because the conditions that underlay Keynesianism had changed or diminished: Fordism was being transformed by computers, financialization was changing the shape of capital accumulation, global markets had arrived, and all these factors were necessitating a global regime of accumulation.

Class Shares of Total Resources

Among other contradictions, neoliberalism and globalization trap the working classes as national classes, subordinate to national state regulation, while capital becomes increasingly mobile and transnational and subject to laws and regulations established at the global level with accompanying economic and political leverage over states. This separation gives enormous advantages to capital and serves to undermine traditional trade-union organizing, not to mention political demands that the organized sector of the working classes may make.

Roughly coterminous with the rise of the "new economy," the global labour force about doubled during 1980s and 1990s, with the opening of China, Russia, and India to more capital investment (Freeman 2005). This increase in labour supply relative to demand and relative to available capital—a growth in the global reserve army of labour—produced downward pressure on global standards of living and wages and salaries, beginning an incremental trend toward global income convergence. It also greatly expanded the possibility of global labour arbitrage, i.e., shifting the use of labour from higher- to lower-cost labour markets and selling the products in the higher. The practice is made possible by the enormous gains in productivity in global production, transportation, and communications associated with post-Fordism, which also allowed for the combination of high productivity and low labour costs. Labour arbitrage takes many forms, but among the most common are outsourcing, offshoring, immigration, temporary work visas, and the lowering of labour standards, the minimum wage, and the age of child labour.

This increase in the global labour market, the reserve army of labour, and arbitraging has undermined the political leverage of the working classes in their national politics. Together these phenomena have also lowered working-class demand for consumer goods, although this has been offset by low interest rates on loans and the lower cost of imported goods and services. Yet the overall point of global labour arbitrage and the growth of the reserve army is to reduce wages to as close as possible to their value or below their value, and to put constant negative pressure on wages and salaries that are above their value. They act in general to deflate working-class incomes, by pitting the working classes in one national or regional market against another.

This pressure is complemented by policies that reduce government health and education programs and transfer payments, put an end to agricultural subsidies and import restrictions, and make legal changes that allow for privatization of various forms of common land tenure and reduction of work standards. The effect is to augment the numbers of the landless and the unemployed/underemployed, to compress aggregate demand even more, to hasten urbanization, to increase emigration and remittances as significant components of GNP, and to enlarge the informal labour sector (unskilled, casual, low-paying jobs). In the end, the slums, *favelas*, or *bidonvilles* of the world are created and expanded; hundreds of millions of people become refugees in a system that does not need them. They become "excluded populations" (Davis 2006), "disposable people" (Bales 2004), the "new helots" (Cohen 1987), and incarcerated "nations" (such as Haiti, Gaza, and Palestine). As such, they also become the fitting subject of security concerns, to be dealt with by police or military forces waging "low-intensity" war.

All of these developments have had an effect on the distribution of the national income between wages and profits. For many decades in the industrial nations, this distribution remained relatively stable. Certainly, between World War II and the mid-1970s, a constellation of forces made for a comparatively steady income and wealth distribution in the industrial nations (Kaldor 1980). By the end of the 1970s, however, growing disparities of wealth and income distribution began to appear throughout much of the world, continuing into the present (Glyn 2006). This shift in distribution corresponded to the gradual ubiquitous adoption of neoliberal policies, which mirrored rapid changes in technology and the gradual shift of political and economic power to the global level.

However difficult it is to measure wealth and income distribution across nations, growing disparities in the share of national income are reported to be rising almost everywhere (Guscina 2006). In the US in 2006, for example, "the share of national income captured by corporate profits ... was at its highest level on record" (CBPP 2007a). "Total employee compensation," including wages, benefits, and state redistribution, was falling in relation to the share of profits. The disparities in income also grew rapidly; the top 1 per cent of households took almost 20 per cent of total national pre-tax income, while the "bottom" 99 per cent garnered about 80 per cent in 2005—about a 2-per-cent rise and fall respectively from the previous year (CBPP 2007b). In Europe, particularly in Germany, France, and Britain, labour's share has fallen over the last 25 years (Glyn 2006: Chapter 5). Japan "witnessed a sharp decline in its national wage share—from 75% in 1980 to 61% in 2005" (OECD 2007). In China, the World Bank revealed that, despite the continuous rapid growth of its economy, "the wage share [of GDP] declined from 53 percent in 1998 to 41.4 percent in 2005" (He & Kuijs 2007). Similar findings have been reported in Australia and Canada, among other nations (Russell & Dufour 2007).

In general, the struggle over shares is central to the reproduction of the whole system; it is a struggle over what amounts to the distribution of the social product and the ability of its classes to survive contradictory demands. It means that there can be economic growth without growth in the share to the working classes, although classes are not monolithic, and so different strata and sectors of capital and labour share the benefits of economic growth and productivity unevenly and according to many factors. It can mean growing impoverishment for certain strata of the working classes (*New York Times* 2010) and a decline of the "middle classes." The significance of an increasing share for capital, however, is that it translates into more of the total social resources open to corporate accumulation. A report by Goldman Sachs in 2006 stated that "The most important contributor of higher profit margins over the past five years has been a decline in labor's share of national income" (Greenhouse & Leonhardt 2006).

Military Expenditures
With consumer demand declining through wage reduction by the early 1980s (offset in part through growing personal indebtedness and cheaper consumer goods and services), foreign markets and state expenditures were left as the two remaining principal sources of demand. Foreign markets, however, were similarly depressed due to structural adjustment or neoliberal policies, not to mention a slow shift of the global centre of manufacturing from the North to the South. This left military expenditures as an important source of demand, one that could be manipulated through state policy.

War and military spending in a capitalist system has always served, among other functions, to moderate overproduction or to increase demand. Aside from maintaining the property relations that divide the working and capitalist classes, war destroys existing capital, and military production creates use-values for destruction by employing overaccumulated capital without flooding the market or requiring market-based demand. Destruction creates new possibilities for accumulation, and war materiel does not necessarily need a market, while being a source of large profits because war production is taken as a necessity and paid for with a premium by the working classes through taxes and state indebtedness.

War destroys capital, and military spending absorbs surplus capital, giving the general process of capital accumulation a certain respite from the crisis gridlock of overproduction and declining demand.

World military expenditures rose throughout the 1980s as part of the effort to move away from the stagnation of the Keynesian period; it declined in the 1990s with the opening up of China and Russia to capital, but then rose again in the first decade of the twenty-first century with the collapse of several successive bubbles. Under the George W. Bush administration, permanent war became part of American foreign policy and state planning—along with the expansion of NATO, a large source of US military sales and increased military activity (National Security Strategy 2002; Priest 1998). That global military spending reached about $1.5 trillion dollars per annum in 2008 means that increasingly large parts of national budgets are excluded from distribution in the form of social goods and services to the world's working classes (Stockholm International Peace Research Institute 2009).

Military and economic power go hand-in-hand; military spending and the fomenting of conflict are one means for ruling strata to maintain their hegemony and access to the world's resources and to increase demand and sustain profit margins in some industrial sectors—in short, to maintain the general conditions of capital accumulation. For the United States, these military expenditures are also related to its dominant position in guaranteeing its currency as the world's main medium of value/wealth representation and medium of exchange.

FINANCIAL SPECULATION

Much of what has happened in the global economy since 1980 can be explained by the argument that in the preceding decades, money capital had come to dominate. Overabundant money capital searches for profitable investment. On the one hand, it moves into the productive sectors and develops them to the point of overcapacity, cheapening products and increasing their quantities beyond market demand. On the other hand, the consequent limited investment possibilities in the productive sector force it to turn increasingly to forms of speculation. Speculation opens up avenues of accumulation, largely in the sphere of circulation where no value is created, but where it is privatized, concentrated, and centralized. The vast and growing amount of money capital in speculative ventures is merely the measure of the relative lack of other investment opportunities. The ensuing policies and practices of governments and corporations have reflected this predicament for capital.

Big Bangs

Many speculative avenues were developed and exploited well before the 1980s (Eatwell & Taylor 2000: ch. 1), but with the end of the Keynesian era, there was greater pressure to enact legislative changes to facilitate these ventures in risk. Among these, in the UK, was the deregulation of the financial markets in 1986 in what was called "Big Bang Day." This unleashing of the markets opened new possibilities for increased speculation, swindling, and centralization of the world's capital pools. In particular, it abolished the minimum fixed commissions, allowed the joining of banks and brokerages, introduced electronic trading, expanded the financial markets, encouraged small investors, and increased fraudulent practices.

Japan, the world's third-largest financial market in the 1990s, moved to deregulate finance in 1997, spreading the changes over two years (Gordon 2003). In the US, a similar "big bang" took place in 1999 with the repeal of the US Glass-Steagall Act, after years of pressure from the financial industry. This Act was actually the US Banking Act, introduced in 1933 to create deposit insurance and place limits on stock-market speculation, partly by separating commercial from investment banking in order to prevent banks from gambling with deposits. Its repeal had similar effects on the US financial markets and institutions as the 1986 UK law, opening the door to many new types of investment "products." These "big bangs" and the others that followed gave new freedom to money capital to engage in a variety of speculative means to augment itself, using vast pools of accumulated capital, with the added competition giving advantages to the largest companies. With few other outlets, superfluous money capital began to flow into the stock markets in search of higher rates of return, to some degree feeding on itself (Tsurumi 2001; Toya 2006; Aslund 2007).

All these changes were promoted or required by new World Trade Organization (WTO) financial deregulation rules. The Financial Services Agreement, which came into effect in 1999, obligated its signing governments to create no new regulations for a long list of financial services, to remove existing regulations affecting the financial sector, to refrain from limiting the development of new financial "products," to avoid setting "limits on the size, corporate form or other characteristic of foreign firms" in the financial sector, and to treat alike domestic and foreign corporations under the framework of WTO regulations (Public Citizen 2009). Here was the heart of the policy changes that were to follow in countries around the world.[7]

Anti-inflation Policies

With the elections of Thatcher and Reagan, Keynesian policies fell into disfavour, and anti-inflationary monetary and fiscal policies were introduced. These amounted to, among other measures, combinations of increased taxes (especially indirect taxes), decreased state subsidies and expenditures, increased interest rates, and wage and price controls. Such policies reflected the rising dominance of money capital, because inflation undermines the value of money, reducing the rate of return on financial assets. Price stability becomes an overriding goal in a financially dominated economy; the constancy of the value of money takes on an importance that it did not previously have. The irony was that the overaccumulation of money capital itself was a significant source of inflation (excess of money supply over demand). The working classes, however, were to pay the price for this situation. To reduce the effect while encouraging the cause, aggregate demand was lowered by the reduction of subsidies and redistribution programs, by caps on wages and salaries, thereby in some measure engineering the rate of unemployment. The value of money and its growth were maintained in part on the backs of the working classes (Jones 1973).

Central Bank Autonomy

The increased autonomy of central banks from political oversight corresponded to the rise to pre-eminence of global money capital. Central banks have many functions,[8] but the origin and history of these are related to overseeing the financial well-being of the national economy. Historically, central banks have served national interests and been subject to political decisions, for better or worse, on the direction of national economic development. There have always been degrees of independence in their operation, goals, and management, but in the 1980s pressure arose to grant much more independence from political decision-making.

Increased independence meant that political accountability was diminished, reducing the possibility of using the central bank as a mechanism of national industrial or growth strategies or monetary policy. Instead, the banks could and did pursue policies encouraging export growth and facilitating foreign investment and integration into the global economy. Increased autonomy also allowed for the continued delinking of the financial sector from the productive sector, giving advantages to the expansion of money capital to the detriment of industrial capital. This uncoupling in turn undermined national economic integrity by creating degrees of exposure to global flows of money capital, bringing a sizeable increase in volatility to national financial systems and foreign purchases of industrial corporations.

Once such a law was passed, the varied powers of the central bank over interest and exchange rates and monetary policy were in the hands of an institution not accountable to national politics. Policy decisions that were central to a national standard of living and economic integrity could now be subordinated to the prevailing demands of global money capital.

Bubble Economics

The "bubble economy," or the growth in the number of large speculative ventures as a mechanism of the financial sector, can be seen as the outcome of the overaccumulation of money capital. With limited investment possibilities in the productive sectors, money capital creates bubbles or inflationary spirals due to its very existence, not to mention from conscious manipulation. Bubbles become mechanisms for restoring profitability when there are few other possibilities; they are the speculative extraction of profit in the sphere of circulation without real growth. They can arise wherever this money capital flows (Brenner 2003).

These flows become the basis of frequent or chronic crises—burst bubbles. Since the 1990s, the list of these bubbles has grown, involving individual corporations, stock market sectors, real estate, commodities, and foreign exchange or currency markets. These crises have affected the economies of whole nations, the savings and pensions of millions of workers, the viability of economic sectors and individual corporations, and latterly the economic stability of the world (Baker 2009).[9]

Asset Stripping

Many of these bubbles involve asset stripping, another form of value accumulation as centralization, i.e., accumulation without value production, or the extraction of profits for the financial sector without investment in the production. In the manufacturing sector, asset stripping is carried out by managers in a position to sell the assets of a firm, pocketing the money as bonuses or dividends, or investing the money elsewhere, leaving a devalued or bankrupted company, and in this way appropriating the value belonging to the shareholders, creditors, and employees. In the financial sphere, the extremely large bonuses paid to money managers may be seen as a form of asset stripping. Here "bonuses," "dividends," "loans," or "management fees" are paid as percentages of "profits" that are a product of financial manipulation or speculation, and that serve as the mechanism for claiming billions of dollars for the managers.[10]

The privatization of state corporations also often involves asset stripping insofar as the real value of the asset is usually higher than what is paid for by the purchaser (corporate or shareholder), thus stripping the state (or taxpayer) of existing value. Asset stripping of the state, or privatization of state enterprises, began in earnest in the UK and New Zealand in the 1980s and then spread to the rest of the world. In the 1990s there was a widespread sell-off in Latin America and Eastern Europe. In both regions, a combination of corrupt governments and legal systems allowed for a massive transfer of public wealth into private hands (Haque 2000; Cull, Matesova & Shirley 2002: 2). Indeed, "by the end of 2002, a total of $1.1 trillion worth of state assets had been sold, with the bulk of revenues going to the industrialized economies" (De Medeiros 2009).

Stripping the state of its assets can involve much more than the privatization of public enterprises. It can also take the form of tax concessions and allowances for certain corporations or individuals, and of deficit financing, with the borrowed funds going to the corporate sector while increasing a range of taxes paid by the working classes. It can also appear as "tax havens," through which corporations and the rich can avoid taxation, thereby restricting the operation of the state and limiting their contribution to the national social resources of the people who create their wealth. It can involve the use of surpluses stored in social-security funds, such as unemployment or accident insurance or pension funds, to cover deficits or even to play the stock market, placing billions of savings and deferred income at the disposal of the marketplace. It can mean simply the privatization of these same funds. In many developing nations, state officials may strip the state through illegal means and launder these funds with the assistance of mainstream banks in the world's major financial centres (Global Witness 2009).

This "selling off the state" has the effect of reducing or eliminating political control over the disposition of social resources and giving that control to the corporate sector. In so doing, it puts large amounts of pooled capital representing the surpluses of national working classes and places those sums into global domains of financial manipulation, while at the same time undermining the possibilities of national development and indebting the working classes through "their" government's national debts.

Looting

Looting is a form of asset stripping and has been an important part of capital accumulation for a long time. It can take several shapes, one of which amounts to the use of "bankruptcy for profit"—a process by which owners or managers extract as much as possible from a corporation for themselves or others, often running up excessive debt loads and then allowing the firm to default (Akerlof et al. 1993). Another is the practice of financial institutions taking excessive risk with "other people's money," skimming off the profits, when there is legislation that a "lender of last resort"—a central bank, the state, and ultimately taxpayers—will guarantee the funds if serious losses should occur. In this way, profits are privatized or "personalized" and losses are socialized, i.e., bailed out by the state. Here is the so-called moral hazard—the knowledge that, because credit is necessary to the operation of the economy or that size matters, negative fallout from undue risks or questionable practices will be covered by state funding (Black 2005).

Accumulation by looting depends on several conditions. It is only possible after high degrees of deregulation have been legislated allowing for maximized leverage and open investment practices. Legislation must also be in place insuring against the loss of deposits to a certain amount.[11] Lax oversight on accounting practices and limited or no penalties for defaults complete the environment (Cull, Matesova & Shirley 2002).

Accounting Scandals

Looting rests on limited or no regulation, loose enforcement of what regulation there is, and "collaborative" and "creative" accounting. "Earnings management" is one of the euphemisms used to describe dubious accounting practices that can be legal or questionable or outright fraudulent, but in all cases outside the spirit of truthful reporting. It amounts to systematic deception in reporting on the revenue, assets, and liabilities of a corporation for the personal gain of managers at the expense of shareholders (Briloff 1972). With the growing necessity to accumulate in the realm of circulation where no new value is produced, the possibilities for value extraction become dependent on the assessment of the existing value. Here lies the rationale for increased pressure to employ such accounting techniques to misrepresent the value of corporations.

Accounting scandals have taken place around the world, but some of the major ones have occurred in the United States. The mere names of several corporations are sufficient to recall the crises of fraudulent accounting—Enron, Tyco International, Adelphia, and WorldCom. Many thousands of investors lost billions of dollars in the failure of these companies. The size of the losses and number of investors involved forced the US government to pass the Sarbanes-Oxley Act in 2002, providing a modicum of "auditing accountability." Despite the losses and the criminal conviction of the accounting firms involved, the Act remains controversial as a "barrier" to international competition.

There are now only four accounting firms or conglomerates that do most of the world's auditing[12]—comprising a significant oligopoly over the global accounting industry. All have been party to scandals involving illegal activity; all have been indicted and convicted of criminal acts with respect to accounting practices in the US and around the world (Emshwiller & Smith 2003).

Corruption

Corruption in the corporate and state boardrooms is not new, and there is no shortage of historical examples. But in a world in which accumulation in the productive sector is increasingly limited, forcing the search for profits to turn to the sphere of circulation, it is to be expected that corruption, as a form of centralization of capital, would increase.

"Control fraud" is one name given to such practices (Black 2005). It involves corporate or government leaders in positions of enormous power, allowing them to perpetuate commensurately large financial crimes. At this level, crime is carried out so close to the dominant levers of power that the chance of prosecution is minimal. The laws and enforcement are weak, and the actions often defined not under criminal but rather civil law.

At these levels, the crimes take the forms of accounting fraud (Enron, Tyco, etc.), faulty consumer products (pharmaceuticals and toxic goods), cartels and oligopolies (secret pricing, market controls, and production restraints), illegal activities (overfishing, environmental pollution, and money laundering), selling off state corporations, restrictions to regulators, insider information, stock manipulation, and tax evasion, among many other forms (Palmer 2009; Global Witness 2009). Looting at this level exceeds by far the value of all other crimes combined (Black 2005).

"Shadow Banking"

With overproduction throughout the manufacturing sphere and profitable opportunities in decline, a vast array of speculative practices and instruments grew in the realm of finance. In the 1980s it was referred to as the invention of "new products" (Pardee 1987), but latterly it has come to be called the "shadow banking" system. Lacking a precise definition, the term generally refers to the practices of a variety of funds, private equity groups, brokers, and other non-bank financial pools and institutions.

They exist largely as mechanisms to evade or circumvent banking or other financial regulations, in particular capital reserve ratios, but they can include any agency or financial manoeuvre intended to profit from fluctuations in prices or to escape from regulation, rather than to purchase for investment. In this sense, the concept of shadow banking can include the use of tax havens and illicit funds. They are also characterized by the search for quick returns, non-transparency, a high degree of leverage, and no deposit insurance or lender of last resort. Shadow banking constitutes an arena of high risk in the financial sphere, to understate the matter.[13]

A sizable part of the shadow banking system is composed of "derivatives"—a wide-ranging concept referring to financial instruments of many sorts "whose value is derived from the value of other assets."[14] There is no value in the instrument itself; it is a speculative contract that can be made on possible changes in prices or rates, but in principle on any change (Eatwell & Taylor 2000: 101). Their mainstream rationale is the management of risk, but for the most part they employ risk vastly expanded for its own sake to profit from the speculation.

They grew rapidly in the 1990s, but more so after 2000 as a result of many factors, including national and global financial deregulation, cheap money policies in the United States and the "subprime" mortgage boom, the falling value of the US dollar, and the continuing increase in money capital in search of profitable outlets. Because they are for the most part contracts between two parties by and large outside of state and tax regulation, not only do they constitute a global black market in money capital, but also the size and extent of these transactions are unclear. There are, however, estimates from the Bank of International Settlements (BIS). From about $100 trillion in 2002, the notional values of derivatives grew to about $596 trillion in 2007 and $684 trillion in 2008, but fell to $605 trillion in 2009 (Bank of International Settlements). To put this into perspective, the notional value of derivatives in 2007 was about nine times the world GDP of $65 trillion, and about 40 times larger than the US GDP of $15 trillion.

The notional value of the derivative is the value of the underlying asset, not the capital that is actually advanced, i.e., the margin, which is usually not more than 10 per cent. Some of the same assets, moreover, may be part of many different derivatives, in other words, counted more than once in these figures. The rapid growth in notional value, however, reveals the speed of expansion and market size; it points to massive leverage of debt in order to make large profits from small changes in the price of the underlying asset, and to potential huge losses for large numbers of people whose savings or pensions are invested in such instruments ("Barings Debacle"; Bryce 2003; McLean & Elkind 2003). It is this multiple usage, enormous leverage, and associated high risk that make derivatives so lucrative for the money managers who accept little responsibility for the losses.

The problems with derivatives are numerous. Despite the best efforts by the BIS, their value is a guess because the contracts are between two private parties and not regulated. The notional value is the underlying asset at the spot price, but what that price will be at the end of the contract is not known. This means that the risk and the price are difficult and perhaps impossible to calculate, and therefore investors suffer not only "asymmetric information" but, more to the point, little or no verifiable information. The large fees for their creation and manipulation are often based on notional value and therefore out of line with the monies actually advanced. The leverage of debt for purchase of derivatives, furthermore, is so great as to limit credit facilities for the real economy and so dampening its activities. The financial institutions issuing derivatives, moreover, can play both sides of the transaction—betting against their own advice to clients who purchase derivatives.

The Credit Rating Agencies (CRAs)

Key to the success of the shadow banking system with its billions of dollars in structured financial instruments is the role of the CRAs. Their main purpose is to rate the credit-worthiness of the issuers of securities of various sorts and the securities themselves (derivatives, bonds, etc.).

Serious controversy arose in the midst of the crisis of 2007–09 over the high ratings given to very risky derivatives, creating a false sense of their safety as investments and helping to increase profits for their issuers. Part of the problem lay in the conflict of interest that defines their activities. For the most part they act in the interests of the providers of money capital, of capital accumulation, by performing an intermediary role between, on the one hand, financial institutions and government, and, on the other hand, these institutions and investors. In the latter case, the credit ratings of the securities and the institution are paid for by the institution, leading to a rating that may be a product of collusion. In the former case, governments are seen not as instruments of capital accumulation, but as sources of revenues for the lender, a source that can be increased with a decrease in the rating of a government's credit worthiness. As a result of the charge of perceived conflict of interest, the main CRAs signed a code of conduct in 2004. Little effect, however, was visible between 2007 and 2009.

Mergers and Acquisitions

With slowing growth rates in the industrial economies and overcapacity in every sphere, mergers and acquisitions (M&As) became one of the main "drivers" of economic activity, one of the routes to "growing value." They really have amounted to a redistribution of value—a centralization of value, however, not a creation of value. It is in the very nature of competitive capitalism that there will be centralization of capital, in part as a product of competition, but also as a means to allow for collusion and manipulation of prices via monopolies, oligopolies, and cartels, in short, to eliminate or reduce competition, and more recently to loot existing firms through leveraged buy-outs and asset stripping.

The slower the growth rate and the greater the overcapacity, the more M&As one would expect to find. While statistics here are merely estimates, they do reveal the growing importance of M&As in the drive of money capital to find sources of profit, even if at the expense of existing capital. According to one study, "M&A in the US during 1995–2005 as a percentage of GDP was the highest ever experienced before or after" (Ahern & Weston 2009). The value of worldwide cross-border M&As, according to the *Wall Street Journal*, stood at $4.83 trillion in 2007, "eclipsing 2006's record total of $3.9 trillion" (*Wall Street Journal* 2008). Although the total value dropped in 2008, it was reported that "the number of deals stood at 11,286—the highest year-to-date figure on record" (Reuters 2008).

A rise in M&As is usually associated with recessions or depressions as a means to profit from weakened or bankrupted firms when productive investment is out of the question, but now they are also a significant part of economic activity during the latest boom and continuing into the recession of 2008–09. This activity suggests an unrelenting search by money capital for "profitable" investment.

CONCLUSION

The crisis of 2007–09 was certainly the largest of a chain of crises over the several decades of the present post-Fordist, neoliberal era. Each was resolved by a variety of new global opportunities for accumulating, particularly in the spheres of circulation (low interest rates, deregulation, asset stripping, and looting around the world). Just what opportunities can yet be opened or expanded remain to be seen, but the several persisting trends underlying this crisis have not disappeared.

Besides the underlying conditions, there were at least two precipitating causes. One was the so-called subprime mortgage defaults, and the other was the speculative spike in oil prices in 2007–08. Little discussed, this unprecedented rise in the price of oil led to a dramatic rise in the profits of oil companies, but at the expense of most of the other sectors of capital. Because oil is so central to the economy, the rise created distortions and strains throughout the whole system, helping to bring down the house of cards built on derivatives. The boom in the

American housing market was predicated on low interest rates, predatory financing, and securitization of subprime mortgages—a combination impossible to sustain in the long run. These trends and precipitating factors constituted the multi-dimensionality of the contradictions that led to the current crisis. But several countertendencies have operated to prevent the crisis from becoming a complete collapse—they allow crises to become periodic or cyclical and a matter of degree. In other words, it is possible to surmount the immediate crisis without solving the contradictions.

One such factor is the continuous introduction of new technology. The higher rate of organic composition of capital restores profitability for the initiating corporation, and expands the market because of lower-priced products, which ultimately helps the whole system to mitigate the crisis. Higher rates of productivity for the means of subsistence also cheapen labour costs; however, they also translate into relatively fewer workers, the potential for overcapacity, and greater centralization.

Another countertendency is the depression of wages below their value. This can be done through legislative means, global labour arbitrage, free trade zones or *maquiladoras*, and military or police states and forms of coerced, slave, and immigrant labour, and attacks on trade unions and collective bargaining. Whatever the means, low wages and a lower total share of total national income translates into more capital for accumulation, although it also means a declining aggregate demand. Aggregate demand, however, can be increased, albeit unevenly across and within nations; more bubbles can be created; more political tensions, wars, and therefore military expenditures can be pursued; and credit facilities can be bailed out by state indebtedness to insure the continuation of the system. All of these developments are evident in the aftermath of the crisis of 2007–09.

If the crisis were the result of these multifaceted contradictions, then, the solution to it would require that they be addressed. The solutions offered so far, however, have been singular in their focus. The main argument advanced by governments is that the credit system must be bolstered so that financial institutions, corporations, and individuals can continue to borrow. If bankruptcies of the major financial institutions and corporations were allowed, the whole system could collapse because every aspect of the economy today depends on credit. It is vital, then, to the system that credit facilities be maintained. The reasoning suggests that there can be a return to the *status quo ante*. There is no long-term vision other than a return to speculative opportunism, as unregulated as possible, and the "bubble" economy.

There is some reluctant talk amongst governments about new regulations, but the very idea of hindering the need to expand speculative opportunities flies against the current structure of economic forces (financialization), not to mention flying in the face of the power of these financial oligopolies over the global economy and world governments. It is difficult to imagine effective regulation of a global economy in which the principal source of profits is found in more or less unmitigated speculation and illicit and extra-legal activities.

To prevent the failure of the system, then, the world's governments stepped in with massive bailouts of some key economic sectors. They amounted to the selective use of state debt to prop up certain corporations considered to be "too big to fail," meaning that their failure to provide credit and industrial employment would threaten the viability of the system. The bailouts not only reflected the power structure of the economy, but also served to heighten the contradictions. They saved certain financial corporations and certain industrial corporations at the expense of others, giving advantages to a few of the largest. Above all, this advantage has increased the power and position of finance in the economy and furthered the plundering and speculative activities of money capital, ensuring its dominance over other forms of capital.

This expansion of state debt has other implications. It is now employed to rationalize the continuation of neoliberal policies to advance the reduction of state redistribution in order to service the debt (for example in health care, welfare, pensions, education, etc.). Such policies, however, dampen working-class demand and exacerbate the chronic problem of oversupply. The use of debt to overcome losses in speculative ventures—that is, the use of public money without adding to real growth—also means that future growth will be undercut by the need to pay off the principal and interest on the debt. This is what happened in the 1980s in various Third World countries, where sizeable debt-loads all but stopped their development and required the dismantling of their public sectors to increase revenues for paying down the debt. This produced enormous hardship on the working classes and led to political and civil unrest, and even military dictatorships.

The use of state debt clearly has limits. The size of the debt is primarily restricted by the ability of the tax base to service it. Taxes can be increased and increases can be hidden, but here too there is a limit determined by the consequent fall in living standards that taxpayers are willing to tolerate. The size is also limited by the confidence of the creditors in the ability of the state to pay back the loan, as well as the designs or intent that creditors may have on the state debt. They may plunder the state as a source of accumulated capital and continuing revenue (debt repayment) until the need for authoritarian government or military dictatorship to take power to prevent threatening working-class (taxpayer) resistance.

There is no solution under capitalism, because the crisis is a crisis of the structure of contemporary capitalism. Recovery is possible, however, and in the past this has come from the destruction of existing capital, lower wages, new markets, and higher rates of profit. War has served well in producing these effects.

Making war and preparing for it as a permanent feature of contemporary capitalism may well be the necessary corollary to a global economy dominated by money capital. Here the search for "profit" is more the search for avenues to extract existing value or revenue streams, rather than the search for avenues to create value. This is a question of expropriating existing capital through mergers and acquisitions (centralization), destruction of pre-capitalist wealth (concentration), privatization of socialized (state) capital, plundering of pooled reserves (pensions, savings, state funds), and the use of state debt to access accumulated capital and to produce revenue streams. While productive capitalism continues to expand, the vastly greater superfluous capital in the form of money capital must increase its search for "profits" in the realms of concentration and centralization and speculation.

To the degree that the main thrust of capitalist "expansion" is in these realms, it is aptly called "casino capitalism" (Strange 1986).[15] In casinos, the dice are loaded and the cards are fixed, and value or money is not created or distributed but "centralized." In the industrial nations, capitalism and liberal democracy now offer few alternatives to restructuring, retrenchment, and centralization. The promise of growth and new possibilities that they once held for the working classes is no longer certain. It becomes increasingly self-evident that the interests of the working classes were never part of the development of capitalism; but now it seems clearer than ever that the centralized or socialized wealth they created, albeit in private hands, is waiting for their management.

NOTES

1 The United Nations Relief and Rehabilitation Administration, sponsored in 1943 by the United States, ultimately involved many of the world's nations in providing economic assistance to European nations after the war.

2 "In 1973 daily foreign exchange trading ... varied between $10 billion and $20 billion per day. The ratio of foreign trading to world trade did not exceed 2/1. By 1980s ... foreign exchange trading reached a daily average of $80 billion, and the ratio to world trade was about 10/1. By 1992 daily trading averaged $880 billion, a ratio ... of 50/1. In 1995 the amount of was $1260

billion, a ratio to world trade of nearly 70/1, equal to the entire world's gold and foreign exchange reserves" (Eatwell & Taylor 2000: 3–4).

3 "The profits of the financial sector represented 14% of total corporate profits in 1981. By 2001–2 this figure had risen to nearly 50%" (Vasudevan 2008).

4 Concentration, following Marx, refers to the private capitalization of many forms of wealth serving as productive means; and centralization refers to the process commonly called mergers and acquisitions, i.e., the amalgamation of many capitals into an ever smaller number of larger capitals (Marx 1977: 776–77).

5 Although widespread use began in the 1980s, growth in the 1990s was extremely rapid, continuing into the twenty-first century and exceeding 1.5 billion users in 2008. This number represents almost one-quarter of the world's population; the rate in increase between 2000 and 2008 was well over 100 per cent in all regions of the world (http://www.internetworldstats.com/stats.htm).

6 In other words, the elements of the historical juncture that allowed for the Keynesian welfare state were coming to an end. These factors included the decline of the raison d'être of the nation-state (a defined territory for national capital), the decline of "returns" from the Third World, the growing transformation of Fordism, legislative attacks on unions and the decline of union membership, the growth of chronic unemployment, and China's adoption of the "capitalist road," along with détente with the USSR and the European communist parties' shift to "Eurocommunism." All of these factors contributed to undermining the rationale for the Keynesian welfare state.

7 WTO Press Release, February 15, 1999: "The WTO's services commitments will enter into force as scheduled.... The combined commitments of the 70 governments cover more than an estimated 95% of the world's financial services activity and eliminate or relax current restrictions...."

8 For instance: creating national currencies, overseeing money supply, controlling interest and exchange rates, acting as lender of last resort, and providing assorted supervisory powers, among other possible functions.

9 "The sheer scale and speed of these flows have produced a succession of major financial crises, which seem to be occurring with disturbing frequency: Latin America's Southern Cone crisis of 1979–81, the developing country debt of 1982, the Mexican crisis of 1994–95, the Asian crisis of 1997–98, the Russian crisis of 1998, and the Brazilian crisis of 1999.... The deregulation of Swedish financial markets in the 1980s was followed by a severe financial crisis in 1992 that saw overnight interest rates exceed 200 percent. This was followed by a long recession. In the fall of 1992 the whole of Europe was convulsed by the financial crisis which hit the ERM" (Eatwell & Taylor 2000: 5). The list is much longer and also includes the US "savings and loan crisis" of the 1980s, the long-term capital management collapse of 1998, the Argentine economic crisis of 1999–2002, the US "Dot-com bubble" crash of 1999–2000, the Enron and WorldCom scandals of 2001, and the "subprime" mortgage crisis of 2007–09.

10 *Wall Street Journal*, January 14, 2010: "Banks Set for Record Pay"—"An analysis by the WSJ shows that executives, traders, investment bankers,

money managers and others at 38 top financial companies can expect to earn nearly 18% more than they did in 2008"—about $148 billion.

11 Another legislative change that created much of the basis of the so-called moral hazard in the US financial arena was the 1980 Deposit Deregulation and Monetary Act. This eliminated the 5-per-cent limit on "brokered deposits" that had been set in 1963, raised the FDIC insurance from $40,000 to $100,000 (further raised to $250,000 in 2008), and gradually removed the upper limit on banks' interest-rate payments. When the S&L crisis hit, the government paid out billions under FDIC obligations.

12 They are PricewaterhouseCoopers, Deloitte Touche Tohmatsu, Ernst & Young, and KPMG.

13 One of the main components of shadow banking is derivatives, which were famously called "weapons of mass destruction" by Warren Buffet in 2002 (Berkshire Hathaway Annual Report 2002).

14 Among the many forms of derivatives are hedge funds, structured investment vehicles (SIV), collateralized debt obligations (CDO), credit default swaps (CDS), and credit-linked notes (CLN).

15 See also Marx, *Capital*, Volume III: "The credit system ... develops the motive of capitalist production, enrichment by the exploitation of others' labour, into the purest and most colossal system of gambling and swindling, and restricts even more the already small number of the exploiters of social wealth" (1981: 572).

REFERENCES

Ahern, K., and J.F. Weston. 2009. "Mergers and Acquisitions in 2007." <http://ssrn.com/abstract=1087111>.

Akerlof, G.A., P.M. Romer, R.E. Hall, and N.G. Mankiw. 1993. "Looting: The Economic Underworld of Bankruptcy for Profit." *Brookings Papers on Economic Activity* Vol. 2.

Aron-Dine, A., and I. Shapiro. 2007a. "Share of National Income Going to Wages and Salaries at Record Low in 2006." March 29. Center on Budget and Policy Priorities (CBPP). <http://www.cbpp.org/cms/?fa=view&id=634>.

———. 2007b. "New Data Show Income Concentration Jumped Again in 2005." October 24. Center on Budget and Policy Priorities (CBPP). <http://www.cbpp.org/files/3-29-07inc.pdf>.

Aslund, A. 2007. *How Capitalism Was Built: The Transformation of Central East Europe, Russia and Central Asia*. New York: Cambridge University Press.

Aronowitz, S., and W. DiFazio. 1994. *The Jobless Future*. Minneapolis, MN: University of Minnesota Press.

Baker, D. 2009. *Plunder and Blunder: The Rise and Fall of the Bubble Economy*. Sausalito, CA: PoliPoint.

Bales, K. 2004. *Disposable People: New Slavery in the Global Economy*. Berkeley: University of California Press.

Bank of International Settlements. Quarterly Reviews. December 2002, 2007, 2008, 2009. <http://www.bis.org/statistics/derstats.htm>.

"Banks Set for Record Pay." 2010. *Wall Street Journal*. January 14.

"Barings Debacle." n.d. RiskGlossary.com <http://www.riskglossary.com/link/barings_debacle.htm>.

Berkshire Hathaway Annual Report. 2002. <http://www.berkshirehathaway.com/2002ar/2002ar.pdf>.

Black, W.K. 2005. *The Best Way to Rob a Bank is to Own One: How Corporate Executives and Politicians Looted the S&L Industry*. Austin: University of Texas Press.

Brenner, R. 2003. *The Boom and the Bubble: The US in the World Economy*. London: Verso.

Briloff, A. 1972. *Unaccountable Accounting*. New York: Harper and Row.

Bryce, R. 2002. *Pipe Dreams: Greed, Ego, and the Death of Enron*. New York: PublicAffairs.

Cohen, R. 1987. *The New Helots: Migrants in the International Division of Labour*. Aldershot: Avebury.

CSE Microelectronics Group. 1982. *Microelectronics, Capitalist Technology and the Working Class*. London: CSE Books.

Cypher, J.M. 1979. "The Transnational Challenge to the Corporate State." *Journal of Economic Issues* 13(2): 513–42.

Cull, R., J. Matesova, and M. Shirley. 2002. "Ownership and the Temptation to Loot: Evidence from Privatized Firms in the Czech Republic.' *Journal of Comparative Economics* 30(1): 1–24.

Davis, M. 2006. *Planet of Slums*. London: Verso.

Debt Bondage or Self-Reliance: A Popular Perspective on the Global Debt Crisis. 1985. Toronto: Gatt-Fly.

De Medeiros, C.A. 2009. "Asset-Stripping the State." *New Left Review* 55: 109–32.

Eatwell, J., and L. Taylor. 2000. *Global Finance at Risk: The Case for International Regulation*. New York: The New Press.

Freeman, R. 2005. "China, India, and the Doubling of the Global Labor Force." Znet: <www.zcommunications.org/china-india-and-the-doubling-of-the-global-labor-force-by-richard-freeman>.

Friedman, M. 1962. *Freedom and Capitalism*. Chicago: University of Chicago Press.

Galbraith, J.K. 1973. "How Keynes Came to America." In P.A. Samuelson (ed.), *Readings in Economics*. New York: McGraw-Hill. 91–96.

"Global M&A Volume Tops $1 trillion—Dealogic." *Reuters*. 2008. April 17.

Global Witness. 2009. "Undue Diligence: How Banks Do Business with Corrupt Regimes." <http://www.globalwitness.org/media_library_detail.php/735/en/undue_diligence_how_banks_do_business_with_corrupt>.

Glyn, A. 2006. *Capitalism Unleashed: Finance, Globalization, and Welfare*. Oxford: Oxford University Press.

Gordon, B. 2003. "Effects of Japan's Financial Big Bang on Consumers." <http://wgordon.web.wesleyan.edu/papers/bigbang.htm>.

Gowland, D. 1983. *International Economics*. London: Croom Helm.

Greenhouse, S., and D. Leonhardt. 2006. "Real Wages Fail to Match a Rise in Productivity." *New York Times* 28 August.

Grossmann, H. 1992. *The Law of Accumulation and Breakdown of the Capitalist System*. London: Pluto Press.

Guscina, A. 2006. "Effects of Globalization on Labor's Share in National Income." IMF Working Paper. <http://www.imf.org/external/pubs/ft/wp/2006/wp06294.pdf>.

Haque, M.S. 2000. "Privatization in Latin America: The Other Side of the Story." *International Journal of Public Administration* 23(5–8): 753–89.

Hawley, J. 1979. "The Internationalization of Capital: Banks, Eurocurrency and the Instability of the World Monetary System." *The Review of Radical Political Economics* 11(4): 78–90.

Hayek, F.A. 1944. *The Road to Serfdom*. Chicago: University of Chicago Press.

He, J., and L. Kuijs. 2007. "Rebalancing China's Economy—Modeling a Policy Package." World Bank. <http://www.worldbank.org.cn/english/content/working_paper7.pdf>.

Henderson, J. 1989. *The Globalisation of High Technology Production: Society, Space, and Semiconductors in the Restructuring of the Modern World*. London: Routledge.

Hogan, M.J. 1987. *The Marshall Plan: America, Britain, and the Reconstruction of Western Europe, 1947–1952*. Cambridge: Cambridge University Press.

Jones, A. 1973. *The New Inflation: The Politics of Prices and Incomes*. London: Deutsch.

Kaldor, N. 1960. *Essays on Value and Distribution*. London: G. Duckworth.

Keleher, R.E. 1998. "Global Economic Integration: Trends and Alternative Policy Responses." In K. Dowd and R.H. Timberlake (eds.), *Money and the Nation State*. New Brunswick, NJ: Transaction Publishers. 305–29.

Kotz, D.M., T. McDonough, and M. Reich (eds.). 1994. *Social Structures of Accumulation: The Political Economy of Growth and Crisis*. Cambridge: Cambridge University Press.

Lilley, P. 1977. "Two Critics of Keynes: Friedman and Hayek." In R. Skidelsky (ed.), *The End of the Keynesian Era: Essays on the Disintegration of the Keynesian Political Economy*. London: Macmillan. 25–32.

Lutz, C. (ed.). 2009. *The Bases of Empire: The Global Struggle against U.S. Military Posts*. New York: New York University Press.

Mandel, E. 1971. *Marxist Economic Theory*. London: Merlin Press.

Marx, K. 1981 [1894]. *Capital*. Vol. III. London: Penguin Books.

——. 1977 [1867]. *Capital*. Vol. 1. New York: Vintage.

McLean, B., and P. Elkind. 2003. *The Smartest Guys in the Room*. New York: Portfolio.

Melman, S. 1974. *The Permanent War Economy*. New York: Simon & Schuster.

Milward, A.S. 2006. *The Reconstruction of Western Europe 1945–51*. Berkeley: University of California Press.

Morgan Guaranty Trust. January 1984. "World Financial Markets."

"The National Security Strategy of the United States." 2002. *The New York Times* 20 September.

Naylor, T. 1994. *Hot Money and the Politics of Debt*. Montreal: Black Rose Books.

"The New Poor: Despite Signs of Recovery, Chronic Joblessness Rises." 2010. *New York Times*. 21 February.

O'Connor, J. 1986. *Accumulation Crisis*. Oxford: Basil Blackwell.

OECD. Employment Outlook 2007. < http://www.oecd.org/document/38/0,3 343,en_2649_33927_36936230_1_1_1_1,00.html>.

Palmer, R. 2009. "Profiting from Corruption: the Role and Responsibility of Financial Institutions." *Global Witness* 31. <http://www.u4.no/document/ publication.cfm?3537=profiting-from-corruption>.

Pardee, S.E. 1987. "Internationalization of Financial Markets." *Economic Review* (February): 3–7.

Priest, D. 1998. "U.S. Military Builds Alliances across Europe." *Washington Post* 14 December.

Public Citizen, Policy Primer. 2009. "The Connection between the WTO's Extreme Financial Service Deregulation Requirements and the Global Economic Crisis." <http://www.citizen.org/documents/ FinancialCrisisPrimer092309.pdf>.

Russell, E., and M. Dufour. 2007. *Rising Profit Shares, Falling Wage Shares*. Canadian Centre for Policy Alternatives. <http://www.policyalternatives.ca/ publications/reports/rising_profit_shares_falling_wage_shares>.

Sayer, A., and R. Walker. 1992. *The New Social Economy*. Oxford: Blackwell.

Sinclair, T.J. 2005. *The New Masters of Capital: American Bond Rating Agencies and the Politics of Creditworthiness*. Ithaca, NY: Cornell University Press.

Stockholm International Peace Research Institute. 2009. SIPRI Yearbook. Summary. <http://www.sipri.org/yearbook/2009/>.

Strange, S. 1986. *Casino Capitalism*. New York: Basil Blackwell.

Tapscott, D. 1996. *The Digital Economy*. New York: McGraw-Hill.

Tapscott, D., and A. Caston. 1993. *Paradigm Shift*. New York: McGraw-Hill.

Toya, T. 2006. *The Political Economy of the Japanese Financial Big Bang*. New York: Oxford University Press.

Tsurumi, M. (ed.). 2001. *Financial Big Bang in Asia*. Aldershot: Ashgate.

Vasudevan, R. 2008. "Financialization: A Primer." *Dollars and Sense: The Magazine of Economic Justice*. <http://brechtforum.org/economywatch/ financialization_primer?bc=>.

Wall Street Journal. 2008. January 3.

Womack, J., D. Jones, and D. Roos. 1990. *The Machine that Changed the World*. New York: Macmillan.

Contributors

DAVID COBURN is Professor Emeritus, Dalla Lana School of Public Health, University of Toronto, and Adjunct Professor in the Department of Sociology at the University of Victoria. Much of his research has focused on the health professions, and on income inequality and health. His work has been published in various journals, including *The International Journal of Health Services* and *Social Science and Medicine*. More recently he has published papers on global health trends and inequality in *The Social Register* (2010), and on political economy and health in *Staying Alive: Critical Perspectives on Health, Illness, and Health Care*, edited by T. Bryant, D. Raphael, and Marcia Rioux (2nd edition; Toronto: Canadian Scholars' Press, 2010).

ELAINE COBURN is Assistant Professor at the American University of Paris and Associate Researcher at the Centre d'analyse et d'intervention sociologiques (CADIS) at the École des Hautes Études en Sciences Sociales in Paris, France. She is the author of more than a dozen articles and chapters focusing on contemporary forms of world capitalism, as well as resistance by global justice movements. She is co-editor of Socialist Studies/Études Socialistes (www.socialiststudies.com) and an editor for the forthcoming International Sociological Association-supported journal *New Cultural Frontiers*.

CLAIRE CUTLER is Professor of International Law and Relations in the Political Science Department at the University of Victoria. She is a graduate of the University of British Columbia (BA; PhD), the London School of Economics and Political Science (MSc), and McGill University (LLB). She focuses on the intersection of international law and international politics, and is interested in developing critical theory in international law. Her contemporary research is on dispute resolution in international law, particularly the trend toward the privatization of global governance and its implications for the future of democratic institutions and processes. Her publications include *Private Power and Global Authority: Transnational Merchant Law in the Global Political Economy* (Cambridge: Cambridge University Press, 2003); *Private Authority and International Affairs*, co-edited with Virginia Haufler and Tony Porter (New York: State University of New York Press, 1999); and *International Economic Regimes and Canadian Foreign Policy*, co-edited with Mark W. Zacher (UBC Press, 1992).

DR. JAMES M. CYPHER is Research Professor in the Doctoral Program in Development Studies at the Universidad Autónoma de Zacatecas (Mexico), an economist and specialist in Latin American Development. He is the co-author of *Mexico's Economic Dilemma* (Rowman and Littlefield, 2010) and *The Process of Economic Development* (Routledge, 2009), and the author of *State and Capital in Mexico* (Westview, 1990). His research on a wide range of topics has been published in approximately 90 journal articles and 25 book chapters. Dr. Cypher has been a visiting professor or researcher at American University (Washington, DC), Universidad Nacional Autónoma de México (UNAM), Universidad Autónoma Metropolitana, Iztapalapa (Mexico), and Facultad Latino Americana de Ciencias Sociales (FLACSO) in Chile. He was for many years Professor of Economics in the California State University system. He is a member of the editorial committee of *International Journal of Development Issues* (Australia) and *Latin American Perspectives* (US). His published research on the political economy of US military spending spans the period 1970–2010.

TONY EVANS is Professor of Global Politics at the University of Southampton. His research has focused on human rights, particularly on the global political economy of human rights. His most recent book, *The Political Economy of Human Rights: Critical Processes* (London: Lynne Rienner, 2010), explores the consequences of globalization on both the theory and practice of human rights. He is now working on a book that examines the intellectual development of Islamic thought as it emerges in the age of communications technology.

DAVID M. KOTZ is Professor of Economics at the University of Massachusetts Amherst. He specializes in the relations among economic ideas, institutions, government policies, and economic performance. His recent work has applied this focus to macroeconomic problems of the US, Russia, and China. He is a co-editor, with Terrence McDonough and Michael Reich, of *Contemporary Capitalism and Its Crises: Social Structure of Accumulation Theory for the 21st Century* (Cambridge University Press, 2010), and co-author, with Fred Weir, of *Russia's Path from Gorbachev to Putin: The Demise of the Soviet System and the New Russia* (Routledge, 2007).

STEPHEN MCBRIDE is a Professor in the Department of Political Science at McMaster University where he specializes in public policy and globalization. His current research includes projects on the private sector role in international trade and investment dispute settlement in NAFTA and the WTO, employment policy regimes in the aftermath of the 2007 financial and economic crisis, and the impact of climate change adaptation and mitigation policies on the world of work. He was formerly Professor of Political Science and Director of the Centre for Global Political Economy at Simon Fraser University.

BOB RUSSELL teaches in the Department of Employment Relations and Human Resources in the Griffith Business School. He is the author of books on industrial relations in Canada, and work transformation in the mining industry. His more recent research on customer service and informational work has appeared in two books: *Smiling Down the Line: Info-Service Work in the Global Economy* (University of Toronto Press, 2009) and *The Next Available Operator: Managing Human Resources in Indian Business Process Outsourcing Industry* (Sage, co-edited with Mohan Thite). He is currently conducting research on tele-health and the transition to digital work environments in partnership with Queensland Health.

KAVALJIT SINGH is the Director of Public Interest Research Centre, New Delhi. He is the author of *Why Investment Matters* (Madhyam Books, FERN, The Corner House, CRBM, 2007). His previous books include *Questioning Globalization* (Zed Books, 2005), *Taming Global Financial Flows: Challenges and Alternatives in the Era of Financial*

Globalization (Zed Books, 2001), and *The Globalization of Finance: A Citizen's Guide* (Zed Books, 1999). His current research interests include global finance, sovereign wealth funds, and capital flows. He regularly writes on such issues in professional journals, magazines and newspapers published in India and abroad.

MARK THOMAS is Associate Professor in the Department of Sociology at York University, Toronto. His research interests are in the areas of political economy and economic sociology, with a primary research focus on the regulation of labor standards at local, national, and transnational levels. He is the author of *Regulating Flexibility: The Political Economy of Employment Standards* (McGill-Queen's, 2009), and co-editor, with Norene J. Pupo, of *Interrogating the New Economy: Restructuring Work in the 21st Century* (University of Toronto Press, 2010). His most recent project, titled "From Labour Rights to Human Rights: Emerging Approaches to Labour Standards in the Global Economy", examines the economic, political, and social factors that shape the regulation of transnational labor standards.

DR. GARY TEEPLE is Professor of Sociology at Simon Fraser University. He is the author of *The Riddle of Human Rights* (Garamond Press, 2005), *Globalization and the Decline of Social Reform* (Garamond Press, 1995; expanded 2nd edition, 2000), and *Marx's Critique of Politics, 1842–47* (University of Toronto Press, 1984), and the editor of *Capitalism and the National Question in Canada* (University of Toronto Press, 1972). His research interests lie mainly in neo-liberalism and the global division of labor, the politics of human rights, the sociology of art, political sociology, and the political economy of Canada.

Index